BATTLE ON THE BAY

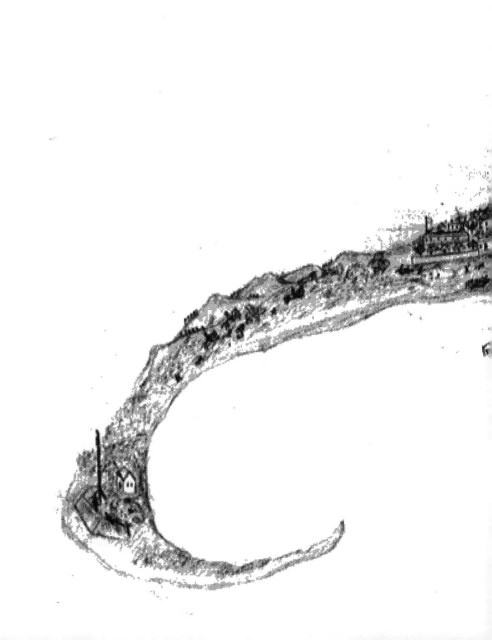

BATTLE
ON THE
BAY

The Civil War Struggle for
GALVESTON
Edward T. Cotham, Jr.

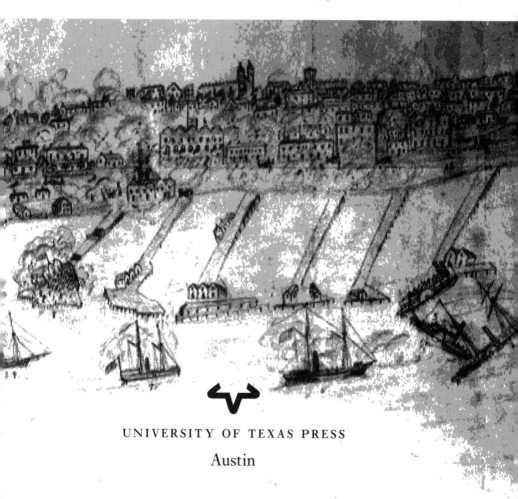

UNIVERSITY OF TEXAS PRESS

Austin

Library of Congress Cataloging-in-Publication Data
Cotham, Edward T. (Edward Terrel), 1953–
Battle on the Bay : the Civil War struggle for Galveston /
by Edward T. Cotham, Jr. — 1st ed.
       p.   cm.
Includes bibliographical references and index.
ISBN 0-292-71204-9 (alk. paper).
— ISBN 0-292-71205-7 (pbk. : alk. paper)
1. Galveston (Tex.), Battle of, 1863.   I. Title.
E474.1.C67   1998   97-4835
973.7′33 — dc21

This book is dedicated to

EDWARD T. COTHAM, SR.

CONTENTS

Acknowledgments ix

Introduction 1

1 The War Is Postponed 7

2 A Safe Condition 13

3 Warming Up for War 21

4 The Island City Chooses Sides 23

5 City in the Sea 26

6 The Blockade Begins 29

7 A Pessimistic Assessment 37

8 Thomas Chubb and the *Royal Yacht* 42

9 The Threat of Bombardment 50

10 Captured by Ferryboats 57

11 The Infantry Arrives 73

12 The Prince and His Players 87

13 From Glorieta to Galveston 100

14 Prince John Plans His Next Production 105

15 The Battle of Kuhn's Wharf 113

16 Cottonclad Victory 124

17 After the Battle 135

18 A Trap Fails to Close 140

19 Still Another Disaster off Galveston 143

20 An Entrenched Camp 148

21 Treated like a Conquered City 160

22 Running the Blockade 168

23 The "Closing Act of the Rebellion" 176

Epilogue 184

Notes 189

Bibliography 219

Index 231

FIGURES

1. Drawing of General Sidney Sherman
16

2. Map of Galveston Island showing Pelican Spit, Fort Point, Virginia Point, Eagle Grove, and South Battery
19

3. Photograph of Hendley Building at 20th and Strand showing Cupola and JOLO Lookout
30

4. Notice of four-day evacuation period dated October 4, 1862
65

5. Photograph of Colonel Isaac Burrell and the officers of the Forty-Second Massachusetts Infantry Regiment
75

6. Photograph of Kuhn's Wharf, 1861
85

7. Photograph of General John Bankhead Magruder
88

8. Photograph of Leon Smith
108

9. Photograph of Morgan's Wharf and steamer traffic, 1861
109

10. Diagram of attack on Kuhn's Wharf
117

11. Photograph of the U.S. Customhouse at 20th and Postoffice
119

12. Drawing of Battle of Galveston by contemporary eyewitness
121

13. Sketch by George Grover of the capture of the U.S.S. *Harriet Lane*
127

14. Detail of *Harriet Lane* capture from Grover sketch
128

15. Diagram of fortifications in the vicinity of Galveston Island
150

16. Sketch by George Grover of blockading Union ships
169

ACKNOWLEDGMENTS

This book would not have been possible without the assistance of Casey Greene and the staff of the Galveston and Texas History Center of the Rosenberg Library in Galveston, Texas. The Rosenberg Library is one of the finest archives and repositories of manuscript materials in the Southwest and fully deserves its excellent reputation.

In addition, I gratefully acknowledge the courtesy and assistance of the staffs of the Center for American History, University of Texas at Austin; the Galveston Historical Foundation; Texas State Archives at Austin; Woodson Research Center, Fondren Library, Rice University; Houston Metropolitan Research Center, Houston Public Library; Library of Congress; Massachusetts Historical Society; Military Division History Research and Museum, Commonwealth of Massachusetts; Boston Public Library; Special Collections Division of the Howard-Tilton Memorial Library, Tulane University; the Wallisville Heritage Park; the Confederate Research Center at Hill College, Hillsboro, Texas; Daughters of the Republic of Texas Library at the Alamo; Special Collections, University of Houston Libraries; Peabody Essex Museum in Salem, Massachusetts; Chicago Historical Society; the Holt-Atherton Department of Special Collections at the University of the Pacific Library in Stockton, California; Clifton Steamboat Museum, Beaumont, Texas; U.S. Army Military History Institute, Carlisle Barracks, Carlisle, Pennsylvania; Concord Free Public Library, Concord, Massachusetts; The Commonwealth of Massachusetts State Library; and the Sam Houston Regional Library & Research Center, Liberty, Texas.

Edward T. Cotham, Sr., W. C. Leroy Rodgers, and Rhett Campbell read early drafts of this manuscript and made many helpful suggestions. The members of the Houston Civil War Roundtable gave me valuable support. Kevin Young and Donald S. Frazier also encouraged this project. Finally, this project owes more than can be acknowledged to the encouragement and help of my wife, Candace.

BATTLE ON THE BAY

Galveston is one of the best-documented, but least-appreciated, American Civil War sites. Although the number of books written about the Civil War seems to be almost infinite, most histories of this conflict ignore the Island City of Texas entirely. This historical anonymity is undeserved. From the appearance off its shores in 1861 of the first blockading Union gunboat to the surrender of the last major Confederate force in 1865, Galveston was the focal point of Civil War activity in the Southwest.

Galveston found itself at the center of this struggle thanks to the geographic forces that stimulated settlement of the island in the first place. The City of Galveston lies at the northeastern end of the island of the same name, across from the southwestern tip of the Bolivar Peninsula. Through the relatively narrow gap between these two points must pass the immense volume of water that is necessary for the tides to alternately raise and lower the water level in the roughly five hundred square miles of Galveston Bay. Physics dictates that at the point of this constriction, the water must pass relatively swiftly, carving out a channel that is deep enough to permit passage of oceangoing vessels. The result is that the eastern end of the island shelters one of the finest natural harbors on the entire Gulf of Mexico.

Because of the inherent natural advantages of this harbor, the City of Galveston was incorporated on its shores in 1838. By 1860, Galveston had grown to be the second-largest city in Texas (only San Antonio was slightly larger). When the Civil War broke out in 1861, therefore, Galveston was not a long-established, decaying port city like many of the other major Southern cities. Instead, Galveston was a relatively new, rapidly growing, and vibrant town, filled with people who were attracted to its seemingly unlimited economic possibilities.

Many of the people who had swelled the population of this new city in the decade preceding the war were not native Americans. Even by the 1860's, Galveston had already become a significant gateway for immigrants to the United States, and many of these new arrivals chose to stay in the Galveston area. According to the 1860 census, almost 40 percent of the non-slave residents of Galveston County were of foreign birth, with the bulk of these immigrants coming from Germany.[1] These immigrants brought with them new arts, skills, and trades that were far different from the occupations commonly associated with the agrarian South.

The Island City these immigrants helped produce was not only very different from other cities in Texas, but also different from other large cities in the South. There is an unfortunate historical tendency to lump all of the large cities of the antebellum South together and treat them as nothing more than extensions of the plantation system. Under this view, Southern cities functioned merely as places where cotton and other agricultural crops grown by slaves were aggregated and exchanged for manufactured goods produced elsewhere. Such a characterization is particularly misleading in the case of Galveston.

To be sure, the Island City did serve as the most important place in Texas at which cotton was gathered and then exported. Of the 300,000 bales of cotton produced in Texas in 1860, over 200,000 were compressed and loaded for export at Galveston. Other prominent exports were sugar (15,000 barrels) and molasses (9,000 barrels). Lesser exports included such diverse items as wool, deerskins, hides, cottonseed, and tobacco.[2]

It is also true that Galveston, like most large Southern cities of the time, had significant connections with slavery. After all, the island had served as a favored destination for smugglers of slaves since at least 1816, when Jean Lafitte and other pirates had made it a major port of call for this illicit trade. It was thus no accident that by 1860, the largest slave market west of New Orleans was located in Galveston. This auction house was owned and operated by John Sydnor, an influential citizen who was also the city's former mayor.

Although the trading of slaves was a significant business in Galveston, these slaves were typically sent elsewhere to live and work. Census records for 1860 reveal that the population of the City of Galveston included 1,178 slaves and only two free blacks. While these slaves and freedmen made up only 16.15 percent of the city's population in 1860, slaves comprised more than 30 percent of the state's total population at that time. Galveston's slaves were predominantly personal or household slaves, who were for the most part well cared for and frequently treated almost as members of the family.[3]

Slave labor and agricultural exports were undeniably important elements of Galveston's growing economy. But to focus only on these aspects of commercial traffic is to miss what was really going on in Galveston just before the war. Because of its situation as the finest natural port between New Orleans and Vera Cruz, Galveston had gradually become a major center of relatively sophisticated manufacturing and service industries catering to the shipping trade. Thus, for example, by 1860, Galveston had two iron foundries manufacturing and repairing ship engines, along with thriving businesses that made sails and rope. The progressive business community had also built a railroad bridge from the island to the mainland, introduced ice, and laid a novel system of gas pipes to provide lighting and cooking fuel.[4]

To accommodate ship passengers, Galvestonians had opened a variety of hotels and entertainment facilities. The city also boasted a number of doctors, lawyers, craftsmen, and other professionals that was disproportionately large compared to its nonslave population of just over 6,000 people in 1860. As befitted the largest professional community west of New Orleans, the city was served by a newspaper (the *Galveston News*) that was the most important paper in Texas and arguably one of the most influential papers in the South. Its editor, Willard Richardson, was a tireless crusader in favor of states' rights, secession, and reopening the slave trade.[5]

Richardson was also justifiably enthusiastic about the Island City's prospects. The 1861 *Texas Almanac* (which Richardson edited on behalf of his newspaper) noted that commercial traffic in and out of Galveston had been growing by an average of 50 percent *per year* during the period from 1858 to 1860, and predicted that "the steady increase in the trade and general business of Galveston leaves no room to doubt that it must ere long rival many of the principal sea ports of the South."[6]

Thus, at the outbreak of the Civil War, Galveston was what today we might call a "boom town," a flourishing new city with economic power and influence that extended well beyond its boundaries. The Civil War would bring many changes to Galveston, as with other Southern towns. But unlike the small towns, river crossings, and farms that through the fortunes of this war often became the scenes of memorable battles, Galveston was not destined to host a campaign involving immense, conflicting armies. Nor was it fated to be the scene of a brief confrontation that lasted a few days and then moved on to some other, usually rural, location. Instead, Galveston had the unique distinction of being a relatively large city that was under the threatening guns of one side or the other (and occasionally both) for almost the entire war.

The reason that Galveston received such attention from the military leaders on both sides of this conflict is not difficult to determine. Desperate to secure a reliable source of cotton for their textile mills, the New England states agitated from the outset of the war for invasion of the Texas Gulf Coast. Because of its railroad connections and port facilities, Galveston was logically a principal target for any invading force with both commercial and military objectives. The same economic and military factors that focused Union attention on Galveston, however, also made it an important place for the Confederacy to defend.

These conflicting strategic objectives led to a struggle for control of the island that culminated in the dramatic Battle of Galveston. On the morning of January 1, 1863, Galveston Harbor was the site of one of the most unusual and poignant battles of the entire Civil War. Among the many unique features of what has been called the "most exciting military event in Texas since the Battle of San Jacinto" and "one of the tidiest little victories of the war"[7] were:

- a successful combined land and sea assault by Confederate forces;
- a battle in an urban setting with artillery and sharpshooters deployed in the upper stories and on the roofs of buildings;
- the successful use of cottonclad steamers loaded with shotgun-wielding sharpshooters to defeat Union gunboats;
- one of the earliest uses of rail-mounted artillery in military history;
- a duel between Confederate field artillery and Union gunboats;
- an unsuccessful charge by wading Confederates against Union troops barricaded on a wharf;
- the explosive destruction by the Union naval commander of his flagship (and inadvertently himself) in an attempt to avoid capture; and
- one of the best-documented cases of a father and son serving on opposite sides in the same battle.

Despite its unique features, there are many reasons why the Battle of Galveston in 1863 has not received the attention lavished on more familiar conflicts in other theaters of the war. Texas was far from the center of military action, not to mention the major media centers (North and South) of nineteenth-century America. More importantly, the strange, almost comical, manner in which this battle was conducted did not lend itself easily to crafting dramatic tales of heroism or martial skill for either side. Finally, the "battlefield" (both land and water) on which this engagement took place was so altered and obliterated by postwar commercial expansion of the City of Galveston that it furnished very limited possibilities for monuments.

This is not to say that the Battle of Galveston was unimportant or uninteresting, or is undeserving of study. On the contrary, as I hope to demonstrate in this narrative, the story of how Galveston fell under Union control, and was then recaptured by Confederate forces who occupied it until after the last Rebel army surrendered, is one of the great untold stories of the war.

Unfortunately, it is a story whose importance has all too often been over-looked. From a military standpoint, the Confederate recapture of Galveston at the beginning of 1863 had enduring and far-reaching consequences. A Union officer captured there ruefully declared that "in not holding Galveston we lost the key to Texas."[8] Reflecting back on the course of the war near its conclusion, Union General Nathaniel P. Banks admitted in a letter to the Secretary of War that Galveston's loss had been a great strategic impediment to the North. If only the Union could have maintained possession of Galveston Island, Banks lamented, it would have rendered entirely "unnecessary" his disastrous campaign up the Red River in 1864.[9] That campaign, by itself, cost almost ten thousand casualties and undoubtedly prolonged the war.[10]

If things had gone only slightly differently, Galveston might now be remembered in Civil War history as the starting point of the great Union invasion of Texas near the end of the war. Instead, it is remembered (albeit dimly) as a haven for blockade runners and as the answer to a trivia question: What was the last major Southern port still in Confederate hands when the final Confederate army signed surrender terms off its shore in June 1865?

On closer reflection, the substance of this question is not really trivial at all. How did Galveston, which as an island would seem to be unusually vulnerable to attack, hold out for so long? Part of the answer is clearly that the Union chose to apply most of its overwhelming resources elsewhere. But a good case can also be made that the Confederacy was more successful in defending Texas than any other state that took part in the rebellion. Yet, at this distance in history, this unusual success is difficult to fully explain.

It was certainly not due to an abundance of military resources, which were almost always in short supply in Texas. Nor can it be attributed to the impact of a single, visionary commander, like Robert E. Lee, who implemented some brilliant plan of strategic defense along the Gulf Coast. Instead, Texas was saved at battles such as Galveston, Sabine Pass, and the series of engagements that comprise the Red River Campaign of 1864, primarily because Union commanders made more critical strategic and tactical errors in the face of determined resistance than their Confederate counterparts.

These errors are only apparent if the events preceding and following the battles are viewed in their proper context. It is unfortunate that the Civil War is often studied as though its battles were staged on a series of chess-boards, where the troops materialized in carefully planned formations, performed their functions, and then exited the board at the end of the game to appear without explanation on some other chessboard at another time and place. But to study a campaign such as the subject of this book in this episodic fashion is to miss what is perhaps the most important part of the story. In order to understand the struggle for Galveston it is essential to examine how each of the major players came to be on this particular stage at the same time; it is also important to learn why other scheduled players missed the performance entirely.

The War Is Postponed

A rumor has reached me that an attack is contemplated by you
upon the Texas troops now encamped on Brazos Island. I will not allude
to the consequences of such an act against the sovereignty of my State. The
fate of individuals on either side is a matter of little consequence compared
with national results affecting the whole country. Civil war with all its
horrors, of which we may not see the end, would inevitably ensue.
EBENEZER NICHOLS,
Commissioner for Texas, to Captain B. H. Hill, U.S. Army, February 22, 1861

On December 20, 1860, South Carolina seceded from the Union, setting off a chain of events that would plunge the country into an internal conflict that will never be forgotten. The firing on Fort Sumter in Charleston Harbor that is traditionally held to mark the beginning of the Civil War did not occur until April 12, 1861, almost four months after South Carolina announced its departure. Although the interval between these two related events is usually treated as the calm before the storm by most histories of the period, it was in reality an extremely active time in the Southwest. In fact, if it had not been for the composure and diplomacy exhibited by one Galveston merchant, the first shots of the Civil War might well have been fired on the Rio Grande in Texas almost two months prior to the attack on Fort Sumter.

This story begins on January 28, 1861, when a convention composed of delegates elected from throughout Texas assembled in Austin to address the issue of secession. They had plenty to consider. In November 1860, Abraham Lincoln (who had not even been on the ballot in Texas) had been elected president, setting in motion the process of dissolution. By the time the Texas Secession Convention first met in late January, six other states (including neighboring Louisiana) had dissolved their ties with the Union. It was clear to all that the states comprising the United States were clearly disuniting at a rapid pace. The question was not whether Texas would secede, but whether it would join the other cotton states in some form of political alliance or resume its former status as an independent republic.

The way in which this question would be answered obviously was of great concern to a coastal and commercial city like Galveston. Naturally, therefore, the city sent prominent and influential representatives to the convention charged with deciding this issue. One of these representatives was Ebenezer B. Nichols, often referred to as "General" Nichols because of his rank in the state militia.[1]

Born in New York, Nichols had arrived in Texas in 1838. A man of vision and boundless energy, he set up a wholesale grocery and general merchandise business with a group of men including William Marsh Rice (founder of Rice Institute), which became the largest business of its type in the city. Nichols and his business associates were farsighted men who were instrumental in building wharves, constructing the railroad, and bringing ice to Galveston.[2] Nichols arrived as a delegate to the Secession Convention in Austin, therefore, with a reputation as an astute and experienced businessman.

The main business of the convention was speedily addressed. On February 1, 1861, an overwhelming majority of the members of the convention (including Nichols and every other member of the Galveston delegation) signed the Texas Ordinance of Secession.[3] Unlike the mechanism by which secession was achieved in most of the other rebelling states, the Texas Secession Ordinance was unique in that it called for a special vote to be held on February 23, 1861, at which the voters could either ratify or reject the ordinance. The results of the vote were then to be tabulated and announced when the convention reconvened on March 2, 1861, a date chosen because it was the twenty-fifth anniversary of the approval of the Texas Declaration of Independence from Mexico.

Symbolic political gestures like the public referendum were important in their own way, but the more practical representatives at the convention (like Nichols) recognized that immediate action would be needed if the new confederation were to have any serious chance of survival. These men had seen to it that as one of its first orders of business the convention had selected a smaller Committee on Public Safety, to which it entrusted broad and somewhat undefined powers.[4] Then, Nichols offered a resolution (which was promptly adopted) permitting the president of the convention to authorize the raising of up to $100,000 to be disbursed under the direction of this Committee on Public Safety.[5]

When it came time to implement this finance resolution, the president of the convention naturally turned to Nichols, as its author, to head up the effort. It would have come as no surprise to the members of the convention that a Galveston merchant took the lead in securing financing for this rebellion. After all, Galveston merchant Samuel May Williams and his firm had been instrumental in financing the Texas War of Independence against Mexico twenty-five years before.[6] In addition, Nichols was known to the delegates as an extremely capable man who had important financial and shipping connections. These connections would soon be tested and prove their worth.

On February 4, 1861, only one week after it had commenced, the Secession Convention adjourned pending the results of the statewide referendum. Most of the representatives went back to their homes to deliver stirring speeches in support of secession. Nichols and the members of the Committee on Public Safety, however, could not afford this luxury. As the convention broke up, Nichols was formally appointed financial agent and commissioner for the State of Texas. He was given written instructions to raise sufficient funds as quickly as possible to finance an expedition of up to six hundred men to seize army supplies on the southern Gulf Coast.[7] As the Committee on Public Safety later admitted, Nichols had been assigned a "Herculean task."[8]

To accomplish this task, Nichols proceeded as fast as he could to New Orleans, where he soon discovered that it would not be easy to raise large sums of money relying upon the credit of a government that was in the process of beginning a rebellion. As Nichols diplomatically summarized the situation, "many considered the undertaking too experimental, however great their patriotism, to give their aid in money."[9]

Using both his financial connections and his most powerful sales pitch, Nichols eventually succeeded in borrowing $10,000 for the Texas secession cause from a bank. He then not only succeeded in borrowing an additional $10,000 using his own credit, but also convinced vendors to provide a substantial amount of supplies without any cash in advance. Most importantly, Nichols procured muskets and ammunition from the governor of Louisiana and contracted with the Southern Steam Ship Company to obtain the services of the steamship *General Rusk* for transportation of troops. Nichols then hurried back to Galveston, where he arrived with the supplies on February 17, 1861.[10]

On the day after Nichols had been appointed financial commissioner, legendary Texas Ranger John S. "RIP" Ford had been appointed to command an as yet nonexistent military force and ordered to proceed to the Rio Grande area to seize arms and munitions and protect against invasions.[11] Colonel Ford raised a force of approximately five hundred men and waited in Galveston for Nichols to arrive with the money, supplies, and ships. Some of

Ford's hastily gathered forces consisted of companies that had informally enlisted in Galveston saloons, giving the phrase "spirit of rebellion" an entirely new meaning.[12]

When Nichols arrived in Galveston on the seventeenth, it was quickly discovered that the *Rusk,* which he had brought with him, was too small to accommodate all of Ford's troops and their supplies. Undaunted, Nichols immediately chartered two additional ships, and the force headed for Brazos Santiago (an island near the mouth of the Rio Grande), at which United States troops guarded a considerable quantity of supplies.[13]

With Nichols and Ford on this expedition was the Galveston Artillery Company. This company, organized in 1840 primarily as a social organization, was the oldest battery in the State of Texas. Its original guns had been obtained from a ship in the Republic of Texas Navy.[14]

Nichols and the forces from Galveston arrived at Brazos Santiago on the morning of February 21, 1861, and promptly took possession of a considerable number of guns and associated supplies. The Texas forces had arrived not a moment too soon. Orders were on their way from Fort Brown (present day Brownsville) directing the officer in charge to destroy all of the public property.[15] But the order came too late; the officer to whom it was directed met the messenger carrying it while coming to Fort Brown to report the Texans' arrival and the abandonment of his post.

The military stores seized by Nichols were soon inventoried. This tedious job was made significantly easier by the fact that the government property at Brazos Santiago had been in the custody of John L. Greer, a U.S. Army ordnance sergeant who promptly resigned and was appointed by Nichols to the same position in the Texas forces. Greer's preliminary inventory showed that the decision to take control of the military property on the Rio Grande had been a wise one. Colonel Ford proudly (if too optimistically) advised the Committee on Public Safety that "the number and character of the pieces taken can not now be given in detail; yet it may be safely asserted that the State of Texas has in her possession a supply of siege guns and mortars amply sufficient to protect all her harbors."[16]

On the next day, February 22, 1861, Nichols proceeded on to Brownsville to see if the troops there were also willing to surrender their posts and public property to the Texas forces without incident.[17] But Captain Bennett H. Hill, in command at Fort Brown, refused to recognize Nichols' authority as commissioner and vigorously protested that he could not surrender United States property without explicit instructions to do so from his government.[18] Threatening to place Nichols under arrest, Captain Hill stated that he considered the Texans' seizure of supplies at Brazos Santiago to be an open act of hostility against the United States.[19] A clash of armed forces appeared inevitable.

The troops with Nichols were fully prepared for a fight. In fact, some of the men were eagerly anticipating their first battle.[20] The situation was tense and could easily have escalated into a conflict that would have started the Civil War (in the Southwest at least) well in advance of the firing on Fort Sumter. But cooler heads prevailed here, and the Texas troops were ordered simply to fortify their positions, avoid provocations, and await developments. Nichols returned to Galveston, where he gathered reinforcements that he placed under the temporary command of Colonel Benjamin F. Terry (for whom the unit known as "Terry's Texas Rangers" would later be named). With these additional troops, Nichols hurried back to the Rio Grande to complete his mission.[21]

The situation at Fort Brown had not changed significantly in Nichols' absence. He arrived on March 1, 1861, to learn that the Texas troops had strengthened their defensive position at Brazos Santiago, mounting several guns from the Galveston Artillery in a fortification that could at best be deemed adequate "under the circumstances."[22] But the United States troops still refused to leave or give up the public property in their possession without orders to do so. An uneasy stalemate had been reached.

Finally, on March 3, 1861, the steamer *Daniel Webster* arrived at the mouth of the Rio Grande carrying several U.S. Army officers, one of whom was Major (later General) Fitz John Porter. Nichols boarded the vessel and met with Porter. He was delighted to learn that Porter carried instructions from San Antonio, where another mission from the Committee on Public Safety had forcibly seized the arsenal and succeeded in obtaining an order from General David Twiggs directing all U.S. troops to leave Texas and deliver all government property to state officials.[23] This ended the crisis at Fort Brown. The remaining military supplies were then peaceably delivered to Nichols in his role as commissioner.[24]

The capitulation of Fort Brown left Nichols with a number of difficult logistical problems. In addition to transporting his victorious forces to other locations, he needed to be able to ship the captured military supplies to a more secure place. Nichols wrote back to Galveston to renew the charter on one of the ships he had borrowed. He also sent back the *Union*, one of the steamers he had chartered on the spot to transport men from Galveston, noting that "[she is] such a miserable old hulk that I would not trust anything valuable on her."[25]

Having arranged for the first shipments of captured supplies, Nichols assisted his adversary, Major Porter, to charter the *General Rusk* to take the United States troops at Brownsville to Florida, and then returned to Galveston, where he briefed members of the Committee on Public Safety on his successful mission. On March 16, 1861, Nichols instructed Colonel Ford to send most of the captured guns and ammunition to Galveston.[26] Unexpectedly, this instruction turned out to be a source of controversy. Ford was convinced that the captured arms needed to stay at the Rio Grande to protect against a potential invasion by Mexico and argued that the diversion to Galveston ordered by Nichols was "imprudent and unsafe."[27] While a number of the guns were eventually sent to Galveston, Ford's resistance to shipment of arms to Galveston meant that the city would have to look elsewhere for additional means to protect itself.

By the middle of March 1861, the preliminary maneuvering in Texas seemed to have gone decidedly in favor of the secessionists. Nichols and his forces from Galveston took pride in the fact that they had given Texas a head start in the Confederacy's fight for independence. Arthur T. Lynn, the British consul in Galveston, confidently reported back to the home office in London that reunification was unlikely:

> Neither can I believe that an attempt will be made to coerce the seceded states back into the union, or if made that it would be successful. . . . I therefore look forward to a peaceable adjustment of the dissensions which now distract this country, and that the Confederate States, though their independence may not now be recognized at Washington, will maintain their separate nationality.[28]

A Safe Condition

This point [Galveston] is plainly the most exposed to an attack
by the enemy of any in Texas. The defenses are imperfect although we have
been actively employed in trying to improve them. Our funds are nearly exhausted
and without aid from the State and ultimately from the Confederacy I apprehend
it will be quite impossible to put Galveston in a safe condition.
GENERAL SIDNEY SHERMAN,
May 22, 1861

While anxiously awaiting word from Ford and Nichols about the results of their expedition to the Rio Grande, the Committee on Public Safety had convened in Galveston to make further defensive arrangements for the coast of Texas. Not knowing where to begin, the Committee had first written to the Commissioner of the State of Louisiana on February 14, 1861, and asked to borrow "spare arms" from one of its "Southern sisters." It was particularly interested in getting back the "Twin Sisters," two cannons that had been used by the Texas forces at the 1836 Battle of San Jacinto, but which had found their way after the war to Louisiana.[1]

When the Committee received an encouraging initial response to this request for arms, James H. Rogers, a member of the Committee, was sent to Louisiana to make the request in person. With the assistance of Braxton Bragg and E. B. Nichols, Rogers succeeded in convincing Governor Thomas Moore of Louisiana to formally request Jefferson Davis to send competent engineers, long-range guns, and ammunition to Galveston. While awaiting a response to this request, Governor Moore agreed in the meantime to ship a thousand stands of muskets to Texas, half of which were sent to Nichols in Galveston. The Louisiana legislature also ordered the Twin Sisters remounted and presented as a gift to the State of Texas.[2]

The Committee on Public Safety was still busy organizing when it unexpectedly received word that a ship in port at Galveston wished to join the rebellion. The revenue cutter *Henry Dodge*, commanded by Lieutenant William F. Rogers of the United States Revenue Service (forerunner of the Coast Guard), had a crew of twelve men who professed loyalty to the South.

During an interview with the Committee, Lieutenant Rogers had expressed his willingness to disobey his current orders, which were to take his ship to New York, and to instead turn his vessel over to the state.[3] The Committee believed that this was too good an opportunity to pass up.

Although the value of the vessel seemed clear, the problem of funding the project appeared insurmountable. The crew of the *Dodge* was due to be paid about $900 for two months' service on March 1. Not having this amount — in fact, the Committee had been forced to borrow $400 just to meet its own expenses — it directed its agent in Galveston not to seize the ship until the second of March, hoping that the United States would pay the crew off on the first and spare the state this added burden.

The plan proceeded as ordered and on March 2, Rogers was named captain of the new Texas Schooner *Henry Dodge*.[4] The economic savings that the Committee thought it had so cleverly ensured in this acquisition did not fully materialize. The United States payment official not unreasonably determined that the crew of the *Dodge* should not be allowed to draw supplies or be paid for the whole month of March since they had turned over their vessel to the enemy on the second day of that month.[5]

In addition, the ship ended up not being as much of a bargain as the Committee had initially believed. After the vessel was turned over, Captain Rogers promptly wrote a letter to the president of the Secession Convention informing him that the *Dodge* urgently needed between $1,000 and $1,200 of repairs to render it efficient as an active cruising vessel.[6] Faced with these complications, the Committee must have looked on its first naval acquisition as a mixed blessing.

In light of the experience with the *Dodge*, it is understandable that one of the Committee's highest priorities was next to try to generate additional revenue to fund its military plans. On February 24, 1861, the Committee had been contacted by the president of a railway company, Abram M. Gentry, who informed them that he had a cargo of imported railroad iron lying in a ship off of Galveston. If he landed it in Galveston as planned, he would be required to pay several thousand dollars in duties to the United States. Gentry volunteered that he would prefer to pay these duties to the State of Texas.

The Committee quickly (and not surprisingly) came to the conclusion that this was its own preference also, and sent Gentry a letter directing him to pay the duties to the state. The letter also purported to authorize him to land the iron at any point he wished on the coast free from any duties demanded by "the old Federal government."[7] Mr. Gentry soon came to rue having made what he considered at the time to be a patriotic suggestion. The customs inspector for the "old Federal government" refused to recognize the validity of the Committee's letter, and it was not until military officials eventually intervened that Gentry finally got his iron released in Galveston.[8]

During its stay in Galveston, the Committee on Public Safety was so busy dealing with one crisis after another that it did not have time to confront the fundamental problem of constructing viable defenses for the island. This failure was eventually rectified by three of its members, who on February 26, 1861, the day after the Committee had adjourned, contacted General Sidney Sherman (see Figure 1) in Galveston and instructed him to head up the creation of military fortifications for the city.[9] This was followed the next day by a letter from President Oran Roberts of the Secession Convention, who, while disclaiming the power to make formal appointments, also asked Sherman to "take the lead" in responding to any emergency that might threaten the security of Galveston.[10] In this manner, almost as an afterthought, Sidney Sherman took the unofficial title of "General" and became the first commander of the Civil War defenses at Galveston.[11]

Despite the informal manner in which he had been chosen, Sherman was the logical choice. He was famous then (as he is today) as the man who led the left wing of the Texas Army in the rout of the Mexican forces at the Battle of San Jacinto; it was Sherman who was credited with first shouting the battle cry "Remember the Alamo!"[12] This fame had apparently cost him the friendship of Sam Houston, his former commander.

After the Texas Revolution was over, Sherman and Houston had become such bitter enemies that Houston had on one occasion in 1859 taken to the floor of the U.S. Senate to read a letter making outrageous charges of cowardice relating to Sherman's conduct at San Jacinto.[13] Two years later, Houston was removed from office by the Secession Convention for failure to take the oath specified by the Convention; thus, Sherman's selection by the unofficial secessionist government for an important military post must have been viewed by Houston as a political slap in the face.

At the time of his appointment, Sidney Sherman had fallen on hard economic times. In the ten years following the census of 1850, the estimated value of his personal assets had fallen from $150,000 to $1,000, largely due to a series of fires and bad investments.[14] Relying principally on his military fame and reputation, Sherman had come to Galveston and, by 1860, had become the jovial proprietor of the Island City Hotel. Organizing defenses for

FIGURE 1. *General Sidney Sherman.*
Courtesy of Rosenberg Library, Galveston, Texas.

the island proved to be an even more challenging job for Sidney Sherman than running a hotel. Short of arms and gunpowder, the general supervised the construction of the best defenses that he could manage with such limited resources.

On March 6, 1861, Sherman wrote to the chairman of the Committee on Public Safety and reported on the status of his efforts to fortify the island. Although the island was far from secure, he had made definite progress. Sherman had taken charge of twelve guns and mortars that had been brought from Brazos Santiago by the expedition under General Nichols and was in the process of designing platforms to mount the guns in batteries. He had also enrolled into the service approximately sixty-eight men from Jefferson County who had arrived too late to participate in the Nichols-Ford expedition to the Rio Grande.

Upon their arrival, Sherman expressed concern that the guns he had received were not of larger size. He also was upset that he had few small arms and not a single pound of gunpowder.[15] The more that Sherman considered the problem of defending the island with the available resources, the more worried he became. On March 8, 1861, he wrote to Judge William Ochiltree (who was then representing Texas in Montgomery, Alabama, during the formative phase of the Confederate government) and candidly predicted:

> Should it become necessary to make a defense here we will find ourselves poorly prepared. . . . Nature has given us very good defenses in our sand banks, but it is important we should have heavier guns, say 68-pounders. One of the committee of the Convention (General Rogers) went to Louisiana to procure guns, but obtained none but one thousand stand of muskets, which had been altered from flint to percussion locks, and are of but little use; in fact, they are not safe. . . . I am preparing to place in battery on the beach what guns we have, but they will be of little use against heavy metal.[16]

Although he lacked sufficient arms, one advantage that Sherman did possess was the advice and assistance of some experienced soldiers who were in the process of switching their allegiance to the new Confederate States. For example, General David E. Twiggs, who had ordered United States forces to leave Texas without a shot being fired, had been jubilantly received when he arrived on the island in early March. The large crowd that turned out to greet Twiggs had hailed him as a hero and, in the words of the *Galveston News*, "paid him those respectful attentions to which he is so richly entitled."[17] While he was in Galveston, Twiggs met with Sherman and advised him regarding the amount and type of captured U.S. supplies that Sherman should attempt to requisition from the arsenal that Twiggs had surrendered in San Antonio.[18]

Another ex–U.S. Army officer, Walter Stevens, was also of substantial assistance to Sherman in constructing the first batteries of the war for Galveston. Stevens happened to be on the scene because he had been on the island helping to design and build its military defenses for the United States prior to the beginning of the war.[19] In 1859, funds in the amount of $80,000 had been appropriated by Congress for the creation of fortifications to defend Galveston Bay. Captain Stevens, who at that time was a thirty-two-year-old engineering officer in the United States Army, had been chosen to supervise the work.

After surveying the possibilities, Captain Stevens began to erect a battery on Pelican Spit (see Figure 2), a low sand bar that now forms part of the southeastern portion of Pelican Island. Reef and shell materials were brought in to be used in the construction of the battery. Commencing in 1860, Stevens also began construction of a large two-story barracks and storehouse on this spit. Before this work could be completed, however, Texas seceded and the work ceased.

Sherman was impressed by Stevens' ability and recommended him both to Texas officials in Austin and Confederate government contacts in Montgomery for the position of captain of engineers.[20] At least in this case, Sherman turned out to be a good judge of talent.

From his modest beginnings as a superintendent over the batteries under construction in Galveston, Stevens went on to have an extraordinary career in the Confederate Army, ultimately becoming a brigadier general and the chief engineer in Robert E. Lee's Army of Northern Virginia.[21] One of Captain Stevens' first assignments after formally joining the Confederate Army was to write a memorandum for Jefferson Davis describing the defensive possibilities of various places on the Gulf Coast (including Galveston) and recommending the numbers and types of guns that should be assigned to each location.[22]

In early April 1861, the Twin Sisters (the two pieces of artillery used at the Battle of San Jacinto), now handsomely mounted on new carriages, were received by Texas as a gift from the State of Louisiana and shipped to Galveston.[23] But, however important their symbolic value, these four-inch guns were found to be "much impaired by rust" and in any event were too small to be of much use in the type of war that Sidney Sherman expected.[24] Therefore, when Sherman wrote to Governor Moore of Louisiana in April

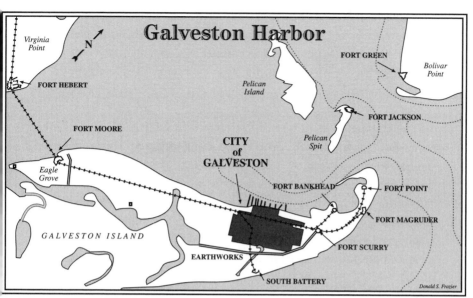

FIGURE 2. *Map of Galveston Island showing Pelican Spit, Fort Point, Virginia Point, Eagle Grove, and South Battery. Prepared by Donald S. Frazier.*

for the ostensible purpose of thanking him for the gift of the historic guns, he used the occasion to plead for more practical guns and ammunition:

> We shall have, by tomorrow, in answer to my call, 1,500 men enrolled [in the service], and I have no powder or lead. We are menaced with the discontinuance of our steam communication with New Orleans, in which event we shall be in a most troublous position indeed.[25]

The deficiencies that Sherman described were quite evident to the citizens of Galveston, one of whom lamented that "in the case of hostilities we are totally unprotected here. There are a number of pieces of artillery here, . . . but there is no powder, no military organization, no leader, no nothing."[26] The mayor and city officials passed a formal resolution to be sent to Governor Edward Clark condemning the "defenseless condition of the City of Galveston." Reminding the governor that "much of the commerce of the State through this City has ingress and egress," they requested that he personally intervene with Jefferson Davis and the Confederate authorities to secure their protection.[27]

Inadequate military supplies were far from the only problem confronting Sidney Sherman in his effort to secure Galveston against attack. There were a number of citizens who refused to recognize his authority, arguing, with some merit, that since Sherman's authority was derived merely from an appointment by the Secession Convention, it ended when that convention adjourned. This was not merely an abstract legal argument; the only person in town with any material quantity of gunpowder refused to accept the validity of Sherman's order directing him to reserve the powder for use by the military.[28]

The volunteers that Sherman had enrolled to defend the city also had their shortcomings. As the general noted in a report to Austin, these volunteers were "inspired by a considerable zeal," but unfortunately felt it "convenient and desirable to be at home at night."[29] A daylight-only defensive force obviously had its limitations. In addition, the formation of even this force had caused severe hardships since they were not being paid and were forced to provide their own uniforms and supplies. As the wife of one of these volunteers complained in an impassioned plea for financial assistance:

> I have perhaps on an average made one dollar per weak [sic] by taking in sewing. . . . Every cent I can get must go to buy uniforms for [the soldiers in my family] we are thirty dollars behindhand in house rent and an empty pantry please tell me what are we to do must poor men (hundreds besides mine) find their own clothes and board and do the fighting for the slaveholders & without a cent?[30]

The pleas of General Sherman and city officials for help in organizing the growing military forces were eventually heard in the Confederate capital. John C. Moore, captain of artillery, was ordered to the island from New Orleans to "plant batteries for its defense."[31] In addition, Colonel (later General) Earl Van Dorn was directed to assume command of the Confederate forces in Texas.[32]

Although Van Dorn's headquarters were officially located in San Antonio, he initially made his temporary headquarters in Galveston because it was widely anticipated to be one of the first places on the Gulf Coast that would be attacked. Under the active supervision of Captain Moore, and sometimes Van Dorn, a line of earthworks surrounding the city was begun, a redoubt (fortification) was constructed on the side of the city facing the Gulf of Mexico, and work was commenced on a fortified camp at Eagle Grove (which guarded the entrance to the railroad bridge connecting the island to the mainland).[33]

Warming Up for War

I have the honor to report that I have this morning surrendered this battalion . . .
to the forces of the Confederate States under the command of Col. Earl Van Dorn.
Two unsuccessful attempts have been made by me to escape with this command. . . . I
was obliged to capitulate under the most favorable terms which I could obtain.

MAJOR C. C. SIBLEY,
Third Infantry, U.S. Army, April 25, 1861

One of the orders that the Confederate high command in Montgomery had given to Earl Van Dorn before sending him to Texas charged him with intercepting and preventing the departure of the United States troops.[1] To accomplish this task, Colonel Van Dorn once again turned to General Nichols and the informal military forces that had been organized by Sidney Sherman in Galveston.

Learning that a large body of Federal troops was marching from San Antonio to Indianola to board ships bound for the North, Van Dorn arrived in Galveston on April 16, 1861, where he promptly called for volunteers to try to prevent this departure. Probably by holding a series of recruiting rallies in a number of popular saloons, Van Dorn eventually succeeded in obtaining the services of approximately 125 volunteers, the bulk of whom were an unruly conglomeration of Irish and German dock workers.[2]

Van Dorn and his men boarded the *Matagorda* at Galveston and left for Indianola. On the morning of April 17, 1861, they discovered a large Union steamer lying at anchor in Matagorda Bay. Ordering his men to get out of sight below deck, Van Dorn personally surveyed both the enemy vessel and the troops on shore. His observations complete, Van Dorn then proceeded back across the bay to Saluria. There, he conferred with Leon Smith, the captain of the *General Rusk,* who had also been sent from Galveston with his ship to lend assistance.

Smith was an experienced mariner who had rendered good service in his vessel while transporting Colonel Ford and his men to the Rio Grande during their expedition two months before.[3] He informed Van Dorn that the Union steamer was none other than the famous *Star of the West,* the ship that had been the target of the first Confederate shots at a Union ship in December 1860 while attempting to come to the relief of Fort Sumter.[4] Although there were many Union troops on shore, the *Star of the West* itself was relatively lightly guarded. A bold plan was quickly devised to capture this vessel and prevent the Union troops from leaving.

As night was falling on the seventeenth, the *General Rusk* moved slowly up to the *Star of the West.* In response to a sentry's challenge, Captain Smith calmly replied that he had Federal troops on board who needed to be transferred. Boarding was made difficult by a gale that had arisen, but with the aid of men from both ships Van Dorn and his troops were eventually transferred to the Union ship. On a prearranged signal, the Confederate boarding party then quickly spread out and took control of the steamer. According to one postwar account, the resulting dialog with the surprised Union captain went as follows:

> "I am Gen. Earl Van Dorn of the Confederate army," [the Confederate commander] suddenly announced to the captain of the ship. "I demand the surrender of this vessel in the name of the Confederate States of America."
>
> "The hell you say!" exclaimed the startled Federal. "I suppose I have no choice, as your men far outnumber mine, but I call this a damned scurvy trick."
>
> "You can consider it the fortunes of war. All things are fair when you play that game," Van Dorn replied.[5]

Because the captured ship had too deep a draft to enter the port at Galveston, it was taken as a prize to New Orleans, where it was welcomed by cheering crowds that lined the banks of the Mississippi River. A crew member from Galveston reported that the reception they received was so enthusiastic that "they turned the city over to us literally."[6] Not long after the capture of the *Star of the West,* Van Dorn also succeeded in capturing another Union schooner (the *Fashion*) and, employing a combined land and sea force, forced the Federal troops at Indianola to surrender and be paroled.[7] With a lot of help from Galveston secessionists, the early maneuvering in Texas had gone decidedly in favor of the Southern cause. This certainly did nothing to discourage the rising tide of Confederate nationalism in Texas.

The Island City Chooses Sides

This Govt. will be overthrown and the Union destroyed. I hope for the
best. . . . But I have strong fears to the contrary; and my best judgment is that
we are doing an unwise & maybe a fatal thing. I have no heart in the cause.
Its responsibility and its glory I leave to others.

WILLIAM PITT BALLINGER,
Galveston attorney, December 30, 1860

From the balcony of Galveston's Tremont House Hotel, on April 19, 1861, Sam Houston made one of the most inspired and courageous speeches of his life. Ironically, this speech was not even delivered until after Houston's remarkable political career had already ended. Just one month before, Houston had been removed from the governor's office by secessionists.[1]

In coming to Galveston to speak, the almost seventy-year-old hero of San Jacinto had entered the lion's den of secessionism in Texas. The news of South Carolina's departure from the Union had been greeted on the island with celebrations and gun shots. Galvestonians were among the most prominent and radical representatives at the convention that had adopted the statewide ordinance of secession. In fact, Judge Robert C. Campbell of Galveston had been the chairman of the committee that presented the ordinance to the Secession Convention by which Texas joined the Confederate States.[2] To make matters worse for Sam Houston, his bitter enemy, Sidney Sherman, was temporarily serving as Galveston's military commander.

Some Galvestonians did not confine their strong feelings on the secession issue to stirring political speeches. When Ferdinand Flake, editor of the local German newspaper, wrote a column criticizing South Carolina's secession, a mob broke into his office, destroyed his printing press, and threw his type into the alley.[3] And when the question of secession was successfully put to a statewide vote of the people on February 23, 1861, Galvestonians voted to secede by the overwhelming margin of 765 to 33.[4] Galveston was clearly not the place to go to find a receptive audience for Houston's pro-Union views.

John Sydnor, then the mayor of Galveston and one of the most active slave traders in this part of the country, joined a committee of Houston's friends who met him as he entered the city and tried to dissuade him from speaking. Houston was determined to speak, however, and not even a shout from the crowd of "here's a rope; hang the old traitor!" could deter "Old San Jacinto" from mounting the steps to the balcony of the Tremont House Hotel and addressing the largely hostile crowd.[5]

Houston began his speech by denying rumors that he had been a traitor to Texas or its interests. Houston admitted that he had heard rumors that a force of United States troops was being organized at Indianola to put him back in office. But, as he told the crowd at the Tremont, he had written to the headquarters of these forces in San Antonio in March and expressly declined and discouraged any such assistance.[6]

Houston did not apologize for his views on leaving the Union. Instead, he defended his previous opposition to secession (by then an accomplished fact) and chided his audience for having rejected "these last counsels of your political father."[7] Finally, Houston denounced those who had jokingly suggested that they could "drink all the blood" that would ultimately be shed in defense of secession, making the following prediction:

> You may, after the sacrifice of countless millions of treasure, and hundreds of thousands of precious lives, as a bare possibility, win Southern independence, if God be not against you; but I doubt it. I tell you that, while I believe with you in the doctrine of State rights, the North is determined to preserve this Union. They are not a fiery impulsive people as you are, for they live in cooler climates. But when they begin to move in a given direction, where great interests are involved, such as the present issues before the country, they move with the steady momentum and perseverance of a mighty avalanche, and what I fear is they will overwhelm the South with ignoble defeat.[8]

Near the conclusion of his address, Houston assured the crowd that whatever course the state elected to follow, "my faith in State supremacy and State rights will carry my sympathies with her."[9] Houston's commitment to support the state he had helped found, in a war he had tried to prevent, was no empty boast; his own son, Sam Houston, Jr., would serve in the Second Texas Infantry Regiment under the command of Galvestonian Ashbel Smith and would be seriously wounded on the battlefield at Shiloh.

Following Houston's defiant but compelling speech, Mayor Sydnor was successful in soliciting three cheers from the crowd.[10] But notwithstanding the general's evidently still potent rhetorical powers, the tide of secession could not be repelled from Texas shores. Ironically, on the same day that Sam Houston delivered his prophetic speech at the Tremont, President Lincoln issued the blockade proclamation that was to have such a profound impact on Galveston and other Southern ports.

City in the Sea

No other county is situated as we are [in Galveston]. On the contrary, they are
the reserve which we must call upon, to come to our aid. Our city is literally in the sea
& may be approached by ships with heavier caliber [weapons] than any of ours.
COLONEL HUGH MCLEOD,
June 26, 1861

As if Sidney Sherman did not have enough military problems to contend with in the organization of defenses for Galveston in the spring of 1861, he also managed to become embroiled in a series of controversies involving shipping and commerce. When it became apparent that a blockade was about to be enforced against Galveston and other Southern ports, merchants in the city unexpectedly discovered that they had differing interests. Those who owned or operated ships in interstate or foreign commerce, particularly those who were in business with Northern firms, did not want to see their ships captured or bottled up in Southern ports. In addition, rumor had it that substantial charter fees were going to be paid by the U.S. government for use of such ships by the military.

Other merchants, whose livelihoods depended upon the shipment of goods to or from Southern ports like New Orleans, became increasingly concerned that all the ships would be withdrawn from this trade by cautious, greedy, or disloyal owners, leading to the cessation of trade and economic disaster. Rumors reached Sidney Sherman's ears that the steamers owned by the Harris & Morgan Line, in particular, were going to be withdrawn and sent to the North to be converted into troop transports. This speculation seemed to be confirmed when a messenger from Sabine Pass reported that one steamer from that line had come into the port heavily laden with coal and would not take on board passengers bound for New Orleans as usual.[1]

When the steamship *Orizaba* of the Morgan line arrived in Galveston, crew members expressed their own suspicions that the ship was headed to the North. General Sherman also was alarmed at this possibility because he had seventy-five or eighty men who needed to return to Galveston from New Orleans after triumphantly delivering the *Star of the West* to that city.

Fearing that his men would not be able to return and help defend the city if he did not act immediately, Sherman detailed thirty volunteers to, as he later described their mission:

> take passage on board of the Steamer *Orizaba* under the command of two discreet citizens who were instructed to take passage as passengers and not to interfere with the regular authorities of the Steamer in any way unless she was diverted from her usual course or there was an evident purpose to use her to the evident disadvantage of the Southern Confederacy. If so they then should take charge of her and bring our troops in New Orleans to this city.[2]

Sherman eventually became so concerned about the possibility of a mass exodus of ships to the North that he issued orders preventing six of the Harris & Morgan Line vessels from leaving Galveston, releasing them only when the State of Texas formally chartered two of them for military service.[3]

Even firms owned by prominent secessionists came under suspicion with respect to the ships within their commercial sphere. General Sherman issued an order, and sent it to the offices of E. B. Nichols & Co. with a pointed note, forbidding any person from communicating with a ship until it had entered the port, the purpose being to prevent anyone at the company from warning a ship to turn around or directing it to go to the North. The result was that the bark *Nueces* was not warned prior to entering Galveston Harbor, where it was then seized on June 3, 1861.

Captain Eldridge, the master of the *Nueces*, was understandably upset about the confiscation of his vessel and protested to anyone and everyone who would listen. The military authorities finally grew tired of these complaints and issued an ultimatum giving Eldridge twenty-four hours to leave the city. Nichols, feeling sorry for the man and partially responsible for his predicament, offered the captain refuge at his plantation on Clear Creek and eventually secured safe passage for him through the Confederate lines.[4]

Sorting out all of the problems that arose from the seizure of ships, as well as working out the details of defending a city with no gunpowder, was too much for Sidney Sherman. By late June, the "General" had resigned in disgust, telling his men that his authority was "embarrassing and insufficient."[5] As if to second Sherman's discontent, Colonel Earl Van Dorn wrote to his wife from Galveston, declaring that the task of preparing adequate coastal defenses for Texas involved a "thousand duties and a thousand annoyances."[6]

After receiving a series of alarming reports from Sherman and Van Dorn,

Governor Edward Clark visited Galveston to evaluate the state of its defenses for himself. In the fashion of politicians throughout the ages, the governor in a moment of unthinking passion vowed unequivocally to a receptive audience that "Galveston must and shall be protected" and pledged the full support of the public treasury and credit to aid its defense. Then, after considering the matter overnight and talking to his advisors, the governor retreated from his commitment, and admitted that he really could do nothing but go back to Austin and consult with the attorney general. A committee of Galveston citizens scolded the governor for reversing his position on financial assistance, predicting with uncanny accuracy that "if this city were once in possession of the enemy, it might cost millions of money & much sacrifice of life to dislodge them."[7]

When the State of Texas did not appear able or willing to provide much assistance, Galveston determined to take matters into its own hands. Because of his skill and reputation as an advocate, attorney William Pitt Ballinger was selected to go to the Confederate capital in Richmond as part of a delegation soliciting artillery for Galveston. After succeeding in this endeavor, he was persuaded some months later to become receiver for the Confederate government, a position that entitled him to seize property and collect debts owed to Northern residents.

Ballinger, like most Galvestonians, followed news of the war with great interest. To get a better understanding of the character of the generals to whom the fate of the rebellion had been entrusted, he consulted men with extensive military experience. For example, Ballinger had breakfast one morning with Sam Houston. As Ballinger's diary records, Houston believed that Gideon Pillow and Sterling Price were the South's best generals, but also had "a good opinion of [General Robert E.] Lee, who has yet had no chance."[8] In the summer of 1862, Lee would, of course, get his "chance" to command the Confederate Army of Northern Virginia outside of Richmond and justify Houston's good opinion.

The Blockade Begins

Now, therefore, I, Abraham Lincoln, President of the United States, . . .
have further deemed it advisable to set on foot a blockade of the ports within [the
rebellious states]. . . . For this purpose a competent force will be posted so as to pre-
vent entrance and exit of vessels from the ports aforesaid. If, therefore, with a view
to violate such blockade a vessel shall approach or shall attempt to leave . . . the
said ports, she will be duly warned . . . , and if the same vessel shall again
attempt to leave the blockaded port she will be captured and sent to
the nearest convenient port for [prize proceedings].
BLOCKADE PROCLAMATION,
April 19, 1861

Undoubtedly the most important Civil War–era structure remaining in Galveston today is the Hendley Building (see Figure 3). Located on the Strand in the city's business district, the building is today occupied in part by the Galveston Historical Foundation's Visitor Center. This historic structure, which still shows the marks of battle on its sides, was constructed in 1858 by the firm of William Hendley & Co., steamship agents. At the time it was built, its three stories made it the tallest and most imposing structure in Galveston.[1]

The Hendley Building originally had a wooden cupola or observatory on its roof from which a good view of both Galveston Bay and the Gulf of Mexico could be obtained. Because of the view available from this observatory, a group of "lookouts" (who called themselves the "JOLOs") was formed at the beginning of the war to keep an eye out for enemy activity. The meaning of the initials "JOLO" has been lost through the passage of time, but it seems likely that the last two letters stand for "lookouts."

Fortunately for modern historians, the JOLOs kept a detailed log that has been preserved in Galveston's Rosenberg Library.[2] This log records not only military activities, but also frequent diversions such as donations of pies by patriotic ladies. It also meticulously records the ship traffic and weather conditions around Galveston during the early part of the war.

The JOLOs consisted primarily of experienced Galveston mariners who

FIGURE 3. *Photograph from 1861 of Hendley Building at 20th and Strand showing Cupola and JOLO Lookout. Courtesy of Rosenberg Library, Galveston, Texas.*

served scheduled watches at their observatory on the roof of the Hendley Building. They affectionately named their lookout "Point Hendley" in honor of their "Grand Commander," Captain Joseph J. Hendley, who with his brother "Uncle Billy" Hendley founded the shipping firm that constructed this building. The membership of the JOLOs changed throughout 1861 as its members either lost interest, were captured trying to run the blockade, or enlisted in the Confederate Navy.

The log kept by the JOLOs, which begins in April 1861, reflects that at least at first, service in this organization often assumed a lighthearted character. On May 7, 1861, two of the JOLOs granted themselves "temporary letters of marque" and went begging on the Strand, where they succeeded through "skillful manoeuvering" in obtaining "one splendid water cooler and two dollars and seventy-five cents in cash."[3] The only real problem experienced by the JOLOs in the early months of the war was that drunken night guards kept damaging the telescope in the observatory.[4]

This did not mean that the duty was always pleasant. For example, one entry reports "a bloody fight going on with mosquitoes — results doubtful."[5] Another entry on June 20, 1861, complains about the boredom associated with waiting for Union blockaders to arrive:

> Lincoln declines presenting himself, why!! we know not, but it is still more evidence that he is not a man of his word as he promised to call on us by the 15th and he has not done so. He must have his hands full elsewhere.[6]

The situation turned grimly serious here when at 1:10 P.M. on July 2, 1861, the JOLO log recorded the appearance of the Union steamer *South Carolina* and the initiation of the blockade. War had finally come to Galveston in earnest and would not end for over four long years.

In one of the curious coincidences that seemed to occur frequently in Galveston during this war, the first meeting with the blockaders was an unexpectedly friendly affair. The schooner *Royal Yacht* was sent out to visit the *South Carolina* and ascertain its purpose. The captain of the Confederate vessel was Thomas Chubb. Chubb was a talkative man and quickly discovered that Captain James Alden of the *South Carolina* had spent part of his service in the same area near Boston from which Chubb had come many years before.[7] Chubb and his party reported that they were received "most courteously" by the Federal blockaders and concluded that Alden was "a man of very decided character."[8]

Alden was also a career naval officer with more than thirty years of naval service. He had served on a wide variety of ships (including the *Constitution*) and had seen action during the Mexican War.[9] When it became obvious that the Civil War was unavoidable, Commander Alden had received secret orders to go to the Gosport Navy Yard in Norfolk, Virginia, and move the *Merrimack* to a safer location. Although his mission to retrieve that vessel was thwarted through no fault of his own, and the *Merrimack* went on to become famous as the C.S.S. *Virginia*, the first Southern ironclad, Alden himself managed to escape after doing significant damage to the soon-to-be-Confederate naval yard.[10]

The loss of vessels at places like the Gosport yard exacerbated the shortage of ships that afflicted the Union Navy at the beginning of the war. Because the United States Navy did not possess enough ships to cover the tremendous expanse of the Gulf Coast, the Union blockade necessarily was predatory when it originated. As soon as the *South Carolina* arrived off of Galveston, for example, Commander Alden began attempting to capture other ships to assist it in its duties. It was not always successful. For example, the first ship that it encountered on July 3, 1861, the day after its arrival, evaded it and entered the port, becoming the first ship to run the blockade into Galveston.

In the next four days, however, the *South Carolina* managed to capture or destroy eleven vessels, the captains of which were unpleasantly surprised to learn that a blockade had been effectuated.[11] This large number of captured or disabled ships is less impressive than it might first seem. All were reported by Alden to be small and have cargoes of little or no value. Three of the captured vessels were deemed to be so unseaworthy that Alden concluded they could not even safely be allowed to lie at anchor.

The disposition of the crew and passengers on the captured ships presented the Union commander with a dilemma. At first Alden tried to force them all to take an oath of allegiance to the United States, threatening to ship them off to Key West as prisoners of war if they declined. One of these prisoners, future Confederate Major General John Wharton, refused, remarking that given his options, "I go to Key West." Once their status as prisoners had been settled, however, Wharton's entire party relaxed as Captain Alden served a cordial lunch.[12]

When the number of prisoners from the captured ships finally got to be so large that the crew of the *South Carolina* could not guard them and still attend to their regular duties, Captain Alden loaded the prisoners on board several of the captured vessels that he had determined to be unsafe and released them. A few days later he did the same thing with another worthless vessel and thirty-three more prisoners. When he reported these activities to the commander of what was then called the "Gulf Blockading Squadron," Alden was reprimanded and told that in the future he should send all of the prisoners who would not swear allegiance to the Union on to the North as prisoners of war.

Instead of releasing the captured ships, Alden was directed that in the future he should sink all prizes of no value so as to "obstruct the navigation of the rebels, using these means as assistants in the blockading service."[13] Deciding that this duty could be made to serve two purposes, he caused one of the recently captured schooners (the *Anna Ryan*) to be towed away from the *South Carolina* and used it for target practice. The lookouts on top of the Hendley Building watched through their telescope as the Union gunners methodically shot away the target vessel's top mast, jib boom, and sails, and were much impressed with the accuracy and range of the demonstration.[14]

On the morning of August 3, 1861, the *Dart,* which was a Confederate pilot schooner that had been captured and used to supplement the blockade, sailed within range of the South Battery (see Figure 2) while returning to the much larger *South Carolina.*[15] The shots that were exchanged between the South Battery and this small vessel were the first hostile shots of the war for Galveston.

Alden viewed the shots fired at the *Dart* as a deliberate challenge and provocation. Late that afternoon, therefore, the *South Carolina* determined to test the intentions and capability of the Rebel battery and intentionally passed within range of its guns. Another exchange of shots lasting approximately half an hour took place, but this time the longer-range weapons of the *South Carolina* showed their superiority and sent shells close to the city itself.

Some of the shells fired by the Union ship went almost halfway across the island, throwing a thirty-two-pound ball into the middle of Broadway, Galveston's main boulevard.[16] The long range of the *South Carolina*'s guns was witnessed by civilians as well as soldiers. Alerted by the morning's activity, virtually the entire town had turned out to see the afternoon action. A circus-like atmosphere prevailed, and the beach was covered with spectators who quickly discovered that an artillery barrage was not ideally witnessed from close range.

A Union sailor on the *South Carolina,* who had observed a beach "black with people and horses & vehicles of all kinds" at the beginning of the engagement, remembered that when the shells began to burst, the beach was soon deserted. "Some of the people who were out to see the Yankee sunk did not stop till they got to Houston," he remarked.[17] Another local historian noted wryly that in the flight to escape the bombardment, "some of the old citizens developed marvelous speed, and left many of the younger generation far in the rear by their fleetness and impatient desire to get beyond the reach of danger in the shortest imaginable space of time."[18]

The members of the viewing public who could not escape quickly enough apparently decided that the next best course of action was to seek cover. The only place to hide on the beach, however, was in or behind several small, wooden bathhouses. J. M. O. Menard, a fourteen-year-old boy at the time, said that the scene reminded him of an ostrich hiding its head in the ground, and described the sight of people crowding behind these tiny bathhouses as "ridiculous and almost beyond description."[19]

Shortly after the firing commenced, a man named Fisher — who was variously described as either Portuguese or Italian — was shot through the body and killed instantly by an errant Union shot. Thus, ironically, a civilian noncombatant (who was probably not even a U.S. citizen) became the first casualty of the Civil War in Galveston.[20]

Two days after this incident, a group of foreign consuls wrote a letter of "solemn protest" to Captain Alden on the *South Carolina* condemning his

> bombardment of this city on the evening of the 3d instant without having given any notice so that women and children might have been removed, and [we] also [protest] against your firing a shell into the midst of a large crowd of unarmed citizens, amongst whom were many women and children, causing thereby the death of an unoffending Portuguese and wounding boys and peacefully disposed persons, as acts of inhumanity unrecognized in modern warfare, and meriting the condemnation of Christian and civilized nations.[21]

In an equally solemn letter to the consuls the next day, Captain Alden responded that he had not intended to harm unoffending citizens. He explained that since the commander of the Confederate battery had "invited me to the contest," it was his duty to see that all noncombatants were out of the way. Alden concluded by observing that it was the "first time I have ever heard that the women and children or unarmed citizens of one of our towns were under the protection of foreign consuls."[22]

Continuing this unusual correspondence campaign, Colonel John Moore, the Confederate commander, wrote a letter to the consuls defending his conduct against Alden's charges and published it in the newspaper. Moore denied responsibility for the incident, explaining that he had previously warned the Union captain, and Alden had clearly understood, that his vessels would be fired upon if they came within the range of the shore batteries. As to Alden's accusation that it was the Confederate commander's job to keep the civilians out of harm's way, Moore responded that he did not feel it was his duty as battery commander to "leave the battery and go out and tell the citizens that [Alden] was a poor shot, and that their lives and property were in danger at the distance of half a mile to the right or left of the object at which he should have fired."[23]

In reporting this incident to Flag Officer Mervine, his immediate superior, Captain Alden stressed that the Confederate battery's firing "was extremely bad, considering the large object that this ship, almost entirely light, presents, for not a shot touched us." [24] Because of the consuls' protest, however, Alden's report was referred to the Secretary of the Navy, who a month later expressed the Navy's complete approval of Alden's course of action.[25]

The JOLOs watched the artillery exchange with the *South Carolina* from their observatory atop the Hendley Building with great interest and kept careful notes of where each shot from the Confederate guns had fallen. They were disappointed and alarmed to see that most of the shots had fallen far short of their intended targets. Several days later they unanimously voted to send a letter to Richmond relating their concerns and asking for heavier guns.

This demonstration satisfies us the enemies' guns are of superior range to ours and unless you can get guns of equal if not superior range to theirs we shall not be able to protect our city and ourselves from bombardment by sea. . . . During this little pass at arms seven of us were in the observatory with our telescopes coolly and calmly looking on to discover where our weak point lay if any existed. And we do assure you there is not a doubt but that our Batteries would have sunk the Steamer in 20 minutes if our guns had been equal in range to theirs.[26]

The citizens of Galveston were not content merely to write letters urging the Confederate government to send them arms. A committee of prominent citizens, including attorney William Pitt Ballinger, was organized and sent to Richmond armed with a requisition for heavy ordnance signed by Colonel Earl Van Dorn.

In Richmond, Ballinger's party obtained some guns, but were told that they would have to get carriages on which to mount the weapons in New Orleans. The trip from Richmond back to New Orleans and then to Galveston turned out to be an ordeal. Bad weather and even worse roads combined to make the transportation of this artillery almost impossible. Ballinger did not return to Galveston until October of 1861, and the guns themselves did not reach the city until the first part of the following year.[27]

The bombardment at the South Battery on August 3, 1861, brought home to Galvestonians the grim reality of the war and initiated a general exodus among citizens and business owners that intensified as it became increasingly clear that the island was a serious Union military target. Many citizens and businesses, including Galveston's principal newspaper, fled to Houston for the duration of the conflict.

Despite the drama of this opening salvo, as the months went by, the blockade began to assume an almost routine character. To break up the monotony, the Union seamen looked forward to the diversion offered by the occasional chase and capture of vessels attempting to run the blockade. Some captures were more challenging than others. On September 11, 1861, for example, a schooner named the *Soledad Cos*, flying the Mexican flag, was intercepted trying to enter Galveston with a cargo of almost twenty tons of coffee.[28] A boarding party was sent to investigate the ship, but returned without much information. The officer leading the boarding party had been told that the vessel's captain was sick in his cabin with yellow fever and could not be disturbed for questioning. Terrified of being infected with this disease, the officer had ordered his men to expedite their return to the *South Carolina*.

Captain Alden was suspicious of the yellow fever story and returned to the captured ship himself with a canteen to investigate the situation and nurse the supposedly ill captain of the Mexican schooner. The ruse was quickly exposed. The captain of the mystery ship was in reality not sick at all; he was a mariner from Galveston whom the *South Carolina* had captured previously.

When carefully examined, the ship itself turned out to be the *Anna Taylor* of Galveston, which had slipped out the San Luis Pass at the other end of the island and gone to Tampico, Mexico. There, it had been the subject of a sham sale transaction and was given a new name. The alteration of the ship's old name had been done so crudely that it could still be read at one end of the ship. The captain of the captured vessel was so disheartened by the loss of his ship that he decided he would rather be sent to the North than face his angry creditors in the South.[29]

A Pessimistic Assessment

There is no doubt but that the defense of Galveston, or any other point on this coast, in the event of a formidable attack, is a very difficult if not an impossible matter; yet an effort must be made in that direction, and this place held as long as possible. It is a cotton port, and if in the possession of the enemy would be a nucleus for the disaffected, of which there are, I am sorry to say, many in this State.

GENERAL PAUL O. HEBERT,
November 15, 1861

Both Earl Van Dorn and Sidney Sherman had written candid letters to their superiors complaining about the inadequacy of the defenses at Galveston and other coastal areas of Texas. But these letters seem positively optimistic compared with the dismal assessments offered by the man who was next appointed to command the Confederate defenses of Texas in late August of 1861.

On the surface, General Paul Octave Hebert seemed to combine all the military and political skills that would be necessary to command a difficult district like Texas.[1] There was no question about his ability as a soldier. He had graduated first in his class at West Point in 1840 and had been brevetted colonel for his gallant military service in the Mexican War. He also had completed a remarkable political career. In 1852 he had been elected the youngest governor of the State of Louisiana. After leaving office, Hebert had used his considerable influence to help his former West Point classmate William T. Sherman become superintendent of the Louisiana Seminary of Learning and Military Academy (which later would become Louisiana State University), and was known as a vigorous supporter of improved transportation and public education.

To his credit, when Hebert received notice that he had been appointed to command the District of Texas, he went immediately to the heart of the problem at Galveston, where he made his temporary headquarters.[2] What he saw disturbed him greatly. Less than two weeks after his arrival, General Hebert reported to the Secretary of War in Richmond that "I find this coast in almost a defenseless state, and in the almost total want of proper works and armaments; the task of defending successfully any point against an attack of any magnitude amounts to a military impossibility." [3]

Hebert was not expected to handle this difficult assignment by himself. Colonel John C. Moore (who had been in charge of the South Battery during its encounter with the *South Carolina*) was formally placed in command of the defenses in the Galveston area.[4] In addition, Commander William W. Hunter, of the Confederate Navy, was assigned to the immediate command of the naval defenses (such as they were) of Galveston.[5] This division in the command structure between army and navy was to result in numerous conflicts and misunderstandings in the future.

On October 7, 1861, General Hebert issued a call to arms directed "To the Men of Texas." Making public his own private fears, he informed the population that it is "more than probable that your State will soon be invaded by the sea-coast," and asked them to organize at once into companies or battalions, clean off their muskets and knives, and be ready to march for the coast at a moment's notice.[6] A more dramatic announcement can hardly be imagined. Newspapers throughout Texas quickly joined in this urgent call for volunteers. But the truth was that because of supply difficulties, Hebert had no real idea what he would do with any additional troops who responded to this call.

A study by the acting chief quartermaster had suggested that while ten thousand troops could be stationed in the vicinity of Galveston, limitations on available provisions meant that only five thousand could be supported on the island itself.[7] In a letter to Richmond, Hebert confided that he would soon have these five thousand men in Galveston "not well armed and equipped, it is true, but as efficiently as circumstances permit."[8]

The more that General Hebert studied the problem of defending the island, the less he could see any solution that could practically be implemented with the resources at hand. This frustration was evident in a letter he wrote to his friend Judah Benjamin in Richmond:

> As an engineer, I can but too well appreciate the defenseless state of the sea-coast, see plainly what is needed generally, but of course can only deplore my inability to remedy the evil. I much fear that I have brought my little military reputation to an early grave.[9]

General Hebert saw one aspect of the military problem of defending Galveston Island very clearly. The city and port of Galveston were located at the far eastern end of the island. If an invading foe landed to the west of the city on the Gulf of Mexico side of the island and then crossed to the bay on the far side, they could seize the railroad bridge to the mainland and completely cut off the Confederate forces in the city (see Figure 2). Therefore, as Hebert perceived things, it was a matter of "military necessity" that any potential invading force be opposed either before it landed on the Gulf shore or not until it reached the mainland.[10]

The point where the invaders would attempt to land on Galveston Island was difficult to predict, and with such an extensive shoreline the Confederates lacked the men and guns to protect the entire coast and prevent a landing. As a result, General Hebert became increasingly convinced that it was pointless to defend the island. Instead, Hebert determined not to seriously oppose occupation of the island, but to instead prepare to defend the only connection to the mainland (the railroad bridge) with all available forces. To avoid the threat of being bottled up on the island, Hebert ordered the planking of the railroad bridge and authorized Commander Hunter to employ a number of ships to transfer the troops to a designated point on the mainland at the end of the bridge in the event it eventually became necessary to retreat from the island.[11]

It gradually became apparent to all that Hebert was preparing to abandon the island to the enemy with at most only a token fight. Understandably, this did not sit well with the city's inhabitants. An attorney employed in the paymaster's office recorded that "everybody is complaining here" and accurately predicted that "these war times will bring out strange things before it is over."[12]

The news that Hebert was preparing to evacuate Galveston reached Austin shortly after Francis R. Lubbock had been inaugurated as the first elected Confederate Governor of Texas on November 7, 1861. Having recently returned from Richmond, Virginia, and a visit with President Jefferson Davis, the new governor was understandably full of patriotic zeal for the cause of the new nation to which Texas had attached itself. This made the news from Galveston all the more disturbing to him.

Believing that General Hebert was not strong enough to make the necessary decisions alone, Lubbock wrote a letter on December 7, 1861, in which he offered to "share with you any responsibility you may be called upon to take in the delicate and arduous duties you are compelled daily to perform." The letter went on to carefully itemize the "delicate" duties that Lubbock believed might become necessary. He suggested that if Galveston could not be defended against enemy attack, as Hebert apparently believed, it should be "entirely destroyed," with the "stock, including horses, cattle, and sheep, to be driven from the island, and every spear of grass burned."[13]

Unlike Lubbock, former Governor (and now General) Hebert was not new to the political arena. He determined that the best course of action was to leak a copy of the new Texas governor's letter as a sort of trial balloon and evaluate the political fallout that followed. To Lubbock's chagrin, therefore, Hebert promptly let it be known to the citizens of Galveston that their governor had recommended the burning of their city. As might be imagined, this interpretation of military necessity was not a popular concept among Galvestonians, and they expressed strong reservations about the wisdom of such a policy.

On December 16, 1861, Mayor Thomas Joseph of Galveston wrote to Governor Lubbock and informed him that the citizens of the city had learned that he had recommended the burning of their city. This, the mayor explained with considerable restraint and diplomacy, had "attracted public attention," causing the citizens to seek clarification of the precise circumstances under which their city would be destroyed.[14]

Governor Lubbock wrote back to Mayor Joseph, clarifying that he had not "ordered" the destruction of Galveston in his letter to General Hebert. Instead, Lubbock explained, he had merely "assured [the general] that, if he deemed the destruction of Galveston a great military necessity, [Lubbock] would most cheerfully share with him any responsibility taken in the premises." A modern politician would almost certainly have softened the tone of his opinion in response to the concerns expressed by some of the most influential citizens of the state. But Lubbock was a man of remarkable conviction, and he did not hesitate to confirm his determination in the strongest possible language:

> Nothing but considerations of great military necessity would cause me to see one stone or plank from the many beautiful buildings that adorn this, our lovely island city, removed from its proper place; but I will repeat what I have said in substance to General Hebert, that I would rather see the city one blackened ruin than that a miserable, fanatical, abolition horde should be permitted to occupy it, gloating over their gains and laughing to scorn our abandonment of so important a strategic point.[15]

In closing, the governor promised to visit Galveston when circumstances permitted to make any other explanation of his views that the people deemed necessary, and was as good as his word.

In March 1862, Lubbock came to the East Gallery of Galveston's Tremont House Hotel and explained to an understandably apprehensive audience that he had not meant to dictate military policy in what the press referred to as his "burning letter" to General Hebert, but had merely intended to confirm the state's stalwart resolve not to furnish aid to a potentially destructive invading foe.[16] Although there is no record of three cheers being given at the conclusion of Lubbock's 1862 Tremont speech, as there had been following Sam Houston's speech there the year before, the governor pronounced himself satisfied with his reception. Galvestonians evidently did not hold a grudge either, since Lubbock lived in Galveston for a time following the end of the war and served as tax collector.

As 1861 drew to a close, the Confederate soldiers assigned to the defenses of Galveston began to realize that this duty would not be completed as quickly as they had first supposed. They began looking for things to do to help them pass the time. Some soldiers learned how to make do with inadequate rations. David Kennard proudly informed his parents in a letter home that he had "lernt [sic] how to make potato coffee and it is the next best thing to coffee that I have ever drank." [17]

To amuse himself, Private Charlie Collings went down to the railroad station to watch the civilians depart with their belongings. In a letter home, he recorded witnessing an elderly French priest use profanity to persuade several nuns to get off an overloaded train.[18] Collings also observed strange rockets and signals at night that he could not explain. He concluded ominously that "there can be no doubt that there is traitors amongst us." [19]

In the fashion of military men throughout the ages, the Confederate defenders of Galveston expended their pay (on the rare occasions when they received it) in less than virtuous pursuits. Collings recorded on the last day of 1861 that "the boys were paid off late yesterday and as might be expected they were going [at] it with a rush — some were gambling — some drunk — others were off downtown, etc. The guard house is full and more coming." [20]

Thomas Chubb and the *Royal Yacht*

*[Thomas Chubb's] life was a remarkably eventful one and
his biography would read like a romance. . . . A recital of the eventful life
of Thomas Chubb would be a part and parcel of the early history of Texas.*

Galveston Daily News, August 27, 1890

One of the most interesting characters in Civil War Galveston was Thomas Chubb. Born in the Boston area, Chubb became involved in the profitable African slave trade in the 1830's. It is not clear that Chubb limited his slaving activities to Africa, however. Disquieting rumors persisted that he had once hired a crew of free blacks in Boston and then sold them into slavery when he arrived in Texas.[1]

In any event, when Chubb became aware of the commercial opportunities created by the Texas Revolution, he put together a cargo of arms and ammunition and sailed for Texas. Part of the gunpowder that was used by Sam Houston's army at San Jacinto probably came from Chubb's cargo. Chubb and Houston emerged from the Texas Revolution as friends.

Not content with a seafaring career, Chubb at one time helped build a theater. He later owned a large circus that traveled throughout the South.[2] But the lure of the sea proved too strong for him. Settling in Galveston, Chubb resumed his career in the merchant marine service.

When the Civil War broke out, Chubb placed himself and his schooner *Royal Yacht* at the service of the Confederacy. Captain Chubb and the *Yacht* first saw service assisting Colonel Van Dorn in the operations around Indianola, after which he was officially commended for providing "material service."[3] Buoyed by this success, he then added a small cannon to the *Yacht* and began policing Galveston Bay.

On July 2, 1861, when the Union gunboat *South Carolina* arrived to initiate the blockade, Chubb and the *Royal Yacht* were sent out under a white flag of truce to meet with the captain of that vessel and determine his intentions.[4] Finally, on October 10, 1861, Chubb, his vessel, and his crew of fourteen men were formally chartered by the Confederacy for a charter fee of $1,350 per month.[5]

The *South Carolina* was relieved of blockade duty by the U.S. Frigate *Santee* on September 17, 1861. To the *Santee* were transferred all of the essential provisions: twenty-three thousand pounds of bread, seventy-five barrels of salt provisions, and twenty-five barrels of whiskey.[6] The captain of the *Santee*, Henry Eagle, was both bold and experienced. Of Irish descent, he had served in the U.S. Navy since 1818, and had made one of the first naval attacks of the war when he helped silence the guns at Sewell's Battery, Virginia, in May 1861.[7] Eagle arrived in Galveston a few months later determined to repeat his success and capture as many ships as possible.

Eagle was not hesitant to take chances in order to make the blockade more effective. On October 27, 1861, he seized the brig *Delta*, which was flying the British flag, and sent it to New York as a prize. He concluded that despite its display of a foreign flag, the vessel's registration was not in legal form and that it intended to run the blockade.[8]

Unlike his predecessor at the Galveston blockading station, Captain Eagle was not content to wait for blockade-running ships to fall into his clutches. He became convinced that a small force could enter Galveston Harbor at night and do serious damage to the Rebel ships anchored there. Eagle's plan was put to the test on November 7, 1861, about two months following the *Santee*'s arrival, when a daring night raid was conducted under the command of a thirty-three-year-old Kentuckian, Lieutenant James Jouett.[9]

Jouett entered Galveston Harbor for the purpose of capturing or destroying the Confederate steamer *General Rusk,* and when this objective proved unobtainable, ended up seizing the crew of the schooner *Royal Yacht.* At the time, only a brief and generally complimentary account of the incident was transmitted to Washington. A more complete picture of what happened during this raid did not surface until Jouett broke his silence and submitted a supplemental report in 1879, eighteen years later.[10]

It is always dangerous to rely on postwar accounts — particularly reports written so long after the fact — to fill in the details of the historical record. Such a course seems particularly treacherous when the postwar accounts make those who provide them seem almost superhuman, while everyone else comes across as nothing more than bumbling cowards. There are enough corroborating details in Jouett's story, however, to make his account more credible than might ordinarily be the case with such a report. In any event, it is such an interesting story that it is worth repeating. The following account of Jouett's expedition assumes the accuracy of its leader's unusual supplemental postwar report, adding some details that can be gleaned from Confederate reports of this same embarrassing incident.

Late on the night of November 7, 1861, Jouett's expedition, consisting of two launches and about forty volunteers, left the *Santee* and headed for Galveston Harbor. Captain Eagle's written orders had directed the raiders to capture the *Yacht* and to use their discretion in regard to making an attempt on the *Rusk*, which was a much larger and more closely guarded ship.[11] Jouett, however, saw this as a chance to do some real damage to the enemy and was determined to capture or destroy the *Rusk* if at all possible.

The first launch in the raiding party was commanded by Lieutenant Jouett, assisted by Gunner William W. Carter. Lieutenant John Mitchell was placed in charge of the second launch. One of the launches had a twelve-pound howitzer. Both boats, however, were supplied with a wide variety of shells, fuses, and incendiary devices that could be used to cripple or destroy any ships that might be boarded.

It was a dark and somewhat "squally" night, and the *Royal Yacht* was anchored at its usual spot on scout duty, guarding the entrance to Galveston Harbor near Bolivar Point.[12] The *General Rusk* was anchored off Pelican Spit, closer to the island and about two miles away. Things went well for the Union expedition at first. The launches, which had left the *Santee* at about 11:40 P.M., took a circuitous route around the *Yacht* and were approaching the *Rusk* without any alarm having been given. Suddenly Jouett's launch grounded on a shoal or spit. Before any warning could be given, the second launch ran into the first boat, breaking a number of oars and causing a loud noise that alerted the Confederate sentries to the raiders' presence.[13]

Jouett's orders specified that he was to return immediately if any alarm was given, so he reluctantly abandoned the attack on the *Rusk* and ordered his men to row back toward their secondary target, the *Royal Yacht*. By this time it was about 2:40 A.M. With the aid of an outgoing tide, Jouett's boats succeeded in reaching the Rebel schooner within a few minutes. Gunner Carter was ordered to fire his gun as the launch approached, but the primer turned out to be damp and the gun failed to fire.

Just as his launch reached the *Yacht* and Jouett was getting ready to attempt to board, the gunner finally succeeded in correcting the problem and fired a shot that he believed pierced the Confederate ship beneath the water line. The recoil, however, pushed the launch a long way back from the schooner and frustrated the initial boarding attempt. In fact, the only man who was prepared for the gun's firing and managed to keep his footing was the gunner himself, who demonstrated great dexterity (and questionable judgment) by leaping up on the deck of the *Yacht* at the same time that he fired his gun.

Since all hope of surprise was now lost, many of Jouett's men began firing their revolvers in the general direction of the *Yacht* while others rowed as hard as they could to get the launch back to where the schooner could again be boarded. Meanwhile, Gunner Carter, stranded on the *Yacht*, hid behind some vertical timbers on the ship's deck. He occasionally fired his revolvers at the members of the night watch on board the *Yacht*, who were themselves busy firing at the shapes only dimly visible on the water below them.

George Bell, the pilot of Jouett's launch, was mortally wounded by a Confederate shot as he tried to swing a grapnel onto the deck of the *Yacht*. As he fell, however, he called out, "Oh Mr. Jouett, they are killing us from the other boat." To his horror, Jouett discovered that Bell was right. Instead of going to the starboard side as they had been directed, the second Union launch had mistakenly gone to the port side and was unknowingly firing into the first launch from only twenty yards away. Jouett yelled at the other launch to cease firing, but could not make himself heard over the noise.

Leaving only four oarsmen to pull the boat back toward the Rebel schooner, Jouett made all the rest of his men lie down in the bottom of the launch to avoid any further injuries from "friendly fire." As the men rowed and ducked, Jouett worried about the fate of Gunner Carter, who had been left alone on the Rebel ship. Finally, after what must have seemed like an eternity, the launch again reached the bow of the *Yacht* and Jouett hauled himself on board.

Yelling down to his men to hurry up and board, Jouett had just turned around to go to the gunner's aid when he was pierced through the arm and side by a boarding pike held by a member of the *Yacht*'s crew who had braced himself in a cabin hatchway. The Confederate seaman tried to twist the pike and throw Jouett overboard, but the pike broke and Jouett disabled his unfortunate assailant by striking him on the head with one of the broken pieces. He then raced to the aid of Gunner Carter, who he discovered was bleeding from a minor wound in the arm, but was otherwise uninjured.

Although Jouett was not entirely aware of the fact, he had caught most of the *Yacht*'s crew unarmed and sleeping below deck. This was not as big an advantage as it might seem, because he lacked sufficient time to conduct any systematic search below deck. Jouett knew that the noise of this engagement would soon attract Confederate reinforcements from the island and that there was not a minute to lose. Hurrying over to the schooner's pivot gun, he tried to light a match to set the gun mount on fire. But by this time, Jouett had lost so much blood from his pike wound that he could not accomplish even this simple task. He felt himself going to sleep from loss of blood, and twisted his shirt tightly to cut down on the bleeding from the wound in his side.

When he recovered enough to again focus on the situation, Jouett observed the impetuous Gunner Carter standing in front of the main hatch with a revolver in each hand. Stepping past him, Jouett yelled down the hatch for the Confederates to come up on deck and surrender. Some of the *Yacht*'s crew were apparently pretending to be asleep, and the remainder did not consider it a good idea to face an unknown foe on deck at night when peremptorily instructed by a strange voice to do so. When the Rebels below deck did not respond to his order, Jouett decided to go down after them. The other members of his crew declined to participate in the search. They had apparently evaluated the situation for themselves and had concluded that going down the hatch of an unfamiliar enemy vessel in the darkness was a very poor idea.

Jouett went down the ladder by himself and had come across a group of potential prisoners when he heard a shout on the deck above him commanding his men to retreat. Alarmed by this development, and knowing that he had given no such order, Jouett raced up to the deck and was surprised to see that all of the members of his boarding party except Carter were in the launch and preparing to leave. Directing Carter to keep a gun trained on the two prisoners who had by this time reached the deck from below, Jouett leaped off the deck of the *Yacht* into his boat and used the flat of his cutlass to berate and beat his men until they again fastened the launch to the Rebel ship and resumed their duties on the deck of the *Yacht*.

Jouett had no sooner gone down the ladder and again reached his intended prisoners below deck when he heard an unknown voice yell "*Santee*," the agreed upon signal for a general retreat. Once again, the wounded and bleeding lieutenant was forced to scramble up to the deck to learn what had happened to his men. This time, however, he was not physically able to reach the launch in time to prevent its departure. By the time he reached the rail, the launch was almost fifty yards away and headed back in the general direction of the *Santee*, leaving the gunner and Jouett as the only Union men on board the Rebel schooner. With a sinking feeling in their hearts, Jouett and Carter could do nothing but scream curses, threats, and taunts of cowardice as they watched their crew depart in the boat. Amazingly, these threatening words had their intended effect, and after a brief pause the launch turned around and came back.

Because Jouett was by this time physically unable to make the trip below deck again, Carter went below and used his revolvers to persuade most of the remaining Rebel prisoners to come up on deck. Only Captain Chubb and a couple of other recalcitrant members of his crew refused to come up and be captured. Knowing that time was growing very short, Jouett then employed a clever ruse. Warning that he was throwing down a lighted shell, Jouett instead lighted and tossed down a "fireball," a nonexplosive incendiary device that caused a great deal of smoke. The trick worked exactly as planned and Chubb and the rest of his men sprang to the deck where they were quickly captured. Jouett wasted no time in setting the *Yacht* on fire, seizing its colors, and heading off for the *Santee* with his prisoners.

It was only after they had left the *Royal Yacht* burning that Jouett could afford to count his losses and evaluate what he had achieved. His pilot had been killed and five other men besides himself were wounded (one of whom died later the next day).[14] But he had captured the entire crew of the *Yacht* (thirteen men) and disabled that vessel. Moreover, he had accomplished all this without the aid of the other launch, which after mistakenly firing on Jouett's boat, had apparently headed back to the safety of the *Santee*.

The trip back to the *Santee* was a long and difficult affair, crowded as the crew was by wounded men and prisoners. At one point in the arduous journey, Captain Chubb turned to the wounded lieutenant and paid him a sincere (and customarily profane) compliment, saying, "I don't know who you are, but d——n me if you ain't a brave fellow, deserted twice by all your crew, and yet got the vessel! You are a man!"

Captain Eagle did not display the lights and rockets that Jouett had requested during the planning of the mission — he said later that he did not want to distract the men from their work. This made the blockading Union vessel virtually impossible to locate until daylight began to break. At about 6:15 A.M., Jouett's exhausted crew finally pulled the launch alongside the now visible *Santee* and Jouett's ordeal ended. As soon as he stepped onto the deck he promptly fainted and was carried below.

Jouett recovered quickly to find that his daring exploit had made him one of the early naval heroes of the war. The commander of the Gulf Blockading Squadron wrote a public letter of commendation for the participants in the raid, which he ordered to be read on the quarterdeck of every ship in the squadron.[15] The Secretary of the Navy, Gideon Welles, also reacted with enthusiasm to reports of the action:

The Department can not in too high terms express its admiration of the daring and successful exploit of Lieutenant Jouett and the officers and seamen under his command. The capture of a schooner, well armed and manned, and with every advantage of resistance, after a desperate encounter, speaks well for the intrepidity and bravery of the captors.[16]

Jouett must have been amused by the secretary's reference to the presumed bravery of his men. Even better than the secretary's praise, however, was an order Jouett soon received detaching him from the *Santee* and directing him to proceed to New York, where he was given his own ship to command. Jouett went on to have a distinguished career in the Navy, playing an important part in the Union invasion of Mobile Bay and eventually rising to the rank of rear admiral in 1886.[17]

General Hebert's reaction to the *Royal Yacht* incident was profound embarrassment, followed by an immediate attempt to shift the blame. Commander Hunter of the Confederate Navy received instructions from Hebert to make a specific report stating whether there was evidence that resistance had been made by the *Yacht*'s crew and whether the capture was the "result of negligence" or instead merely the "want of proper vigilance."[18] Hunter could report only that since the *Yacht* had been assigned the duty of warning of enemy approach it had, by definition, failed in that duty when the ship itself was captured without giving any advance signal. He also reported that the vessel showed evidence of a significant struggle, including thirty-seven musket ball holes, a broken pike, and a variety of U.S. Navy shells and weapons.[19]

The *Royal Yacht* had been left in flames, and the Union forces assumed that it had been destroyed. But despite a great deal of damage, the vessel survived. The *General Rusk* arrived just in time for its uncommonly brave commanding officer (Leon Smith) to put out the fire before it burned through the chest holding the ship's ammunition.[20]

As for the crew of the *Yacht*, they were initially placed in double irons on board the *Santee*.[21] Chubb was taken to New York, where he was imprisoned at Fort Lafayette. At first, he was condemned as a pirate and it appeared that he might be executed. Through diplomatic channels, the Confederate government notified the Union authorities that it would retaliate against Union prisoners if Chubb were killed. As a result of this threat, Chubb was eventually exchanged.[22] Upon Chubb's return to Galveston in the spring of 1862, he was presented with a new six-pounder cannon for the *Royal Yacht* and awarded the courtesy title of "Commodore." The *Royal Yacht* was then restored to active condition under his careful supervision.[23]

Chubb was never afflicted by the vice of false modesty, and his imprisonment had certainly not taught him humility. After having returned from captivity only about a week earlier, the Commodore delivered a speech in front of the Tremont House Hotel in which he claimed that he and the brave crew of the *Royal Yacht* had killed eight members of the Union boarding party and wounded seven more during their desperate and heroic defense of that vessel. His experience in Northern prisons, he reported to the assembled audience, had convinced him beyond doubt that the Yankees were "moving Heaven & Earth for our subjugation." [24]

"Commodore" Chubb again became chief of the harbor police and under flags of truce resumed his visits to the Union fleet during the negotiations preceding the Union capture of Galveston in October 1862. The blockaders were surprised to see Chubb and his vessel reappear and greeted him with astonished comments such as "Why, there's Captain Chubb!" and "Yes, this is Captain Chubb, that was hung for a pirate; and this [pointing to the schooner] is the *Royal Yacht*, that was burned and sunk, all as good as new!" [25]

Despite its seemingly miraculous recovery in 1861, bad luck seemed to follow in the wake of the *Royal Yacht* for the remainder of its military career. Although it sailed from Houston on New Year's Eve 1863 as part of the improvised Confederate armada that was to be victorious at the Battle of Galveston, the *Royal Yacht* ran aground on Red Fish Reef and played no part in the fighting. [26]

Commodore Chubb was remembered by the Union soldiers and sailors whom he encountered primarily for his rapid and profane manner of speech. A sailor on the *South Carolina* wrote in 1861 that Chubb "can talk more in 5 minutes than any man or woman I ever heard could in 5 hours." [27] A member of the Forty-Second Massachusetts Regiment, which Chubb visited frequently after its capture at the Battle of Galveston, recalled that the Commodore "was much given to boasting, and could utter more oaths in one sentence than any man the prisoners ever heard." [28]

Later in the war, Chubb was placed in charge of a Confederate navy yard at Goose Creek near the upper part of Galveston Bay. In the summer of 1864, something called a "torpedo boat" was being constructed under Chubb's supervision to attack the blockading Union fleet. Because of the scarcity of necessary materials, the war ended before this curious vessel could be completed. [29]

The Threat of Bombardment

It was finally discovered that the only object of the [bombardment]
threat was to frighten the people into a surrender of the city without a fight;
and not being able to accomplish this, the blockaders have remained very quiet
ever since. However, the citizens suffered almost as much from the threat
itself as they would have done from the execution, while the enemy have
doubtless suffered far less. It was, indeed, a cheap way of inflicting
injury upon us, though they accomplished nothing for themselves.

WILLARD RICHARDSON,
Owner, *Galveston News*

As the new year of 1862 dawned, the situation in Galveston did not look promising. The invasion of Galveston Harbor and the capture of the crew of the *Royal Yacht* two months before had demonstrated beyond question that the island was not adequately defended. The artillery that had been requisitioned had not all arrived, and the experimental attempt to manufacture some artillery locally had been put on hold when two of the new guns cast in Galveston exploded during a firing test.[1]

The frantic sense of insecurity manifested by General Hebert in his earlier reports to Richmond was now shared by the general population. The feeling of invulnerability that had characterized public rhetoric at the beginning of the war had gradually disappeared, to be replaced by feelings of helplessness and resignation. After reading a particularly discouraging newspaper report, Captain Elijah Petty wrote to his daughter that "It seems now that we cant whip any thing and if every Department of our Government is as weakly governed as this I do not wonder at our mishaps and defeats for I do tell you that there is not enough energy here [in Galveston] to pull a setting goose off of her nest nor honesty enough to save even a pound of pickled beef."[2]

Because they lacked confidence in the military's desire and ability to make an effective defense of the island, civilians continued their exodus to the interior at a rapid pace. Every train and steamboat to Houston was loaded to capacity with citizens and their belongings.[3] In early January, William Pitt

Ballinger reported from Houston that many former island residents were now living there, some in "miserable shanties." He lamented after a visit to the island that "Galveston has the most abandoned & desolate appearance that can be conceived. I felt relieved to get away. It was positively painful."[4] As bad as conditions on the island seemed during Ballinger's visit, however, they were soon destined to get even worse.

Events were coming together in such a fashion that Union attention was to be drawn to Galveston at the very moment that Confederate attention and resources were to be diverted elsewhere. As is usually the case, economics played an important part in causing these pressures. Commercial interests in New England had argued since the outset of the war for the occupation of the Gulf Coast of Texas as a means of acquiring access to the cotton that their mills needed to function.[5] Even more importantly, these business interests had political allies in high places.

Governor John Andrew of Massachusetts, for example, had written to Assistant Secretary of the Navy Fox in November 1861 contending that the "next demonstration" should be made upon the coast of Texas, arguing that this would provide a "way out for cotton." The governor observed that Galveston was only six hundred miles from Lawrence, Kansas, and Saint Joseph, Missouri, and that a railroad connecting these places would isolate the cotton states and "flank the whole rebellion."[6] The military was not unaware of these political and economic concerns. In the orders issued to General Benjamin Butler concerning the attack that was being planned on New Orleans, Butler was given the not so subtle hint that "a feint on Galveston" might facilitate the capture of the city.[7]

The occupation of Galveston also became increasingly important to the Union as a means of enforcing the blockade. A conference for the consideration of measures for effectively blockading the Gulf Coast had concluded as early as September 1861 that cutting off commerce to the Island City was critical, noting that an "efficient blockade of Galveston is, in fact, the blockade of the coast of Texas."[8]

In order to devote more attention to the western part of the Gulf of Mexico, the U.S. Navy divided its blockading forces into separate western and eastern components. David Glasgow Farragut was put in command of the West Gulf Blockading Squadron, which was assigned to blockade a vast territory extending from the western part of Florida to the Rio Grande.[9] The adopted brother of Commander David Dixon Porter, Farragut was over sixty years old, with naval experience stretching back to the War of 1812.[10] Despite the fact that he was a Southerner by birth, Farragut was fiercely devoted to the Union. When Confederate sympathizers had tried to convince him to join their cause, he had flatly refused, warning: "Mind what I tell you: You fellows will catch the devil before you get through with this business."[11]

When he left the North for the Gulf of Mexico, Farragut was well briefed on his new assignment. He had every intention, as part of that assignment, of occupying Galveston as soon as possible. On March 12, 1862, shortly after he had reached his new squadron, Farragut wrote confidently to Captain Eagle of the *Santee*, assuring him that "Galveston will be looked to at my earliest convenience." In the meantime, Farragut said, he did not wish Eagle "to either burn or fire on the town unless they fire on you first, but do not hesitate to return the fire for fear of injuring the town."[12]

Unlike the Union Navy, which primarily for economic reasons was beginning to devote considerable attention to the island, the Confederate Army's high command was reaching the conclusion that Galveston needed to be stripped of its defenses and troops in order to support the war effort in other states. On February 24, 1862, Secretary of War Judah Benjamin wrote to General Hebert, explaining that due to the "recent disaster in Tennessee," he was instructing Hebert to send to Arkansas all of the troops in his command except those absolutely necessary to man the batteries. "No invasion of Texas is deemed probable," Benjamin noted, but if it does occur, "its effects must be hazarded."[13] As Benjamin stated several weeks later in a letter to Governor Lubbock on this same subject, the Confederacy "must leave the coast exposed as the least of the two evils and strike heavy blows at [Union] armies in the interior."[14]

Recognizing the increasing weakness of the city's defenses as troops and arms were diverted to the interior, the Confederate commander of the island began making contingency plans for its evacuation. Battery commanders were instructed that if the enemy should try to take the island by force it would probably be necessary for them to spike their guns, destroy all military equipment that could not easily be transported, and fall back to the railroad depot.[15]

Sensing an opportunity, and being an aggressive man by nature, Captain Eagle of the *Santee* decided to attempt a bold bluff. To give credit where it is due, this bluff had not been entirely Eagle's own idea. In a cheerful note on May 2, 1862, Commander Farragut had advised Eagle that, in light of the surrender of New Orleans, it "would be well to demand the surrender of Galveston. Tell them it is only a matter of time, and I will be along your way soon."[16] Adding his own definition of "soon," on May 17, 1862, Eagle sent the following message ashore to the commander of the Confederate forces:

In a few days the naval and land forces of the United States Government will appear off the town of Galveston to enforce its surrender. To prevent the effusion of blood and destruction of property which would result from the bombardment of your town I hereby demand the surrender of the place, with its fortifications and all batteries in its vicinity, with all arms and munitions of war. I trust you will comply with this humane demand.[17]

Colonel Joseph Cook, who was in charge of the Confederate defenses on the island at this time, was instructed by General Hebert to stall for time while evacuating and spiking some of the more exposed batteries.[18] Thus, entirely by accident, Cook hit upon the perfect reply. He proposed sending a note back to Captain Eagle informing him that "whenever the naval and land forces of the United States shall make their appearance off Galveston I shall answer their demand." [19] With Hebert's approval, the reply was sent and Captain Eagle's bluff was effectively called.

Eagle, however, did not give up so easily. He decided to take his threat to the next level and notified the foreign consuls that since his demand for surrender had been refused by the military authorities, he had no choice but to give them four days to remove their families and property from the city. After this deadline, Eagle warned, "the bombardment will commence at my earliest convenience." [20]

This threat had its intended effect on the consuls. To their frantic request that he designate some easily recognized point of refuge (such as the Ursuline Convent) that would not be bombarded, Eagle responded:

No person can deplore more than myself the misery that would result from the bombardment . . . ; yet it is a duty that will become necessary to enforce [the city's] surrender. It is not in my power to give you any assurance of security during the bombardment, for it is impossible to tell what direction the shot and shell will take.[21]

Although the remaining residents of the island were understandably in a panic due to the threatening tone of Eagle's communications, General Hebert (who was in Houston) was not convinced of the sincerity of that threat. In a dispatch to Colonel Cook in Galveston, he reiterated that there was to be no surrender under any circumstances. As a former politician, however, Hebert was careful to leave himself a way out, admitting that although the city would never be surrendered, there was still the possibility that there might be "an abandonment in [the] face of a superior force." [22]

To respond to the emergency, Hebert issued a controversial proclamation placing a number of counties, including Galveston, under martial law. He also ordered all excess provisions removed to the mainland, which caused a problem that had not been anticipated. Part of Hebert's order required excess cattle and horses to be either removed to the mainland or destroyed.[23] Although such an order must have sounded like a wise precaution when it was drafted in Houston, it proved very difficult to implement as a practical matter. As the commander of the state militia on the island complained to his superiors in Austin, the "coast guard of 25 men cannot get the cattle off the island, it is a physical impossibility, the [railroad] bridge is in constant use by trains, no transportation can be had for them, and they cannot be crossed over the bay."[24]

Fortunately for the residents of Galveston, not to mention the cattle, the twenty-third of May (Eagle's deadline) came and went without the occurrence of the threatened bombardment. Provost Marshal J. C. Massie continued the movement of excess supplies and stock off the island, however, and soon was able to boast to a newspaper that "after a few more days the enemy can have all that is left; and if they can make much use of it, they may have my head for a football."[25]

Although Captain Eagle's attempt to secure the surrender of Galveston without a shot had not succeeded, it had come close enough to persuade him that the city would be abandoned if only a little more force could be displayed. On June 4, 1862, Eagle wrote to Commander Farragut and urged him to send three gunboats and one mortar boat, saying that with this added force "I will make the attempt to enforce [Galveston's] surrender, and think the town will be given up in preference to having it destroyed."[26] Farragut was occupied with other operations, however, and Eagle did not get the chance to test his theory.

The Union bombardment threat prevented any form of commerce from taking place. As one Confederate soldier observed, this was a great change from the port's former level of activity:

Two years ago this bay was almost covered with vessels of all shapes, sizes, colors and classes, with sails steam and oars: moving in every direction; now but two or three are seen lying at the wharves, or moving leisurely along. Now and then a steam boat moaningly whistles as if calling in dispair [sic] for its lost companions. . . . Now the wharves are vacant, and the streets almost deserted. . . . [A] few lounging soldiers and yawning shop keepers are found on the sidewalks, the former seeking to kill time instead of Yankees, and the latter waiting for an opportunity to *"fleece"* the needy customer.[27]

As the days following Eagle's deadline stretched into weeks, and then months, it became evident that the threatened bombardment and invasion were not imminent. Slowly, residents began to filter back into the city from which they had fled.[28] The rest of the summer of 1862 passed uneventfully, with the exception of a dispute between the state and Confederate authorities about whether some rope-making machinery should be removed to the interior.[29]

One other event of interest during this period between invasion threats concerned some unusual letters written by Galveston's French consul. Because it was an important port city, Galveston hosted representatives of all of the major (and many of the minor) European powers. As was not uncommon in those days, Benjamin Theron served on the island both as consul for France and vice-consul for Spain. In the middle of August he wrote two identical letters, addressing one to Sam Houston and the other to Governor Francis Lubbock.

Theron's letters requested each of the recipients to inform him "confidentially" whether they believed that Texas had acted wisely in joining the Confederacy. The letters further solicited an opinion on the question of whether the reestablishment of Texas as a republic would be in its best interests. Houston appears to have ignored the letter, but Lubbock prepared a reply firmly stating his opinion that Texas was better off in the Confederacy than as an independent entity.[30]

Governor Lubbock was highly suspicious of the Galveston consul's motives in writing this unusual letter and forwarded it to Jefferson Davis with a note warning of what he believed might be an "incipient intrigue." When essentially the same questions were later asked by a French consular official in Richmond, Judah Benjamin, by then secretary of state, became convinced that a French conspiracy to separate Texas was at work. He directed that Theron be expelled from the Confederacy. An explanation of Benjamin's expulsion order destined for France was intercepted by Union blockaders. Theron's letters, which were attached as part of the captured correspondence, then created a sensation when they were published in Northern newspapers.

Although Confederate officials in Richmond continued to insist that Theron must leave Galveston, the consul was well regarded by local Confederate officials, and they delayed implementing this directive. Pleading ill health and a series of other excuses, Theron managed to postpone his expulsion from the Confederate States until the order was rendered moot by his death in Galveston in 1864.[31]

With the threat of bombardment apparently removed for the time being, the only person whose morale did not improve was General Hebert. At the end of August 1862, he wrote perhaps his most discouraging letter yet to Governor Lubbock, complaining that orders from the Confederate War Department had operated to "paralyze my efforts and strip me of means of defense." Tired of raising regiments of troops that were then sent to other states, Hebert informed Lubbock that he was applying to go to Arkansas and command some of these regiments himself.[32] Lubbock and others familiar with the situation were not sorry to see him go.

Thomas North summarized the feelings of most Texans when he described the departing General Hebert in these unflattering terms:

He proved to be a man of no military force or practical genius, though a West Pointer, and had enjoyed the advantages of military associations in Europe, the reflex of which appeared rather to damage his usefulness than otherwise. He brought with him so much European red-tapeism, and being a constitutional ape, that he preferred red-top boots, and a greased rat-tail moustache . . . to the use of good practical sense. . . . Everybody became tired and disgusted with the General and his policy. He was too much of a military coxcomb to suit the ideas and ways of a pioneer country; besides, he was suspected of cowardice.[33]

Captured by Ferryboats

*You will proceed down the coast of Texas with the other vessels, keeping a
good lookout for vessels running the blockade, and whenever you think you can
enter the sounds on the coast and destroy the temporary defenses, you will do so and
gain the command of the inland navigation. Galveston appears to be the port
most likely for you to be able to enter, if the forts are not too formidable.*

REAR ADMIRAL DAVID G. FARRAGUT,
Orders to William B. Renshaw, September 19, 1862

In early October 1862, Commander William B. Renshaw arrived at the entrance to Galveston Bay with an unusual assortment of Union vessels. His
objective was the capture of Galveston. Captain Eagle had reported that
based on his experience threatening the city in May, it could be taken with
three gunboats and a mortar boat. But the *Santee* (Eagle's ship) was suffering from a "frightful" outbreak of scurvy and had to be sent home.[1] After
capturing the city of New Orleans and conducting a series of operations
around Vicksburg earlier in the year, Rear Admiral Farragut finally decided
that he could spare a portion of his "mortar flotilla" (Renshaw's force) to test
Eagle's idea and satisfy his previous pledge to pay Galveston a visit.

The unusual collection of ships under Renshaw's command had seen more
than its share of action. His flagship, the *Westfield*, and its sister ship, the
Clifton, were both large ferryboats that had been withdrawn from the Staten
Island run and sold to the U.S. Navy. Because these ferryboats were designed to carry heavy loads, yet operate in relatively shallow coastal waters,
they seemed to be perfect for operations along the Gulf Coast. This kind of
versatility did not come cheap, however. Cornelius Vanderbilt had sold the
Westfield, which was 215 feet long and had a displacement of 822 tons, to the
Navy for approximately $100,000.[2]

Also part of Renshaw's fleet was the *Owasco*, which had only been commissioned in January 1862. The *Owasco* was one of the "90-day gunboats,"
ships that had been ordered by the U.S. Navy as an emergency measure.
Often built of unseasoned timber because of time pressures, these ships
nevertheless were of great service to the Union war effort.[3]

The other large gunboat that accompanied Renshaw's expedition, the U.S.S. *Harriet Lane,* had a very distinguished service record. As one historian has commented: "For hard fighting, long and continuous service, and for variety of experience, perhaps no American war vessel can compare with the *Harriet Lane.*"[4] What is perhaps the most interesting thing about this ship is that most of this impressive experience was not gained in connection with the U.S. Navy.

In 1857 Congress approved funds for the construction of the first side-wheel steamship for the Revenue Cutter Service (today known as the Coast Guard), which is the oldest seagoing military service in the United States. The new ship was carefully designed to be one of the most advanced warships of its time.[5] Howell Cobb of Georgia, then secretary of the treasury and later a Confederate major general, christened this vessel the *Harriet Lane* in honor of the niece of President Buchanan who had served as official hostess during Buchanan's administration.

Immediately after its launch, the *Lane* was assigned to the difficult service of capturing slave ships and combating smuggling and piracy. But in 1858, when the U.S. Navy conducted a military expedition against Paraguay, the *Lane* turned in an excellent performance in the narrow and winding Paraguay River.[6] Then, in 1859, the *Harriet Lane* was ordered by Secretary Cobb to conduct a secret expedition to the waters around Galveston, "to aid in curbing the slave trade moving there."[7]

When it was not engaged in military operations or fighting the slave trade, this ship was also used for a wide variety of ceremonial duties. In 1860, for example, the *Lane* entertained a Japanese royal party and was later placed at the disposal of the Prince of Wales during his visit to America.[8] When war broke out the following year, the *Harriet Lane,* as the only side-wheel steamship in the Revenue Cutter Service, was once again summoned to assist the U.S. Navy.

On the evening of April 11, 1861, the *Lane* and several other ships arrived at the sand bar outside of Charleston Harbor. Their mission was to relieve the Union troops besieged in Fort Sumter. The steamer *Nashville* was spotted attempting to enter the harbor, and the captain of the *Lane* (at that time John Faunce) feared that it was bringing aid to the Rebel forces. He therefore ordered a shot fired across the *Nashville*'s bow to force it to stop and reveal its intentions. This shot is sometimes argued to have been the first shot of the Civil War.[9]

None of the ships in Renshaw's armada had an easy time getting to the Gulf of Mexico, where their primary wartime service was to be. After all, ferryboats were not constructed for the purpose of crossing great distances in the open ocean. Nevertheless, they proceeded to sea and, after no little difficulty, reached the Gulf Coast. As one naval history writer described the situation:

> Off they gamely waddled. Like the bee, which is held aerodynamically incapable of flight yet flies anyhow, the ferryboats did not understand that they could not go into the open ocean, and they steamed obliviously forth.[10]

Even the *Harriet Lane,* which unlike the ferryboats had been designed to function in the ocean, had difficulty reaching the South. In the fighting around Hatteras Inlet in August 1861, it had run aground and was nearly lost. In the passage shortly thereafter from Washington to Key West, a rifled shot from a Confederate battery had damaged its port wheel and wheelhouse.[11] Although this damage was easily repaired in Philadelphia, it did emphasize an area of vulnerability on this ship that would later play an important part in the ship's subsequent difficulties at Galveston.

During the naval operations that resulted in the capture of New Orleans, the *Harriet Lane* served as the flagship of David D. Porter, who commanded the Union mortar flotilla.[12] In addition to the *Lane,* the ships under his command in this flotilla included the *Owasco, Westfield,* and *Clifton.* In the spring of 1862, the first job assigned to the flotilla was to tow larger warships over the sand bars at the mouth of the Mississippi River, enabling Porter to boast that his vessels had "succeeded in getting over the bar the heaviest vessels that ever entered the Mississippi River."[13]

The mortar flotilla was next used in connection with the operations designed to capture New Orleans. Downriver from the city, two Confederate forts, Fort Jackson and Fort St. Philip, guarded the Mississippi River from opposite banks. The ferryboats were primarily used to tow a number of mortar schooners (floating batteries) into position to shell these forts. For five days, Porter's mortar schooners lofted shells at the forts to soften their defenses.

On the morning of April 24, 1862, while it was still dark, Farragut's squadron of gunboats passed the forts and, after defeating the Confederate naval forces, proceeded up the river to capture New Orleans. This left the still dangerous forts to be handled by Porter and his mortar fleet, which had stayed behind to accomplish this important task. Porter demanded the surrender of the forts, but his demand was refused.[14] He therefore resumed firing on them with his entire mortar fleet.

At midnight on April 28, 1862, a Confederate officer was brought to the *Harriet Lane* with news that the forts were finally ready to surrender.[15] The terms of capitulation were signed on board the *Harriet Lane,* with Commander Renshaw of the *Westfield* and Lieutenant Wainwright of the *Harriet Lane* serving as additional witnesses.[16] The signing of these terms was not without incident.

Admiral Porter and the Confederate and Union officers who were going to sign the capitulation were all sitting at a table below deck on board the *Harriet Lane* with the terms before them. Porter had signed the paper, as had Commander Renshaw of the *Westfield.* Lieutenant Wainwright of the *Harriet Lane* was about to sign, when he was suddenly called on deck by one of his officers. He returned almost immediately and informed the group of a dangerous new development.

One of the Confederate river defenses associated with the forts was an ironclad named the *Louisiana.* The engines on this vessel were so unsatisfactory that it had been anchored and was being used as a floating battery. What Wainwright had learned was that the *Louisiana* was now in flames and was drifting down the river toward the mortar flotilla. To make matters worse, there did not appear to be room for the flaming vessel to pass between or around the Union ships.

In an account written after the war, Porter described the events that followed this discovery:

> "This is sharp practice," I said to the Confederate officers, "but if you can stand the explosion when it comes, we can. We will go on and finish the capitulation. . . ." [The Confederate officers] coolly signed their names in as bold a hand as if they were not momentarily in danger of being blown up. Then we all sat quietly awaiting the result. In a few moments an explosion took place that fairly shook us all out of our seats and threw the *Harriet Lane* over on her side, but we finished the terms of capitulation. The *Louisiana* had blown up before reaching the flotilla.[17]

As later events would demonstrate, exploding ships seemed to be a hazard that afflicted Renshaw's mortar flotilla wherever it went.

After Porter and the *Harriet Lane* had taken a cruise to scout out possible avenues to attack Mobile, they accepted the surrender of Pensacola, Florida, and returned to the mortar flotilla on the Mississippi River.[18] The flotilla then went up the river and participated in an attack on the Vicksburg batteries. Flag Officer Farragut wrote to the Secretary of the Navy that the mortar squadron had "opened in fine style upon the enemy," and observed that only a small number of casualties had occurred on these ships as a result of what he termed "accidental shots." [19] Porter himself reported that a "kind Providence seems to look out for this little fleet." [20]

This "kind Providence" was tested on July 15, 1862, when the Confederate ironclad ram *Arkansas* entered the Mississippi River and steamed through the entire Union fleet, its iron casemate protecting it from the fire of numerous ships. One of the schooners in the mortar flotilla, the *Sidney C. Jones*, was lying in a defenseless position, having run aground several days before. Commander Renshaw of the *Westfield*, who was in temporary command of the flotilla, signaled the officer in charge of the stranded vessel to be ready to destroy it if the Confederate ram approached.

An artillery officer was brought on board the *Jones* to make the necessary preparations to blow the ship up if it became necessary. At this point there appears to have been some confusion, because as Renshaw was returning to see to the schooner's condition, it abruptly exploded. Although the two men responsible for the destruction of the *Jones* later claimed that Renshaw had ordered them to destroy her without any further signals or conditions, Renshaw denied these assertions. Claiming that he had merely ordered them to be ready to destroy the ship *if necessary*, Renshaw ordered that the men be sent home, and recommended their dismissal from the service. [21]

The operations that led to the capture of New Orleans and the assault on Vicksburg's batteries had been hard on the vessels comprising the mortar flotilla. Renshaw reported at the end of August that many of the flotilla's ships would require significant repairs before they would be in efficient service condition. In addition, he noted, the crews of all of the vessels were so "enervated by the climate and constant use of salt provisions" that they would need some time off with regular provisions before they would be ready for their next assignment. The *Westfield* alone, he observed, had some twenty cases of fever and twenty men suffering from scurvy. [22]

After receiving this kind of report, Farragut was at a loss regarding what to do with the mortar flotilla. Although they had originally been commanded by David Porter, they now appeared to be operating as a virtually autonomous unit. Farragut wrote to Washington for clarification of his authority and was told that Renshaw and the rest of the mortar squadron were his to command. [23] Still not entirely comfortable with this odd assortment of ships or its eccentric commander, however, Farragut decided to use them to pay the visit to Galveston he had long promised. After all, he must have reasoned, Captain Eagle of the *Santee* had assured him that such a force could easily take the city without a single shot being fired. Following a month's recuperation, Renshaw and his ships were ordered to Galveston.

Despite a great deal of initial confusion, the Union Navy's capture of Galveston went almost exactly as Eagle had predicted. At around 6:00 A.M. on October 4, 1862, the *Harriet Lane* was sent over the sand bar at the entrance to the harbor under a flag of truce.[24] A shot was fired from the Confederate fort at Fort Point, which guarded the entrance to Galveston's harbor, to draw the steamer to a halt until its purpose could be ascertained. Captain Jonathan Wainwright of the *Lane* sent a messenger to shore in a small boat to let the Confederate authorities know that he had an important message to deliver from the commander of the Union naval force. The Union messenger was assured that a proper representative would be summoned to receive it.

Since there was no boat at Fort Point, it became necessary for the Confederate representative to leave from the city. He was delayed by a series of problems and did not set sail from the dock until about 1:00 P.M. When the representative finally did leave, he was sent out in a small sailboat that seemed to have enormous problems making any progress toward the waiting Union ship. Angered at what he viewed as unjustified delay, Wainwright decided that no response was going to be forthcoming and turned around and went back to discuss the situation with the rest of the Union fleet.

Renshaw was not pleased that the *Lane* had sent a boat ashore, and was even more unhappy to learn that, having done so, Wainwright had not waited for the sailboat, which was still making its pitifully slow way across the bay flying what appeared to be a white flag. But Renshaw was also tired of wasting time; he got under way with his whole force to meet the boat. As might be expected, the Confederate fort at Fort Point, seeing the whole Union force converging on the small sailboat, became alarmed and opened fire.

Although the Confederate battery at Fort Point appeared formidable, it only had one real gun (a ten-inch columbiad), the rest being merely painted logs. The guns from the Union gunboats made quick work of disabling the one real piece of artillery in this fort. Then, in accordance with his previous orders, the Confederate battery commander spiked what was left of his gun and set the small barracks afire as he abandoned the fort.

Seeing this exchange of shot and shell, the Confederate representative in the sailboat, still flying the white flag, determined that this might not be the best time to receive the Federal message and turned back to port. The guns from the city were now firing at the Union ships also, but their shots fell far short. By now, Renshaw had become embarrassed at what he saw as a simple misunderstanding and gave the signal to cease firing. He then anchored and hoisted a white flag of truce. Almost immediately, the Confederate sailboat turned back around (again) and finally came alongside the *Westfield*.

Renshaw was not an easy man to get along with, and the day's events had tested his patience and made him even more direct than usual. He demanded the unconditional surrender of the city and said that he expected an immediate answer. His exact words, as reported to General Hebert in San Antonio, were that he would either "hoist the United States flag over the city of Galveston or over its ashes."[25]

At about 3:30 P.M., the truce boat returned to the city to give Colonel Cook the Union commander's message and obtain a response to Renshaw's demand. Based upon the report Renshaw had received as to Eagle's previous experience, and his assessment of the poor quality of the defenses he had so far encountered, the Union commander had every reason to believe that his demand would be accepted. He was therefore surprised when the truce boat returned (more quickly this time) and instead conveyed Colonel Cook's absolute refusal to surrender.

The Confederate messenger told Renshaw that there were women, children, and aliens in the city and argued that no bombardment should be commenced until these persons had all received an opportunity to leave the city. He also dropped vague hints about the presence of yellow fever in the city, something that greatly influenced Renshaw's decision not to immediately attempt to send marines to occupy the city as he had originally planned.

After a spirited argument about whose fault it would be if noncombatants were injured during a bombardment of the city, Renshaw finally agreed to allow a period of four days for evacuation. The agreement was expressly conditioned upon the Confederate commander's commitment not to use this period to increase the city's defenses. And here, on a day that had consisted of little else but a series of misunderstandings, occurred the greatest miscommunication of them all.

The Confederates felt safe in giving this last assurance since they had no intention of *increasing* the defenses of the city. To the contrary, the delay gave them the perfect opportunity to complete their withdrawal to the mainland. Colonel Xavier B. Debray had arrived in Galveston to take charge of the situation on October 5, 1862. He had concluded, as General Hebert had previously ordered in his contingency plans, that "Galveston can not be defended, and a fight in this city would be a useless braggadocio against forty guns, or about [that many], at 1 mile from the wharf."[26] Debray ordered

Colonel Cook to retreat to Virginia Point (on the mainland), taking with him as much in the way of military supplies as he reasonably could salvage.[27]

Colonel Cook implemented the instructions that he had been given with alacrity and was later able to report that in addition to moving all but one of the guns, "all machinery of any value was removed."[28] By the expiration of the four-day deadline, Cook had relocated from the island to Virginia Point all of his troops with the exception of a small force located at Eagle Grove, the fortification that defended the entrance to the railroad bridge that stretched from the island to the mainland.

Cook's efficiency in removing military property did not go unnoticed by the enemy. When Renshaw saw the Confederate batteries being relocated, he and his officers protested, arguing that the terms of the truce provided for maintenance of the *status quo*. Colonel Cook responded that his understanding of the agreement was that it prevented only increases in the city's defenses. Since the agreement was not in writing, and since Renshaw was still afraid of the danger of contracting yellow fever if he sent forces ashore to enforce his interpretation, the Union naval forces decided not to interfere with Cook's movements.

After Cook had completed his withdrawal operation, Colonel Debray inspected the Confederate defenses at and around Virginia Point and pronounced them to be generally adequate. He found only one serious defect. The fort at Eagle Grove had been designed in such a way that it was not protected from a surprise attack at night. Debray's mild rebuke to Cook that such an attack is "always disgraceful for a commander who did not prevent it" is ironic in light of later events in the Confederate recapture of Galveston.[29]

Colonel Cook had posted public notice of the four-day truce period (see Figure 4) and warned the citizens of Galveston to leave the island. In obedience, yet another general exodus began to Houston and other inland destinations. The situation turned chaotic at the railroad depot as train after train was loaded with women and children and their household effects. On October 6, 1862, two days into the truce, noted local physician Samuel B. Hurlbut became the only fatality associated with the Confederate evacuation and Union occupation of Galveston when he was killed while helping his family to board a train to Houston.

Private Thomas Stanley, a soldier who had made a reputation as a prize fighter prior to the war, got into a scuffle at the station with military authorities who were trying to arrest him. He drew a pistol and fired at his pursuers, missing all of them but striking the unfortunate Dr. Hurlbut (who

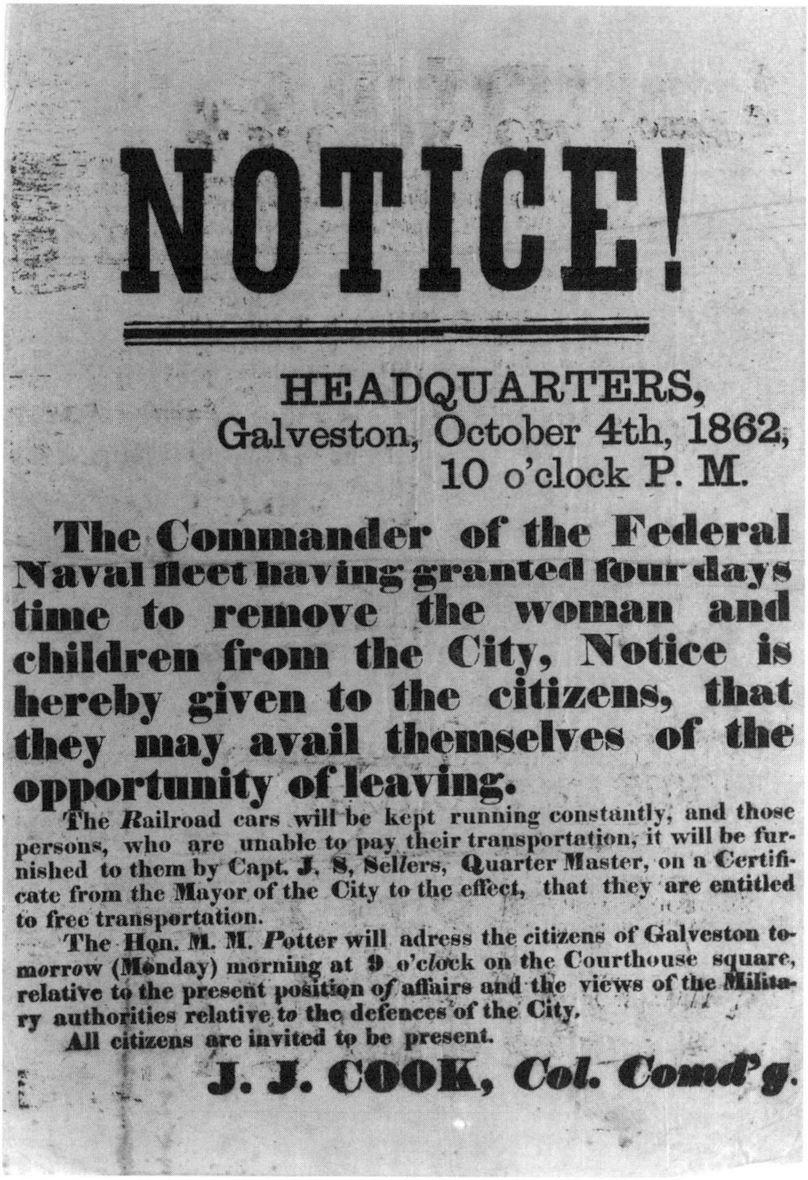

NOTICE!

HEADQUARTERS,
Galveston, October 4th, 1862,
10 o'clock P. M.

The Commander of the Federal Naval fleet having granted four days time to remove the woman and children from the City, Notice is hereby given to the citizens, that they may avail themselves of the opportunity of leaving.

The Railroad cars will be kept running constantly, and those persons, who are unable to pay their transportation, it will be furnished to them by Capt. J. S. Sellers, Quarter Master, on a Certificate from the Mayor of the City to the effect, that they are entitled to free transportation.

The Hon. M. M. Potter will adress the citizens of Galveston to-morrow (Monday) morning at 9 o'clock on the Courthouse square, relative to the present position of affairs and the views of the Military authorities relative to the defences of the City.

All citizens are invited to be present.

J. J. COOK, Col. Comd'g.

FIGURE 4. *Notice of four-day evacuation period dated October 4, 1862. Courtesy of Rosenberg Library, Galveston, Texas.*

was entering his carriage after placing his family on the train) in the back of the head with a fatal shot.

When Stanley was finally subdued, he was almost lynched on the spot by the angry crowd. The military authorities managed to spirit him off to Virginia Point, where he was closely confined.[30] Two days later, as the truce period expired, Dr. Hurlbut was buried with Masonic honors at the Trinity Episcopal Cemetery in a ceremony that was made even more dramatic by the fact that Union naval forces were entering the city at precisely the same time as Confederate members of the local Masonic lodge conducted the funeral service on the outskirts of town.[31]

A despondent William Pitt Ballinger wrote in his diary that it was a "black day in our history. Galveston is in the power of the enemy." Although there had been a lot of bold talk about making a stand in the city and opposing any landing by the Union forces, Ballinger recognized that such talk had been "all gas." Like many other island residents, Ballinger felt "deeply grieved and humiliated" by the fact that his city had been given up without any serious fight.[32]

As a Union marine described, the first destination of the Union occupying force in October 1862 was the Customhouse that had been completed just before the war:

We found the wharves of the town guarded by the firemen in full uniform, by orders of the Mayor, and on our landing they escorted us to the custom-house. The Mayor here received us, and expressed his pleasure at seeing the City about to pass into Union hands. He delivered the keys to Captain Wainwright, of the *Harriet Lane,* who immediately took possession of the building and proceeded to the roof with a proper guard and raised the flag. The battalion presented arms as the colors were flung to the breeze, and the crowd of spectators expressed their delight in various patriotic remarks. Altogether it was quite a gala occasion for the marines and sailors, and when we marched back to the boats nearly every one of our muskets was decorated with flowers, which the women and children gave to us. Of the people of Galveston we must say, that a more respectable and well-behaved set we have never seen. Not a single sentry had to be detailed to keep the crowd back from the line. The modest distance kept by the ladies showed their good breeding and the conduct of the numerous youngsters was a good example for the youth of northern cities.[33]

In a letter to Admiral Farragut notifying him of the city's abandonment, Commander Renshaw estimated that the Rebel force opposing him at

Virginia Point and Eagle Grove numbered up to about five thousand men (a considerable exaggeration). He suggested that his mortar schooner, and the rifled guns on the ferryboats, could now be used to support an infantry attack on the Confederate position, but only if the ships were first lightened as much as possible to avoid running aground.[34] In the event that the army could not spare the substantial infantry force that he anticipated would be required to overcome the Confederate position, Renshaw offered his opinion that two to three hundred men should be able to hold a credible position on the island.

On the Confederate side, Colonel Debray was worried about an entirely different plan of attack. What Debray was concerned about was not that the Union forces would assault Virginia Point directly (where he was comfortable with his fortified position), but that the enemy would simply bypass his position, making a landing at one of the many undefended portions of Galveston Bay or the river systems that emptied into it. Being cut off from Houston, the Confederate forces would then be forced to attempt to fight their way through, in all probability losing the precious guns that they had finally managed to assemble at Virginia Point.

Debray did not see any military value to the protection of Virginia Point, asking headquarters in San Antonio, "Is Virginia Point a strategic position worth keeping after Galveston has been evacuated, or should it be abandoned and our artillery be removed if the enemy gives time, to protect obstructions at the mouth of our rivers?"[35]

The response that Debray received from General Hebert to his inquiry about the importance of Virginia Point was far from comforting. A short note from headquarters advised that, upon reflection, the general now viewed Virginia Point also to be "as untenable as the island." Hebert's letter enclosed a two-sentence order from San Antonio dated November 3, 1862, directing Debray to take his guns and retreat toward Houston whenever he had reason to believe that an attack might be made on his line of communication with Houston.[36]

Dismayed by the pessimistic tone of this communication, Debray countered with a letter dated November 6, 1862, in which he proposed not only to hold Virginia Point (with the aid of some requested reinforcements), but to try to reoccupy Galveston.[37] But this was far too ambitious a gamble for the pessimistic Hebert. Debray's plan was rejected. Within a month, however, a new Confederate commander would arrive on the scene to whom such a proposal made sense.

The news that Galveston had been taken by the Federals without a fight was received with alarm by Governor Lubbock, who it will be remembered had recommended burning the city before surrendering it. By October 12, 1862, he was on the scene at Virginia Point, offering suggestions to both army and navy officers. Lubbock had little patience for military bureaucracy, particularly in such dire circumstances. After talking with Colonel Debray, he became concerned that the Confederates had virtually no naval forces to scout enemy positions and guard against troop movements by water. Lubbock decided to do what he could about this problem.

At the beginning of the war, the State of Texas had acquired the steamer *Bayou City*, which was captained by Henry Lubbock, the governor's brother. The problem with this ship was that it was poorly equipped and had an inadequate crew for serious military service. Not deterred by these obvious defects, the governor ordered the *Bayou City* to occupy a position where it could "watch the movements of the enemy." He directed Captain Lubbock to operate his ship in such a fashion that "your name and that of your vessel may be one of terror to the detested Yankees." After giving these instructions, the governor then sent a letter to Commander Hunter begging him to formally take the vessel into the Confederate naval service.[38]

Looking around for a crew and supplies for the *Bayou City*, Governor Lubbock discovered that the cutter *Dodge* (the first ship acquired by the Texas secessionists) was now lying in a decrepit condition in the San Jacinto River. He knew that better use could be made of the resources assigned to this vessel and inquired sarcastically of General Hebert, "I am told that there is a very good crew under pay on board of [the *Dodge*]. In God's name, what does a vessel not intended to be used need with a crew?"[39] Eventually, through a combination of persuasion and persistence, Lubbock succeeded in having the *Bayou City* purchased for Confederate service at a cost of $50,000.[40]

Commander Hunter, the Confederate naval officer assigned to Galveston, examined the *Bayou City* and said that he not only considered it unsuited for a gunboat, but believed that it was of no use whatsoever except as a lookout boat.[41] As later events would prove, however, the governor's belief that the ship could be made useful was entirely correct.

While Lubbock worried about equipping the *Bayou City*, the Union forces celebrated their success. The news of Renshaw's "easy conquest" of Galveston and other places in the vicinity was received with delight by Admiral Farragut, who forwarded notice of it to Washington with a letter boasting that "All we want, as I have told the Department in my last dispatches, is a few soldiers to hold the places, and we will soon have the whole coast."[42]

Farragut also wrote to General Benjamin Butler in New Orleans, begging for a small force to hold Galveston. After all, he suggested to Butler, it "is on a slip of land and can be held with a very small number of troops and one gunboat."[43] Privately, however, Farragut confessed to Renshaw that he feared he would "find difficulty in procuring the few troops we require to hold the place."[44] By the end of October 1862, however, Farragut was again confidently predicting that Butler would soon send Renshaw a regiment (about a thousand men) to occupy the city.[45]

Since Commander Renshaw did not possess sufficient forces to effectively occupy the entire city until infantry support arrived, he landed a few marines on Pelican Island to protect the barracks that had been built before the war at that place. He also elected to make only a token demonstration of his authority by sending armed observation parties into the city during daylight hours. The principal mission of these landing parties was to exhibit Union control by displaying the United States flag at the Customhouse. Fearing Confederate guerilla activity, the Union naval forces prudently retreated to the security of their vessels at night.

At least one Union naval officer was impressed with the City of Galveston. Captain Jonathan Wainwright of the *Harriet Lane* reported that "the town is well built, containing many fine stores and dwelling houses, together with other structures, which could be converted into quite formidable strongholds, and easily held against anything less than artillery, from which the guns of our vessels would prove an ample protection." He joined in Renshaw's request for infantry, noting that "the place can easily be held by a regiment with the aid of one or two vessels in the harbor."[46]

The civilian residents of Galveston did not fare well during the city's Union occupation. The gas factory had closed, so the city was almost completely dark except for the dim light supplied by candles and oil lamps. The markets were often devoid of food, and what food there was went for staggering prices. Wives and children wrote to Confederate soldiers to inform them of their dire circumstances and plead for monetary assistance.[47]

Although there was relatively little interaction between the Union fleet and the citizens of the town, Captain Wainwright nevertheless made a favorable impression on the remaining inhabitants of Galveston. Wainwright was a handsome man in his early forties. Like his superior, Commander Renshaw, Wainwright had flowing sideburns and a huge moustache. In addition to his appearance, his kindness to the suffering inhabitants of Galveston made him popular with the civilians remaining in the city.[48]

In early November he ordered some machinery to be removed from a foundry because he feared the Confederates might come in one night and take it back with them to Virginia Point. It then came to his attention that one of the ladies in the town (Mrs. Caroline Mason) was almost beside herself with worry that her husband and son might be blamed for tipping the enemy off about the need to remove this equipment. In an unusual gesture, Wainwright went to the trouble of writing a letter for Mrs. Mason confirming that her family had been completely uninvolved with his decision to remove the equipment.[49]

While Renshaw did not have an easy time maintaining control of the city with so few men, he did not allow his attention to be diverted (as had previous Union naval commanders) by pointless arguments with the foreign consuls. On one occasion, the consul for Austria, Saxony, Holland, and three other small nations wrote the Union commander a letter wanting to know if the consul's slaves would be regarded as contraband if they escaped and claimed protection from the Union fleet.[50] Renshaw replied with a rare display of wit that he saw no reason to make an exception for the consul, particularly since the institution of slavery was not recognized by any of the six governments that the consul purported to represent.[51]

Rumors of a planned Confederate attack began reaching the ears of Commander Renshaw in early November 1862. In response, he ordered the crew and marines on the *Westfield* mustered on deck and delivered a speech. Renshaw urged all of his crew to be vigilant, particularly at night, predicting with uncanny accuracy that "If we are attacked at all it will be by boats drawing very little water, and they may come upon us without coming through the channel; and their object will be to board us." After complimenting the men on their previous service, Renshaw concluded that if the Confederates "catch us napping they may succeed; but if we are wide awake when they come, I'll be d——d if they will."[52]

Despite its relatively shallow draft, the *Westfield* had encountered severe difficulty maneuvering in the shallow waters around the Texas coast. In October, for example, it had gone aground while surveying the upper part of Matagorda Bay. A month later it ran aground on Pelican Spit.[53] This odd habit of going aground at inopportune moments was to have tragic consequences for this vessel and its captain only a month later.

On the night of December 1, 1862, an incident on the wharf closest to the Union fleet caused consternation among the Federal forces.[54] Thomas Barnett, known to Galvestonians as "One-Armed Tom," was an English veteran of the Mexican War who had lost an arm to a cannon shot and was serving as a Confederate scout in the city.[55] Fortified by a shotgun in his remaining arm and a number of alcoholic beverages on the inside, Tom Barnett decided to visit the wharf late at night and see what might be seen.

When challenged by a sentry, Barnett undiplomatically advised the sentry to "go to hell." An exchange of fire ensued and Barnett ran for cover. This unexpected gunfire drew the excited attention of the Union gunboats, which were concerned that this incident might be the precursor to a full-scale Rebel attack. They began firing randomly into the city, but stopped when it became clear that no such attack was occurring. Some inhabitants of the city took cover in wells to avoid injury.[56]

Despite the fact that this shelling did little serious injury either to citizens or property, one sensationalistic journalist reported to a Houston newspaper that "one woman had her clothes torn off, but escaped injury."[57] Acting Mayor George Grover protested to Confederate authorities that Barnett had acted irresponsibly in provoking this bombardment and received a formal apology. Despite (or perhaps in tribute to) this provocation, Tom Barnett was regarded affectionately by Galveston's citizens after the war and served for many years afterwards on its police force.[58]

Incidents like the episode with Tom Barnett made the Union Naval forces jumpy and led to problems. One night, for example, the two-and-one-half-story Henry Schirmer residence came under intense scrutiny from the Union warship *Harriet Lane*.[59] The officers on the *Lane* noticed that a light shining from the upper window in the house appeared to alternately dim and flicker. They incorrectly interpreted these lights as some unique form of coded signal directed at the Confederate forces on Virginia Point.

Several warning shots were fired from the *Lane* when the light did not cease, and a Union patrol was sent out to investigate the signals. As the elder Mr. Schirmer was being escorted back to the Federal fleet, he explained to his captors that there was no ceiling between the second floor of his house and the roof. It turned out that the light that was shining out of the top window was actually coming from a lamp located on the second floor. In reality, the "signaling" that had been detected was nothing more than family members moving about in front of the light in the living quarters on the second floor. This explanation for the unusual phenomenon was apparently convincing to the Union naval forces, and Mr. Schirmer was eventually released unharmed.

As emphasized also by a confrontation with Galveston's butchers, noises and lights at night were of particular concern to Renshaw and his fleet. To the west of the cemetery, on the outskirts of town, was the area in which the city's butchers did their slaughtering. To make sure that the meat supplied to the market was fresh in the morning, this activity had historically been performed before dawn by the light of lanterns. One night, the Union naval forces fired on these lights, supposing them to be Rebel forces. Legend has it that the result of this uneven battle was that one of the butchers dropped his lantern and killed his horse in the ensuing darkness and panic.

Naturally, after this incident the butchers refused to perform their jobs until they could do so under working conditions that did not include being fired upon. When fresh meat became a pressing necessity to his fleet, Commander Renshaw finally relented and issued an order that prohibited firing at the butchers in their work area. Safe from Union weaponry, the butchers of Galveston resumed their work.[60]

By the end of the first week of December 1862, the excitable Commander Renshaw's nerves were on edge. The Tom Barnett incident had convinced him that the Rebels were up to something. But there seemed to be little he could do about it. The infantry reinforcements that had been promised at the end of October, and again early in November, had not arrived. Rumors of various Rebel plots continued to reach Renshaw's ears, and he began passing them all along to Farragut with the assurance that withdrawal ought to be considered since the reports had come from a "reliable person."

The admiral had heard enough. On December 12, 1862, he scolded Renshaw in the strongest of terms and told him to hold his position at all costs:

Has it come to this, that four gunboats, armed with 8, 9, and 11 inch guns, are to be driven out of a harbor by the report of some "reliable person" that preparations are making to drive them out of the harbor? Are you willing, captain, that I should make such a statement to the honorable Secretary [of the Navy]—that we have abandoned the ports of Texas because of reports that they were making preparations to drive us out? I trust not. The gunboats must hold Galveston until the army arrives, and I have no doubt when you are attacked you will make a defense that will do credit to the Navy as well as to yourselves.[61]

Farragut had apparently calmed down three days later when he wrote Renshaw to inform him (again erroneously) to stop worrying, because General Butler was immediately sending down one thousand to two thousand men to help him occupy Galveston.[62] The large Union infantry force that Farragut promised turned out to be less than three hundred men, who arrived as a much anticipated Christmas present to Renshaw near the end of December 1862.

The Infantry Arrives

*It does not follow that every man who enlisted in the army is entitled
to credit for so doing. "Bummers" and shirks were plenty. When a thousand
men are got together there must be a percentage of this element among them.
The most worthy and deserving men do not have much to say about their
army experience, and never drag it into prominence for selfish reasons.*

SERGEANT MAJOR CHARLES P. BOSSON,
Forty-Second Massachusetts Infantry

On Christmas morning, 1862, three companies of the Forty-Second Massachusetts Regiment (approximately 260 men), who had arrived at Galveston
the day before, landed and fortified a position on Kuhn's Wharf. Although
Commander Renshaw was undoubtedly relieved that the infantry had finally
arrived, he must also have been disappointed that the number of troops was
so much smaller than the thousands he had been told to expect.

The Massachusetts troops, none of whom had ever been under enemy
fire before, had not even occupied the wharf for a full week before they were
captured in the Battle of Galveston. The questions that almost spring forth
from these facts are: Why did only three companies of inexperienced troops
make it to Galveston and why were they located on a wharf? To even attempt
to answer these questions it is necessary to review the background of this
regiment and its difficult journey to the South.

Massachusetts was probably the most motivated and best prepared for
war of any Northern state. Making it the center of the antislavery movement, abolitionists like William Lloyd Garrison had been agitating there for
years prior to the actual conflict. Its governor, John Andrew, was a devoted
slavery opponent who had raised funds to help defend John Brown and was
in favor of using the war as a tool to defeat the forces of slavery once and
for all.[1]

In addition to having a sincere and lasting commitment to the Union
cause, Massachusetts had a well-developed militia system that was rapidly
and efficiently turned into a vehicle for furnishing troops for the Union war

effort. When Lincoln called for volunteers in April 1861, the first armed troops to answer his call were from this state. By the end of the war it had contributed seventy-seven infantry regiments and over 152,000 men to the United States Army. It also raised the second-largest number of naval recruits from any state.[2]

In the summer of 1862, Governor Andrew notified the militia that they would be called into service for nine months, letting them enlist additional men to get up to full strength. This mobilization·was intended to delay the necessity of implementing conscription and to use the experienced state military organization to help train the raw recruits that enlisted.[3] In theory, this combination produced units that could be effectively sent to the field at an earlier date. In practice, it did not always work out that way.

The Second Regiment of the Massachusetts Volunteer Militia was an old and established militia organization. Since there was already a Second Massachusetts Regiment of three-year troops in the Army, however, the regiment was redesignated the Forty-Second Regiment when it was called into service. The men went into camp on August 26, 1862, starting with about one hundred volunteers. The period from that date until November 11, 1862, when the regiment was complete, was spent drilling, instructing, and (primarily) recruiting. The basic problem in filling its ranks was that out of the ten companies that would form the new regiment, there were seven existing companies, most of which were not even close to being full.

Volunteers for military service in Massachusetts tended to want to join with others from their own town or area to form a separate and distinct company. Although the Forty-Second Regiment could accept three more such companies, it had experienced difficulty in filling up the existing companies. Four of these companies were so slow in recruiting that they were eventually disbanded and their men dispersed among the other companies. By the time the regiment had completed recruiting, the members of the old Second Regiment were a minority.

Because the members of the new regiment were not very familiar with each other, the election of officers was a difficult process. Isaac Burrell (see Figure 5), a forty-two-year-old wheelwright from Roxbury, was finally elected to continue as colonel since he had held that rank in the old regiment and was the best-known man. The office of lieutenant colonel was a much closer election, but in the end Joseph Stedman, a twenty-eight-year-old civil engineer from Medfield, was elected. He edged out his competitors when the three companies from Worcester County (the swing votes) corresponded

FIGURE 5. *Photograph of Colonel Isaac Burrell (third from right) and the officers of the Forty-Second Massachusetts Infantry Regiment. Courtesy of Rosenberg Library, Galveston, Texas.*

with a military academy where Stedman had been a tactics instructor and received a strong recommendation.

At the beginning of October 1862, there was almost a mutiny or, as one of the men put it, a "general skedaddling for home," in Burrell's new regiment.[4] The subject that unexpectedly caused such discontent was uniforms, or more precisely, the lack of them. As fall approached in New England, the weather began to cool. No coats had been issued to the regiment, and the soldiers began to demand to be properly clothed. This problem appeared to be solved when a shipment of garments finally arrived on October 10, 1862.

Instead of solving the problem, however, the new shipment merely angered the troops further. The coats were black as night—not the regulation blue that the men had been told by their officers to expect. And even worse, certain men in the regiment who had been employed in the textile industry declared after examining the coats that they were made of the "poorest shoddy." As Jarvis Baker of Company "I" recalled, the situation was tense:

> The wrath of the men knew no bounds. Were we considered the scape-goats and scum of society? Had we been detailed to act as pallbearers for the rest of the army or were they to serve for our own funeral robes were questions that could not be answered.[5]

Colonel Burrell defused the potentially explosive situation by informing the troops in a loud and indignant voice that the offending garments would be returned and proper ones demanded.

When the field and staff officers were commissioned on November 11, 1862, Colonel Burrell had reason to be proud of his regiment. By and large it consisted of dedicated and well-educated men from all segments of society. The regiment drilled and trained in camp at Readville, Massachusetts, until November 21, 1862, when it departed for service under General Nathaniel Banks.

Burrell's regiment had originally been assigned to go to North Carolina, but the colonel of the Fifty-First Regiment expressed a preference to serve there and offered to switch assignments. Colonel Burrell was willing to do so because it meant serving with General Banks on what he thought was shaping up to be a large (and possibly lucrative) expedition to the South. In this casual manner, and totally as a matter of chance, the Forty-Second Regiment took the first steps on the road that would lead some of its members to Galveston.

Serving with General Banks would certainly have seemed a mixed blessing to an impartial observer. Nicknamed the "Bobbin Boy" because of his work in a textile mill at a young age, Banks had been elected to Congress and had served as governor of Massachusetts until January 1861, when President Lincoln appointed him a major general of volunteers.[6]

While he had undoubtedly held a number of high political offices, it was equally true that General Banks had not distinguished himself as a military leader. As Banks would prove time and again throughout the war, he had virtually no talent as a soldier. What he did have, however, and what Burrell was apparently drawn to in late 1862, was raw political power and a unique talent for raising men and money.

The importance of these skills was certainly not lost on Washington, and in October 1862, Secretary of War Edwin Stanton let it be known to the governors of the New England states and New York that Banks was organizing a large expedition to land on the coast of Texas. The governors enthusiastically pitched in, particularly when the administration did nothing to correct the misimpression that many of the troops that were being raised would also serve as pioneers and settlers who would reopen the cotton trade to Northern mills.[7]

Banks was not actually destined for Texas; on November 9, 1862, he had received secret instructions to replace General Ben Butler as commander of the Department of the Gulf in New Orleans. His real mission was to cooperate with the Navy in an attempt to open the Mississippi River.[8] To add to the deception that Texas was the objective, however, on November 14, 1862, Andrew Jackson Hamilton was appointed Military Governor of Texas and directed to accompany what became known as the "Banks Expedition."[9] The deception was a complete success. Neither "Governor" Hamilton nor the troops comprising the expedition knew that they were going to New Orleans until the ships began steaming up the Mississippi River.[10]

When Burrell agreed to the switch that made his regiment part of the Banks Expedition, he learned that it was scheduled to leave out of New York City. On the afternoon of November 21, 1862, therefore, the regiment boarded railroad cars and traveled to Groton, Connecticut. At Groton, the men marched aboard the steamer *Commodore,* which belonged to Cornelius Vanderbilt.

The stress of parting from loved ones was soon left behind in the comfortable environment of this ship. With the card playing, dancing, singing, and cutting up that went on throughout the trip to New York, many of the men did not get to sleep at all. Unused to army rations, many of the men also consumed what was intended to be three meals' worth of rations for their first meal. Delayed by the fog, the regiment finally arrived in New York in a hungry and tired condition.

Landing at Williamsburg, the regiment was greeted by the citizens of the town with cheers and food. They then marched nine miles at night to a camp where they found no tents available and had to sleep in the stalls of a nearby race course. The next day the men were issued tents, and displayed their ingenuity by building crude stoves and ovens to protect themselves against the bitter cold.

While in this camp, some of the officers and men were granted leave, and others informally granted themselves leave, to visit New York City. Many of these men had never been to such a large city before and were in awe of its size and opportunities for mischief. One of these new soldiers, Alexander

Hobbs, recorded in his diary that on Thanksgiving Day, he went to the city and had a good dinner of turkey, chicken, and plum pudding, after which he visited P. T. Barnum's Museum.[11] Back at camp, the rest of the regiment also had turkey and chicken. The complaints of nearby farmers about missing poultry for several weeks thereafter destroyed all mystery about this holiday feast's origin.

The food was not usually this good. The government, in its wisdom, had paid private contractors to prepare cooked rations on the basis of a set price per ration. The results were predictable. The rations were of uniformly low quality, and the numbers reported as served were grossly inflated. As Sergeant Major Bosson recorded:

> [The contractor] must have realized a very large amount of greenbacks by the operation. Frequently the food was not fit for the dogs to eat. Not once could the coffee be drank without creating a nausea. . . . To such a pitch had the feelings of men been wrought by this one item of bad rations, when the post commissary building caught fire one day, not a soldier would lend a helping hand to quench the flames until it was announced that the post hospital was over the cook-house.[12]

Colonel Burrell was so angry about this scheme that when it came time to depart from this camp, he refused to sign a receipt for the rations, telling the contractor the whole thing was a fraud. Finally, a compromise was reached under which the colonel gave a receipt for one-third of the rations originally claimed by the contractor to have been issued.[13]

At noon on December 2, 1862, orders finally came from General Banks for the Forty-Second Regiment to proceed to Brooklyn to board transports for the South. Arriving at the designated embarkation point, Colonel Burrell discovered that there was only one small transport and even it was not ready to be loaded. Some of the men spent the night in private houses that were generously opened to the troops. Most were quartered in the nearby armory of the New York National Guard, from which the more exuberant promptly attempted to escape by digging tunnels and crawling through ventilators.

Although most of the regiment behaved moderately well during this waiting period, two color-sergeants decided to take the Massachusetts and United States colors on a tour of the bars in the area. As if this were not bad enough, they left the regimental flag behind in what was described as a "low groggery," where it was fortunately discovered by the merest accident and restored to the regiment just before it shipped out. These men probably would have been the subject of a formal Court of Inquiry if events in Galveston had not intervened.

On the morning of December 3, 1862, two more transports arrived and embarkation commenced. It quickly became apparent that the regiment could not be accommodated on the three transports that had been provided. After some argument, a fourth transport was obtained. Distributed among the four transports, the regiment left for what its men expected to be their destination with "Governor" Hamilton and General Banks in Texas. To ensure secrecy, the transport captains were directed to sail forty-eight hours out to sea and then to open their sealed sailing orders. When opened, the sealed orders directed them to rendezvous at Ship Island, off the Mississippi coast, where they were then instructed to proceed on to New Orleans.

As it turned out, the division of the regiment into separate parts had critical consequences for the Battle of Galveston. Most of the regiment left New York on four transports: the *Charles Osgood*, the *Shetucket*, the *Quincy*, and the *Saxon*. Of these four transports, only one ever reached Galveston. Since the story of each of these vessels contributed substantially to the outcome of the events at Galveston, their journeys will each be briefly summarized.

The *Charles Osgood* was altogether an "unfortunate vessel." An old propeller vessel that before the war used to run on Long Island Sound, it was fitted up with a false deck made of wood and canvas to cover the area where the troops slept and cooked their meals. The undesirable feature of this deck was that it tended to be swept away by any serious seas. The problems with this vessel were compounded because the *Osgood*'s captain was an inexperienced mariner, who had never been south of Virginia.

As far as navigation instruments went, the captain had only a small compass. The ship had no charts, no chronometer, and no life preservers. It undoubtedly was not even seaworthy by modern standards. It was damaged so much by heavy seas in the Atlantic during its trip down the coast that the captain had to take it up to Philadelphia for repairs. Fortunately, at Philadelphia the captain finally obtained proper charts, life preservers, and an experienced navigator.

None of the troops on board the *Charles Osgood* was allowed to go ashore at Philadelphia because it seemed likely that if allowed to do so, none would return. In fact, when the vessel ran aground briefly during the passage out, some of the men walked back to Philadelphia, got drunk, and did not return. The soldiers that did make the voyage were themselves not entirely sober. Lieutenant Martin Gorham of Company "K" was rumored to have been so drunk throughout the trip south that Gorham "didn't know his head from his heels half of the time."[14] On December 16, 1862, the steamer finally reached the open sea and arrived at Key West a week later.

The *Charles Osgood* had a disquieting habit of running aground and did not reach New Orleans until 2:00 A.M. on January 1, 1863. By then, the action at Galveston was already in progress. The *Osgood* left New Orleans for Galveston January 2, 1863, but encountered the *Clifton* the next day before getting very far. From that vessel, the troops learned the bad news of the events that had taken place on New Year's Day in Galveston. They promptly turned around and went back to New Orleans.[15]

The *Shetucket* was also a very old propeller freight boat that had been operating out of New York. As with the *Charles Osgood*, a "false deck" had been built on top of its regular deck out of poor quality, unseasoned lumber. This deck was designed to shield the passengers (roughly two hundred men) from the rolling sea. The reality was that in a rough sea the waves penetrated the deck and soaked the men's bunks, requiring them to use rubber sheets to protect anything of value.

Life on board a troop transport like the *Shetucket* was in some ways even more regimented than it had been in camp on shore. Men were expected to present themselves for reveille promptly at 6:00 A.M. and were scheduled for regular guard duty at specified intervals. The officers also had important duties to perform. Written orders issued on board the ship required each officer on a daily basis to "see to it that every soldier washes his face and hands [and] combs his hair as this is necessary for the general health of all on board."[16]

On the third night out, the ship ran aground due to pilot error. The pounding of the waves against the sides of the stationary vessel made an ominous sound. Some of the men aboard had been to sea before and knew that the ship could not take such punishment very long. They were on the verge of taking the ship's small boat and heading for shore when they were stopped by an officer with a revolver. Finally, a long ocean swell lifted the damaged ship off the shoals and enabled it to get back out to sea, where it then commenced taking on water through its damaged hull.

The *Shetucket* was so damaged by this incident that, upon reaching Fortress Monroe the next day, it was ordered to Norfolk for repairs. The men used this opportunity to go ashore and cause all manner of trouble for the unprepared citizens. At one point, a local military official jokingly threatened to send a battery to fire into the ship if the men rang the church bell one more time. On the afternoon of December 21, 1862, the ship finally put to sea. Short of coal and water, the captain headed for Hilton Head.

Unfortunately, the *Shetucket*'s captain seriously miscalculated his course. On December 25, 1862, he was intercepted by Union gunboats while inadvertently attempting to run the blockade into Charleston Harbor. The Union naval officers were said to have employed "strong language" to berate the *Shetucket*'s captain for his stupidity, and claimed that they would have sunk him despite his flag if not for the troops on board. After getting further directions, the embarrassed captain finally reached Hilton Head. The men were granted shore leave on December 28, 1862, at Beaufort. As the experience of the other ships confirmed, letting the men off of the ship was almost always a serious mistake.

The troops had seen the incompetence of their ship's captain and the inadequacies of his ship; they voted not to go back on board again until matters were fixed. The local provost marshal and his force had to be called out to use their bayonets and other weapons to drive the reluctant voyagers back on board by the appointed time. The officers on board were not at all surprised by this mutiny. In fact, given the condition of the ship and the repeatedly demonstrated incompetence of its captain, they considered it creditable that the men had endured these hardships as long as they did.

The *Shetucket* did not arrive at Key West until January 2, 1863, where it was met by the gunboat *Sagamore*. When informed of the day the *Shetucket* had left New York, the officer on the *Sagamore*'s deck replied: "Where in h[e]ll have you been all this time?" The slow vessel did not finally reach New Orleans until January 11, 1863.

The *Quincy* left New York on December 4, 1862, the first ship to get away. It ran into a gale that caused the men to become so seasick that many said later they did not care whether they lived or died. As if the danger from the tossing ocean were not enough, the heavy seas caused hot fat from the stewpans to be tossed out on the deck, where it burst into flame.

Designed to operate on lakes instead of the ocean, the *Quincy* was old and in poor shape. Within a year following this trip, both this ship and its captain would be lost making this same run. But on this voyage, on December 8, 1862, a leak in the boiler was discovered, and the captain was forced to put in to Port Royal for repairs.[17]

During the next eight days, while repairs were being made, the troops were put ashore on Hilton Head. Unlike the passengers on some of the other transports, the men of the *Quincy* generally behaved themselves well and went back aboard the ship without trouble when it was finally time to leave. The ship then made a relatively quick run down to Fort Jefferson on Tortugas, where provisions and coal were taken on board.

As luck would have it, however, while leaving Tortugas for Ship Island, the *Quincy* collided with another ship in the channel and had to put back into port for several more days of repairs. Patched together once again, the ship then continued on its way to Ship Island. This comparatively pleasant part of the voyage was interrupted when a private died of fever. There was a short delay while he was buried at sea. As if by common agreement, the men ceased playing cards and began reading their Bibles, a study that occupied them only for the rest of that particular day. The *Quincy* did not arrive at New Orleans until December 29, 1862, where it was met by a heavy fog that delayed unloading until the next day.[18]

The last of the regiment's four transports, the *Saxon*, was the only one to reach Galveston in advance of the Confederate attack on January 1, 1863. It left New York on the morning of December 5, 1862. Called the "Headquarters" because it carried Colonel Burrell and the rest of his staff, the *Saxon* had the same difficulties with heavy seas at the beginning of its journey that were experienced by the other vessels. One of the soldiers, a farmer from Medfield, described the "utter misery" of the scene that greeted him when he went below deck:

> Two hundred and fifty men packed like so many hogs into one small room, where there was hardly room for half the number to be upon their feet at once, almost all seasick and some frightened half out of their wits for fear we should go to the bottom. Ever and anon some unlucky fellow, not succeeding in getting a good hold, when the vessel gave a sudden lunge, would be thrown from his bunk and sprawled in the filth upon the floor.[19]

Despite this rough passage, the *Saxon* proved to be the fastest and safest of the whole group of transports. It arrived off of Key West on December 11, 1862, with nothing more exciting to report than the theft of some cabbages and the sighting of a group of whales. Taking on fresh water and coal, the ship set out for Ship Island. On the dark morning of December 12, 1862, the *Saxon*, like each of the other transports, had severe navigational problems. It had run past the initial line of defenders and was inadvertently attempting to run the blockade into Mobile Bay when it was brought to a halt by a shot from a blockading gunboat and advised of its mistake.[20]

Correcting this dangerously erroneous course, the *Saxon* made good time, arriving at New Orleans on December 17, 1862. That afternoon, the ship was directed to take the troops up the river to Carrolton, where the men went into camp beside a soldiers' graveyard. Because the *Saxon* had made the trip so much faster than the other transports—it was almost two weeks before the next ship was to arrive—only Companies "D," "G," and "I" went into camp with the regiment's officers.

On the afternoon of December 18, 1862, while these three companies were setting up camp, Colonel Burrell received orders from General Banks to proceed to Galveston "forthwith." Supposing that "forthwith" meant right away, Burrell made immediate preparations to leave that same day. It turned out, however, that the *Saxon* needed repairs and did not leave until three days later. As the transport anchored opposite New Orleans, Colonel Burrell went ashore to obtain what he anticipated would be some specific and important last-minute instructions from General Banks. After all, Burrell must have thought, he and his men had come all the way from Massachusetts to help their gallant former governor with his critical mission.

When Burrell reported to headquarters, however, he found only one officer, a quartermaster, who assured him that detailed written instructions had been prepared but that they could not be located. He advised Burrell to take his time getting to Galveston, and to consult with Commander Renshaw when he got there. There, the officer assured Burrell, he had only to wait briefly for the written instructions and the balance of his regiment, both of which had been lost but would be sent to him as soon as they were found. Burrell's men were happy to learn that they were heading for Texas. Private George Fiske wrote in his journal that "Galveston is our destination, and we like the idea of going to Texas very much. It is a healthy country, and I think we shall have as pleasant a time there as anywhere." [21]

The trip to Galveston was without incident, and the *Saxon* arrived at the island on Christmas Eve. It was at this point that a critical mistake was made. When Renshaw had originally suggested to Admiral Farragut a plan for occupying the city, he had advised keeping the army force on Pelican Island, where there was already a comfortable barracks.[22] Similarly, in asking General Butler for troops, Farragut had stressed that since the requested infantry regiments would be isolated on Pelican Island, and protected by gunboats, their "protection must be perfect." [23]

When Burrell and his men arrived, however, Commander Renshaw had changed his mind and "strongly urged" the infantry to instead land in the city and take up a position on Kuhn's Wharf. Although the reason for this change can only be guessed, Renshaw probably wanted the infantry stationed onshore to provide his gunboats some measure of protection at night. Although Burrell expressed a strong preference to follow the original plan and occupy a more protected camp on Pelican Island, in the absence of any written orders from headquarters he felt that he had no choice but to be guided by the advice of the naval commander. After all, Burrell reasoned, Renshaw had been on the scene now for almost four months and was familiar with the situation. In addition, Burrell was also assured that in the event an attack was threatened, his men could be taken off the wharf in no more than five minutes' time.[24]

Thus it was that on Christmas Day, 1862, at approximately 10:00 A.M., Colonel Burrell and the three companies of the Forty-Second Massachusetts Regiment that had come with him on the *Saxon* landed on Kuhn's Wharf (see Figure 6) at the foot of 18th Street. The wharf was a large one, about four hundred feet long and twenty feet wide. It had a two-story storehouse at its end that was quickly converted into a barracks, hospital, and storage facility. About half the men then entered the city to survey the town they were theoretically intended to occupy. They were struck immediately with the deserted appearance that the city presented. They found all the stores closed, and thought the people looked ragged and hungry.[25]

Despite the peaceful appearance of the city, Colonel Burrell was all too aware of the exposed condition of his small garrison. He immediately began taking the best precautions that could be taken to protect his position on the wharf. One of the first things he did was to barricade the inside wall of the storehouse facing the city with sacks of plaster and other materials that he found abandoned in the structure. This, he hoped, would protect the men against shots from the city. Next, to protect the sentries and pickets that would be patrolling the entrance to the wharf, Burrell directed some of the planks from the wharf to be pulled up and made into a breastwork. Not only did this make a very acceptable defensive work, but the missing planks made it virtually impossible for a large force from the shore to rush down the wharf to attack the storehouse.

In unloading and taking an inventory of the ammunition, a disturbing discovery was made. While Company "G" had been issued rifled muskets, the other two companies with Burrell had been issued only regular smooth-bore muskets. But in the rush to load the four transports, most of the ammunition placed on the *Saxon* was of a type that would only work in the rifles possessed by Company "G." Fearing that it might harm morale to tell the men of their predicament, Colonel Burrell decided to keep the shortage of ammunition a secret and instructed the men not to fire their weapons unless expressly authorized by their officers.

After defensive preparations were completed, Colonel Burrell went on a scouting mission in the *Harriet Lane* with Captain Wainwright. Looking at

FIGURE 6. *Photograph of Kuhn's Wharf, 1861.*
Courtesy of Rosenberg Library, Galveston, Texas.

the Confederate fortifications at Eagle Grove and the railroad bridge, Burrell judged them to be "well built." He noted that in addition to a gun at the draw in the middle of the bridge to the mainland, there was a "strong battery, mounted with heavy guns" at Virginia Point. He estimated the Confederate force in the immediate area to be about two thousand.[26] Burrell learned that Wainwright had launched a few shells at the Confederate fort at Eagle Grove to get its range, but had made no serious attack because Renshaw was afraid to move before the rest of the Union infantry arrived.[27]

After he had surveyed the island, Burrell immediately began preparations (never completed) to make an assault on the Rebel works guarding the railroad bridge. Other than some friendly advice from Wainwright, the Navy gave him no cooperation in this effort. Commander Renshaw had left the bridge intact largely because of his concern that the remaining inhabitants of the city would suffer if it was destroyed. He also believed that when the Union invasion of Texas ultimately began, as Renshaw confidently anticipated, the bridge would save his ships the tedious task of transporting Union supplies and artillery from the island to the mainland.

In addition to fortifying Kuhn's Wharf, Burrell's troops also went on scouting missions in the city. Although the first of these missions had as its stated objective the location of some stoves with which to heat their quarters, the men took full advantage of this convenient opportunity to satisfy their other personal needs. One Union soldier recorded in his diary (later captured and published in a Galveston newspaper) that on one foraging expedition "most of the boys spent their time in stealing property out of the stores. They took everything they could lay their hands on." [28]

Another soldier, Jarvis Baker, remembered that "some articles found their way back to camp that could hardly be called necessities," in particular tobacco, brown sugar, molasses, and some Confederate money. Although taken by the Massachusetts soldiers primarily as a souvenir, the latter item was soon to come in very handy during their imprisonment. [29]

As December 1862 drew to a close, the Union infantry began hearing the same rumors that Renshaw had heard regarding a Rebel plan to retake the city. Although privately uneasy about this prospect, Commander Renshaw publicly proclaimed that as far as the naval forces were concerned the very idea of such an attack was ridiculous. Burrell, however, took the rumors seriously, and strengthened his defenses accordingly. Commencing on the afternoon of December 30, 1862, and continuing until midnight of that night, Burrell directed his men to construct a second breastwork, closer to the storehouse, protected with cotton bales. The men also were forced to sleep on their arms, a situation that the troops found to be "extremely disagreeable." [30]

On his right as he faced the shore, Colonel Burrell noted that another wharf extended along his flank about one-eighth of a mile distant. To protect against a flanking fire from this direction, he needed another barrier. Looking down at the water he spotted a low, flat wooden raft that had been used by men engaged in caulking operations near the waterline of a ship. With a great deal of effort, the raft was hoisted out of the water and placed on its side perpendicular to the end of the second breastwork. The men grumbled mightily at all this work. But as later events would prove, this protection on their flank and the other defenses that the Massachusetts troops had improvised on this wharf provided substantial protection and undoubtedly saved many lives. [31]

The Prince and His Players

["Prince John" Magruder] is handsome, perfectly uniformed, insistent,
impatient and theatrical, and he always appears at a gallop. Despite a slight
lisp, he loves to talk and he writes ceaselessly to his superiors. A certain aptitude
for independent command he possesses, and with it ability to bluff an adversary.
After winning much applause for the first Confederate victory in Virginia, he
gradually becomes entangled in a large military organization, which irks
him unreasonably. In the end, when his great opportunity comes,
he shows a weakness not uncommon in war — an excited,
overzealous desire to do all his work in person.
DOUGLAS SOUTHALL FREEMAN,
Lee's Lieutenants

In October 1862, orders were issued in Richmond replacing General Hebert as head of the Confederate District of Texas, New Mexico, and Arizona.[1] The new commander, General John Bankhead Magruder (see Figure 7), was an entirely different sort of man. As events in Galveston would soon prove, Magruder was an aggressive and bold fighter, who was not afraid to take chances to achieve a valuable objective. This style, which was just what the Texans had ordered, had been developed over a long and unusual military career.

Born in Virginia, Magruder graduated fifteenth out of his forty-two-member West Point class in 1830.[2] He was far from a model student, coming within four demerits of being expelled during one of his years at the academy. Initially assigned to the Seventh Infantry, Magruder exchanged assignments with his good friend Albert Miller Lea, and went into the First Artillery. Lea volunteered to switch with Magruder to please Magruder's lady friend, who wished to "remain in more civilized society."[3]

The next few years were relatively uneventful and Magruder began to doubt his desire for a military career. To overcome the boredom, he turned to heavy drinking. Magruder's drinking habits were the stuff of which legends are made. On one occasion, while staying at a hotel in Baltimore, he returned too late and found the door to the establishment locked. Finding the

FIGURE 7. *Photograph of General John Bankhead Magruder.*
Courtesy of Rosenberg Library, Galveston, Texas.

door to the adjacent stage office unlocked, however, Magruder collapsed on a pile of mail sacks and fell into a deep, inebriated slumber.

In the morning, the stage driver came to pick up his cargo and noticed that the manifest reflected only one passenger. Concluding that the unconscious Magruder must be that passenger, the driver picked him up and loaded him on the stage. During the bumpy ride to Washington, Magruder still did not awaken, and the exasperated driver finally left him on a bench near a hotel in Washington. When he finally awoke, Magruder had no idea where he was. He considered simply asking his location, but did not do so because he feared that he would be thought insane.

After having breakfast and a rejuvenative tonic, Magruder went for a long walk. Seeing the Capitol, and some other familiar Washington landmarks, Magruder now seriously began doubting his own sanity. Finally, he ran into a former classmate who worked at the Topographic Bureau. Together, they figured out what had happened. This incident caused Magruder to swear off drinking, but only for what appears to have been a very brief period.

Magruder became known as "Prince John" to his army companions because of his elegant uniforms, theatrical manners, and dramatic pretensions. Sometimes this reputation served as an unfortunate distraction. He was "so brilliant and gallant in social life," observed one general officer who served with him, that he "received less credit for his remarkable genius for war than he deserved."[4] The stories and anecdotes about Magruder's social skills and humor are almost endless.

On one occasion, for example, he invited several visiting British officers to dinner. Knowing that they expected only a very crude and primitive function, Prince John decided to put on a show. He rented or borrowed gold plate, cut crystal, and elegant furniture for the occasion. When the guests expressed astonishment at these opulent furnishings, Magruder apologized for what he described as their shabby appearance and explained that this was only the poorer stuff that had escaped an unfortunate shipwreck on its way from Florida.

Being military officers themselves, his guests next asked what the pay of an American officer was, since it apparently allowed him such a high standard of living. Magruder pretended to think about the question for a moment and finally responded, "Damned if I know." He then referred the question to his "servant" (borrowed for the occasion), who also professed complete ignorance of such an unimportant detail.[5]

The Mexican War brought Magruder his first real taste of combat, and cemented his reputation for theater in military circles. While serving with

Zachary Taylor's army near Corpus Christi, Texas, he was ordered to build a stage on which to present productions to divert the soldiers from patronizing the area's saloons and gambling houses. Magruder's plays were a huge success. For one of his productions, Magruder attempted to stage *The Moor of Venice*, starring David Dixon Porter's brother as Othello. The leading female role was originally assigned to James Longstreet, but he proved to be too tall for the part. The ingenious Magruder looked around the camp and next substituted Ulysses S. Grant in the role. Unfortunately, he too ultimately turned out to be unsuitable for the part, and a professional actress was brought in from New Orleans.[6]

In addition to staging plays, Magruder saw plenty of hard fighting in the Mexican War. He started his service with Zachary Taylor in the assault on northern Mexico, and then served under Winfield Scott in the march from Vera Cruz to Mexico City. He emerged from this war as one of the most famous artillerists of the conflict, having been brevetted lieutenant colonel for bravery. Serving under Magruder in this conflict was a young West Point graduate named Thomas J. (later to become known to the world as "Stonewall") Jackson. Jackson expressed satisfaction at his assignment, noting that "if any fighting was to be done, Magruder would be on hand."[7]

Two battles in the campaign for Mexico City made particularly vivid impressions on Magruder. At the Battle of Contreras, Magruder and his battery created a valuable diversion while a flanking force came up behind the Mexican position, creating such panic and confusion that the enemy troops broke ranks and fled. When they reached the fortifications at Churubusco, however, a bloody battle ensued in which the Mexicans repelled a series of American frontal assaults, inflicting heavy casualties. The contrast between the tactics and casualties at Contreras and Churubusco was not lost on Magruder. As he would learn again in the Civil War, a well-executed diversion and flanking maneuver was often preferable to a charge into the teeth of a heavily fortified position.

Winfield Scott's final campaign leading to the capture of Mexico City was a masterpiece of military misdirection and deception. Since Magruder viewed himself as a protege of "Old Fuss and Feathers," as Scott was known, the lessons he learned in this campaign about deceiving an enemy as to a commander's true intentions made a strong and lasting impression on him. Magruder's experience hauling guns across Mexico also persuaded him that light field artillery, because of its mobility, could be made to operate effectively in almost any circumstance.

After the Mexican War was over, Magruder was transferred to California, where he and a friend opened a saloon and resumed bad habits. Here he also met a steamboat captain named Leon Smith, whom he was to meet again in Texas in 1862, with important results.[8] Following his service in California, Magruder then received a variety of temporary assignments around the country, including a tour of duty as commander of the Artillery School for Instruction at Fort Leavenworth, Kansas.

In March 1861, Magruder returned from an assignment in Europe to find his native country deeply divided by the coming war. The onset of this sectional conflict, and its division of family and friends, affected some professional soldiers more than others. One evening in Washington, for example, Magruder had a long talk with his friend John C. Pemberton. Pemberton, who was from Pennsylvania, confided that he had just received a letter from his mother threatening to disinherit him if he joined the Confederate Army. In the same mail, the unfortunate Pemberton had also received a letter from his wife, who threatened to leave him if he did not join the Southern forces. Turning to Magruder, he pleaded for advice, saying, "What course shall I take?"

To lesser men, this moral dilemma would have presented a weighty problem. To Magruder, however, the answer was obvious. "What course shall you take?" said Magruder, "Why, take a drink," he responded. After Magruder and Pemberton had taken this "course" for quite a distance, the unfortunate Pemberton decided to cast his lot with the South, later to become known as the Confederate commander who was forced to surrender Vicksburg.[9]

When Virginia seceded on April 17, 1861, Magruder resigned his commission in the U.S. Army and offered his services to his native state. Less than a month later, Magruder found himself in charge of all of the Rebel forces on the Virginia peninsula between the York and James rivers. There, he opposed General Benjamin Butler, who was in charge of a large Union force at Fortress Monroe and was eager to march up the peninsula and seize Richmond.

With a Union force of approximately 4,400 men, Brigadier General Ebenezer W. Pierce headed inland in early June. At "Big Bethel," Magruder and Daniel H. Hill, with approximately 1,200 Confederates, defeated these Union forces in an engagement of a size that would a few years later only be regarded by Virginians as a mere skirmish. But in June 1861, the people were anxious for victories, and Magruder appeased this desire by furnishing the first land battle (and victory) of the war. Foreshadowing a strategy that he would successfully employ again at Galveston, at Big Bethel Magruder dismounted some of his cavalry regiments and used them as infantry with their double-barreled shotguns.[10]

After the battle, Magruder turned in a series of reports praising virtually everyone involved in gallant terms. The newspapers had a field day; the *Richmond Dispatch* declared the battle at Big Bethel to have been "one of the most extraordinary victories in the annals of war."[11] The publicity that Magruder personally received was largely undeserved, but the result was that he was promoted to brigadier general.

The authorities in Richmond realized that the peninsula leading to the Confederate capital continued to be vulnerable to enemy attack. At their request, Magruder spent the remainder of 1861 designing and supervising the construction of an elaborate series of defenses below Yorktown, partly using impressed slave labor.

On March 24, 1862, he wrote to Confederate Secretary of War George W. Randolph, who had been his chief of artillery at Big Bethel, and warned about a large Union force gathering at Fortress Monroe.[12] Although Magruder was initially accused of seeing phantoms, it soon became apparent that the large army he was reporting was no illusion. What Magruder was seeing was the advance guard of General George McClellan's Army of the Potomac, over 100,000 Union soldiers, which had landed on the peninsula and was determined to take Richmond before the Confederates could mobilize to oppose them.

Magruder's line from Yorktown to the James River, and the manner in which he defended it, were a masterpiece of creativity. Building dams on the Warwick River, he flooded some of the lowlands to prevent the movement of the Union Army. Drawing on his theatrical training, Magruder then had his men (only about ten or eleven thousand strong) make a large number of wooden guns out of logs and mount them on wagon carriages to simulate mobile artillery.

To further give the impression of vast Confederate forces, Prince John also directed his men to build extra campfires at night, and choreographed elaborate spectacles during the day in which men marched in circles and sounded bugles. As one of his soldiers recalled with obvious pleasure after the war: "Here, there, everywhere, by night and by day, [Magruder] showed himself to the enemy in a magnifying glass, not only exaggerating the numerical proportions of his army, but in making illusive and confusing dispositions of his troops in carefully concealed changes, and in transformations as deceptive as a juggler's tricks."[13]

Richmond diarist Mary Chesnut recorded that it was wonderful to see how Magruder "played his ten thousand before McClellan like fireflies and utterly deluded him."[14] Magruder's deception was indeed a great success. Convinced that he was facing a gigantic opposing Rebel force, the over-cautious McClellan remained bottled up on the peninsula south of York-town for over a month.

While directing this extravaganza from his headquarters at Yorktown, the romantic Magruder must certainly have been struck by the fact that his defenses were located on the same field at which George Washington had defeated the British in the siege that led to the end of the Revolutionary War. As a Virginian, and an artillerist by profession, he was undoubtedly fa-miliar with the story of Washington's final attack on the British lines, in which Washington himself was sometimes said to have been given the honor of firing the first American gun to signal the beginning of the grand as-sault.[15] Perhaps it was here that Magruder first began dreaming of the day when he himself could fire the first shot in a grand assault.

After Magruder developed problems in dealing with a superior officer, orders were issued in May 1862 assigning him to the command of the Trans-Mississippi District, which embraced all of the lands west of the Missis-sippi.[16] There was only one problem: Prince John did not want to go. Preferring to stay in Virginia where the action was, Magruder exerted all his influence to get the order suspended until after the coming battles with McClellan. The assignment was withdrawn.[17] If Magruder had known what was in store for him in what would eventually become known as the "Seven Days' Campaign," he probably would have headed for Texas without delay.

Things started off well enough for Prince John. The new commander of the Army of Northern Virginia, Robert E. Lee, decided on a bold plan of at-tack in which Magruder was to play an important part. McClellan's army was divided by the Chickahominy River, with two-thirds of this Union army south of the river and about one-third of it, under Fitz John Porter, to the north. Lee's plan was to concentrate his forces on the north side of the river and attack Porter's isolated detachment. But such a plan had one obvious drawback. Concentrating most of the Confederate Army against Porter meant that on the southern bank of the Chickahominy there remained only a token force (less than twenty-five thousand men) between the bulk of the Union Army (more than sixty-five thousand men) and Richmond. The key to Lee's whole plan was the assumption that the small Confederate force he was leaving on the south side of the river could somehow manage to hold off the timid McClellan while Lee concentrated on Porter.

Without hesitation, Lee chose Magruder to command the army opposing

McClellan south of the Chickahominy and ordered him to keep the Union Army occupied. Prince John and his players were more than ready for the job. As General D. H. Hill wrote after the war:

During Lee's absence Richmond was at the mercy of McClellan; but Magruder was there to keep up a "clatter." . . . No one ever lived who could play off the Grand Seignior with a more lordly air than could "Prince John." . . . During the absence of Lee he kept up such a clatter that each of McClellan's corps commanders was expecting a special visit from the much-plumed cap and the once-gaudy attire of the master of ruses and strategy.[18]

To occupy the Union troops opposing him, Magruder revived the play that he had performed so brilliantly in defending Yorktown, ordering troops to move back and forth to simulate activity, and even having slaves from Richmond march around in circles beating drums.[19] Officers shouted orders to nonexistent units and artillery fire was occasionally directed at the Union lines to put them in fear of an attack by what seemed to be large forces massing against them. Magruder's demonstrations were an unqualified success. Unhinged by what he thought were two large forces operating on both sides of the Chickahominy, McClellan moved his base south to the James River and began to retreat.[20]

It is at this point that Magruder's troubles began. As events were shortly to prove, Magruder functioned best when he could allow his creativity free rein. As one of Lee's staff officers summarized the situation: "Magruder belonged partly to that class of men whose genius, being unshackled, was capable of achieving the most brilliant results; but when overshadowed by authority became paralyzed."[21] Moreover, by this time, June 28, 1862, Magruder had slept very little within the past several days and was seriously ill with acute indigestion. Compounding the problem, the medicine with which he was treating this ailment contained morphine, to which he appears to have been allergic.[22]

On June 29, 1862, Magruder caught up with the retreating Federal army near Savage's Station. Confused about the instructions he had received from Lee, and preparing for a Union attack that never came, Magruder waited for reinforcements and did nothing until about 5:00 P.M. Then, making what is commonly considered to be the first use of a rail-mounted gun, he finally opened his attack with a thirty-two-pounder Brooke naval rifle known as the "Land Merrimack" because of its protective armor.[23] Mounted on a railroad car, the gun had been designed for the purpose of preventing the flow of McClellan's supplies along the railroad line. Despite the gun's novelty, it proved relatively ineffective when its unprotected sides were raked by Union sharpshooters, necessitating its withdrawal back up the railroad line toward Richmond.[24]

Although Magruder did ultimately order an attack by two brigades at Savage's Station, it was not properly supported and had no real impact. General Lee was disappointed by Magruder's failure to attack more vigorously, writing (in what must be regarded as a stern reprimand coming from the mild-mannered Lee) that "I regret much that you have made so little progress today in the pursuit of the enemy" and warning that "We must lose no more time or he will escape us entirely."[25]

On the next day, Magruder got lost due to poor local guides and confusing orders, which resulted in his troops marching all day and into the night without firing a shot.[26] On the morning of July 1, 1862, Magruder arose early, still ill and exhausted after only one hour's sleep, and attempted to sort out the confused lines that his troops had formed during the night. The Union Army, protected by a large force of artillery, was crowded on the top of nearby Malvern Hill. In a strategic decision that he would repeat (with similarly bad results) at Gettysburg, General Lee had determined to make a frontal assault on the enemy's position.

Magruder's instructions were to go down the "Quaker Road" and form his troops on Stonewall Jackson's right flank.[27] In what must be counted as an unbelievable stroke of bad luck, Magruder got lost. As it turned out, there were two roads in the area that were referred to by the designation "Quaker Road," and Magruder's three local guides directed him down the wrong one.[28] After finally being redirected by Generals Lee and Longstreet, a "Galloping Magruder" showed up at the appointed meeting place about 4:00 P.M. As historian Douglas Southall Freeman described his demeanor, Prince John was "all ardor, all excitement, and altogether ignorant of the situation on his immediate front."[29]

General Lee's instructions to Magruder had been exceedingly vague. Robert H. Chilton, Lee's adjutant, informed Magruder that Confederate artillery was going to bombard and soften the enemy's lines. Then, when the Union lines broke, as Chilton confidently deemed "probable," Lewis Armistead's brigade had been ordered to charge with a yell. Chilton told Magruder that when he observed this charge he was to "do the same." Chilton's order did not set any specific objectives and did not specify the forces with which Magruder was to make his charge.[30]

Armistead's brigade had some temporary success against Union skirmishers. Uncertain whether this action qualified as the charge described in Chilton's order, Magruder sent a message to Lee informing him of this temporary advance and awaited further orders. Apparently convinced by Magruder's message and other evidence that McClellan was in the process of retreating again, Lee sent back a message directing Magruder to "advance rapidly" and "press forward your whole line and follow up Armistead's success."[31]

Magruder had difficulty getting the cooperation of other commanders to make the assault, probably because they had been suffering much of the day under the fire of the immense concentration of Federal artillery located on Malvern Hill. They realized, as Magruder apparently did not, that an attack into the strength of this Federal position would result only in a foolish waste of life. Although Magruder did not know it, the guns on Malvern Hill had been carefully positioned by Henry Jackson Hunt, who had studied artillery tactics under Magruder at Fort Leavenworth, Kansas.[32]

With Lee's scolding about his failure to attack at Savage's Station still ringing in his ears, Magruder was determined that this time he would make a "vigorous" attack. The result, however, was a piecemeal and uncoordinated advance up the hill into the teeth of the well-positioned Union artillery. Heavy guns from Federal gunboats along the James River also pounded the advancing Confederates. As General D. H. Hill later described the tragic result:

> I never saw anything more grandly heroic than the advance after sunset of the nine brigades under Magruder's orders. Unfortunately, they did not move together and were beaten in detail. As each brigade emerged from the woods, from fifty to one hundred guns opened upon it, tearing great gaps in its ranks; but the heroes reeled on and were shot down by the reserves. . . . Most of them had an open field half a mile wide to cross, under the fire of field artillery in front, and the fire of the heavy ordnance of the gunboats in their rear. It was not war — it was murder.[33]

As General Hill correctly observed, the action at Malvern Hill had turned out to be an unmitigated Confederate disaster. Magruder knew that he had not enhanced his reputation in this campaign, and was more than ready for a change of scenery. He wrote to his friend George Randolph, now secretary of war, on the day after the battle, and informed him that he was now ready to command the Confederate Trans-Mississippi Department as he had originally been ordered in May.[34] Lee promptly relieved him of command, and Magruder characteristically began to beg the government for arms for his new department.[35] He had already started the long journey to his new post when he received an ominous directive from President Jefferson Davis to return immediately to Richmond.[36]

Faced with the failure of Lee's army to destroy McClellan's forces, and the terrible casualty figures suffered in battles like Malvern Hill, the politicians and press were looking for a scapegoat. Magruder made a convenient target, and scandalous allegations started against him almost immediately. Some said that he was drunk, others that he had ignored orders or exhibited cowardice on the battlefield. There is no reliable evidence that Magruder had been drinking during this campaign. The rumors to this effect apparently originated in the general's illness and his unfortunate prewar reputation.[37]

Battered brutally by such charges, usually from anonymous sources, Magruder wrote a lengthy and detailed defense of his actions. This report included the affidavits of his guides, as well as a surgeon who swore that the general did not look drunk and did not hide himself from enemy fire as had been suggested.[38] Lee forwarded the report to the War Department with the lukewarm endorsement that while he regretted that Magruder did not overcome the obstacles facing him more readily, "General Magruder intentionally omitted nothing that he could do to insure success."[39]

Lee's failure to vigorously defend Magruder was probably not due to the press of other business. Robert H. Chilton, Lee's adjutant, had secretly written a letter to Inspector General Samuel Cooper in which he complained that Magruder was an "utterly incompetent and deficient" commander and suggested that General Lee himself would confirm this opinion if asked directly by the president. Chilton's letter was probably motivated by more than honest patriotism. After all, it had been Chilton's poorly worded order to Magruder that had been partially responsible for the debacle at Malvern Hill. His strong criticisms of Magruder to Cooper may have been nothing more than an attempt to shift the blame that he feared might eventually attach to his own actions.

Without consulting Lee or Magruder, Cooper forwarded Chilton's letter directly to President Davis, and it is this letter that probably caused the initial suspension of Magruder's assignment and his recall to Richmond. In relaying Chilton's letter, Cooper told Davis that Magruder was a "partially reformed drunkard" who in his experience would "as surely return to his cup as 'the dog to his vomit.'"[40] These were strong words and they had their intended effect on the president.

By the middle of July, Magruder's assignment to command the Trans-Mississippi Department had been officially revoked. He arranged a personal interview with President Davis to discuss the nature of the scandalous charges by Chilton and others against him, and sent the president a copy of his detailed report and affidavits.[41] Magruder's arguments were apparently not persuasive enough. On July 13, 1862, Major General Theophilus Holmes was assigned to the Trans-Mississippi command that had originally been assigned to Magruder.[42]

It took several months for the anti-Magruder tide to recede in Richmond. He did not receive his assignment to the Southwest until October, and when it finally did come it was to command only the District of Texas, New Mexico, and Arizona, and not the whole Trans-Mississippi Department as he had originally been offered. By this time, the nature of the assignment was less important to Magruder; his inactivity had caused so many rumors to circulate about his situation that any assignment at all was a vast improvement.[43]

Although Magruder must have viewed his transfer to Texas under these circumstances as a serious blow to his reputation and prestige, he was actually the logical man for the job. After all, the defenses of the Texas Gulf Coast at this point in the war would have to rely principally on artillery (his specialty) to repel Union ships. In addition, as General Hebert had continually emphasized to Richmond, the man who commanded in Texas must be able to overcome overwhelming odds with limited resources.

After his performance on the Virginia peninsula in early 1862, there was probably no officer in the Confederate Army who had more experience in fooling a more numerous and powerful enemy than Magruder. Robert E. Lee had implicitly recognized this skill when he had recommended that Magruder be assigned to command the defenses in Texas earlier in the year.[44]

Although he was a good soldier, Magruder did not have General Hebert's administrative skills, and he certainly was no politician. Edmund Kirby Smith, who as head of the Trans-Mississippi Department would later oversee Magruder's actions in Texas, privately summarized his new subordinate's flaws in characteristically blunt fashion:

Magruder has ability and great energy; he acts by impulse, commits follies, and has an utter disregard for law; he has no faculty for drawing around him good men, and his selection of agents is almost always unfortunate; he has no administrative abilities, though he is active and can do a large amount of work; he would be a better commander of a corps, though no reliance could be placed upon his obedience to an order unless it chimed in with his own plans and fancies.[45]

When Magruder's revised assignment was made public, the people of Texas were naturally eager to learn anything and everything they could about the new man who was to control their military destiny. One thing in his favor was that Magruder was said to be related to some well-known Texas pioneers, including some prominent Galvestonians.[46] But the reviews Magruder received from Virginia were mixed. As one Confederate soldier serving there later wrote home to his mother in Galveston, Magruder "is not one of our great generals. In these parts he is considered only a second-rate general; not comparable to Lee, Jackson, Bragg, Longstreet." The soldier then delicately inquired, "Does he let whiskey alone now? That was a very serious failing with him while in command on the Peninsula."[47]

In November, Magruder finally arrived in Houston, where he was greeted by signs hailing him once again as the "Hero of Big Bethel." Instead of press reports castigating him as a coward and a drunkard, as in Richmond, the Texas newspapers focused on his singular record of military achievement. He was the toast of the town in Houston and quickly won the hearts of Texans anxious to believe they had at last found a military leader worthy of their support. Texas Ranger John S. "RIP" Ford wrote later that he spoke for many in saying that Magruder's arrival "was equal to the addition of 50,000 men to the forces of Texas."[48]

The confidence in him exhibited by the Texans was contagious. Magruder again became the aggressive and bold commander who had insisted in 1861 that with five thousand men he could take Washington, D.C.[49] Placed once again in an independent command, Prince John decided to do the one thing that the enemy might not expect from a new commander: attack.

The question of where to attack was an easy one for Magruder to answer. He saw immediately that Confederate control of Texas was the key to holding the Trans-Mississippi region, and that Galveston Island, with its port and railroad connections, was the key to controlling Texas. As he later told his superiors:

> In a word, in my judgment, Texas is virtually the Trans-Mississippi Department, and the railroads of Galveston and Houston are virtually Texas. For whoever is master of the railroads of Galveston and Houston is virtually master of Texas, and this is not the case with any other part of Texas.[50]

Magruder would need men and arms to recapture Galveston, however, and they would have to come from a very unlikely source.

13

From Glorieta to Galveston

Except for its political geographical position, the Territory of New Mexico is not worth a quarter of the blood and treasure expended in its conquest. . . . As for the results of the campaign, I have only to say that we have beaten the enemy in every encounter and against large odds.

GENERAL HENRY HOPKINS SIBLEY,

MAY 4, 1862

By the time that General Magruder arrived to assume command of the District of Texas, New Mexico, and Arizona, the latter two portions of the district had ceased to have much meaning. The Confederate campaign to seize these two territories, and perhaps expand the Confederacy all the way to California, had been a dismal failure. The forces that had been a part of this effort, however, were not only still in existence, but would play a major role in Magruder's campaign to recapture Galveston. Probably no other troops in either army fought under such geographically separated and diverse conditions during the war as did the Confederate troops who first conquered and then abandoned the Confederate Territory of Arizona.

In December 1860, John Robert Baylor and his brother began riding across Texas raising volunteers for a "buffalo hunt," a thinly disguised effort to recruit men for service in the coming rebellion.[1] On August 1, 1861, Baylor announced the creation of the Confederate Territory of Arizona (which included a good part of the present State of New Mexico), with himself as governor.[2]

In December 1861 Baylor was joined by Henry Hopkins Sibley, a former U.S. Army officer in New Mexico who had resigned and obtained Jefferson Davis' permission to organize an expedition to extend the Confederacy to the West. Sibley had with him less than four thousand men, consisting of the Fourth, Fifth, and Seventh Texas Volunteer Cavalry Units, but did have under him some excellent regimental commanders. Several of these men would figure prominently in the action at Galveston. Lieutenant Colonel William R. Scurry was in charge of the Fourth Texas; Colonel Tom Green the Fifth Texas; Lieutenant Colonel John S. Sutton the Seventh Texas; and

Major Charles Pyron headed a battalion of Baylor's Second Texas Mounted Rifles.

Tom Green had first seen combat as a private of artillery at the Battle of San Jacinto. He had gone on to see action opposing raids by Comanches. During the Mexican War he had fought at Monterrey under Captain Jack Hays of the First Texas Mounted Volunteers. Prior to the Civil War he had been serving as clerk of the Texas Supreme Court. He was greatly admired by his troops, who affectionately referred to him as "Daddy."[3]

William Read "Dirty Shirt" Scurry was another experienced soldier. A Tennessean who had relocated to Texas in his early twenties, Scurry had served in the Republic of Texas Army and had also fought in the Mexican War at Monterrey. Scurry was a prominent lawyer, had served as a delegate to the Texas Secession Convention, and was noted as both a poet and orator. There is some dispute regarding the origin of his nickname. Some say that it was merely an observation on the soiled clothing he wore while campaigning across Texas in favor of secession. Another explanation is that he earned this title because such a garment was the only thing that he could find to signal his desire for a truce at the Battle of Glorieta Pass.[4]

Pyron was from Alabama, but had settled in Texas at an early age. Like Scurry and Green, he also had served in the Mexican War. By the time of the Civil War, however, Pyron had become a farmer and rancher. He had his work cut out for him in commanding the rough and often uncontrollable forces organized by Baylor.[5]

Joining forces with Baylor, Sibley's Brigade headed up the Rio Grande and defeated a large Union force under Colonel Edward R. S. Canby on February 21, 1862, at the Battle of Valverde. Although the Confederates lost valuable mules, cattle, and supplies in this encounter, they inflicted more casualties on the Union forces than they themselves suffered and managed to capture six guns. These guns were proudly referred to thereafter as the "Valverde Battery."[6]

At this point, things appeared to be going well for the Confederate expedition. By early March of 1862, Sibley and his men had captured Albuquerque and Santa Fe, and seemed to be on the verge of controlling all of the New Mexico territory. Things came undone, however, in the vicinity of Glorieta Pass, not far outside of Santa Fe.[7]

After a series of bitterly fought engagements during the three days from March 26 through 28, 1862 (leading to its claim to be the "Gettysburg of the West"), Scurry's men had won the field at Glorieta Pass. But, while the fighting was taking place on the twenty-eighth, a company of Colorado troops had come up over a mesa and had destroyed the entire Confederate supply train, leading Scurry to signal for a truce and assess his limited options. The invasion had come to a sudden and unanticipated halt.[8]

The Confederate forces returned to Santa Fe and began a long, desperate retreat to Texas. Short of supplies, shadowed by Union forces, and abandoning all but the most necessary supplies, Sibley's Brigade continued its grim retreat. On April 25, 1862, the first survivors reached the Rio Grande near Mesilla, and began the march across West Texas that ended at last in July when they reached San Antonio. Less than 1,800 men remained of the much larger force that had moved up the Rio Grande with Sibley.[9]

As usually happens with an unsuccessful campaign, the charges of misconduct and incompetence lingered long after. Sibley himself was accused of drunkenness and cowardice during the failed expedition. He spent the fall of 1862 defending himself against these charges and did not join his regiment until it was transferred to Louisiana in 1863.[10]

Even those who did not follow the expedition up the Rio Grande were not immune from its troubles. Lieutenant Colonel Arthur Pendleton Bagby, for example, a West Point graduate and son of an influential Virginia family, became the subject of a very strange disciplinary proceeding.[11] Bagby had been assigned to stay behind at Dona Ana to hold that place with the aid of a small garrison of men from the Seventh Texas Mounted Volunteers. The boredom associated with this duty proved too much for Bagby, and on April 16, 1862, while allegedly intoxicated, he drew his pistol on Captain Hiram Burrows, a Methodist minister. Burrows did not see the humor in this incident and preferred charges.

A lawyer by profession, Bagby attempted to resign from the army to avoid having to answer the charges. The Confederate government, however, was desperate for experienced officers like Bagby and refused to accept his resignation. It was decided instead to convene a Court of Inquiry in Austin on September 15, 1862, with Colonel Tom Green as president. The court found that Bagby had been drinking, but not to the extent that it disabled him from performing his duties. The court did not address the charge having to do with conduct to the prejudice of good order and discipline (i.e., pulling a gun on a minister), because Green—an experienced lawyer himself—was conveniently able to find that the court lacked jurisdiction. The Court of Inquiry apparently did Bagby's reputation no lasting damage. The decision of the court was published on October 23, 1862, and a little over three weeks later Bagby was promoted to colonel of the Seventh Regiment of Texas Mounted Volunteers.

After a well-earned rest, the Sibley Brigade gathered again at Millican, Texas, near Hempstead, in November 1862. Depleted by casualties and desertion, about 50 percent of the brigade consisted of new conscripts who filled the ranks to the original number and requirements. None of the soldiers knew or cared where General Sibley was. As one of his soldiers remembered, "it was generally supposed that he crawled into a jug hole and pulled the jug and hole in after him." [12]

By this time, the original leader of the expedition, John R. Baylor, was also out of the picture. In March of 1862, then-Governor Baylor had advised that an attempt be made to lure the Apaches into a peace negotiation and then kill them. When Jefferson Davis learned of this infamous policy, he stripped Baylor of his authority to raise troops.[13] Baylor then decided (erroneously) that General Magruder, being fresh from Richmond, might have some influence with President Davis. Therefore, at the end of 1862, Baylor traveled to Houston and wrote a long letter to Magruder in justification of his Indian policy, which Magruder dutifully forwarded to Richmond.[14]

The Sibley Brigade's next assignment and destination seemed to be a moving target that varied from day to day. In September 1862, it was directed to report to General Richard Taylor at Opelousas, Louisiana. Then an order, later countermanded, came from General Sibley instructing the brigade to meet him in Richmond, Virginia.[15] At the end of November, the brigade was ordered to the vicinity of Vicksburg.[16] As late as December 23, 1862, even General Magruder professed to have received conflicting indications as to the place to which the brigade was ordered to report.[17] None of these orders made any real difference. The fact was that the brigade had no money and no credit with this district of the army. It needed General Magruder's cooperation to travel any significant distance.[18]

Given his plan to recapture Galveston, Magruder was certainly not inclined to cooperate with any effort to move the Sibley Brigade out of his district. In fact, shortly after his arrival in Texas, Magruder had instead begun bombarding officials in Richmond and Little Rock with requests to leave the Sibley Brigade at his disposal to defend the coast.[19] He used the rumor (untrue, as it turned out) that the Banks Expedition was headed to Texas to justify detaining these troops in the vicinity of Houston. Then, in preparation for the supposedly imminent arrival of Banks, Magruder moved the Sibley Brigade to Harrisburg.[20]

On December 21, 1862, Magruder reported to Governor Lubbock that, despite his many requests to the contrary, the Sibley Brigade was almost certainly going to be sent to General Taylor in Louisiana, and noted that his delaying tactics would not be able to hold the troops in Texas much longer.[21] Magruder's prediction eventually proved accurate. He later received an order dated the day following the Battle of Galveston expressly denying his request to further delay the brigade's departure for Louisiana.[22]

The main problem confronting Magruder with any potential use of Sibley's Brigade in an attack on Galveston was that these troops were poorly armed. During their nightmarish retreat from New Mexico, many of the veterans had sold or bartered their weapons to civilians to obtain desperately needed food and clothing. The new men who had joined the brigade since its return to Texas had no arms at all. Magruder had brought with him from Virginia only one thousand Enfield rifles and two hundred other assorted guns.[23] This was enough to equip a small force, but certainly not sufficient to prevail against the sort of infantry force that might be on its way to Texas. In the end, he really had no choice. Magruder realized that it was now or never; if he was ever going to use any of these troops in an offensive operation against Galveston, it would have to be now.

14

Prince John Plans His Next Production

Gen. Magruder will attack the Yankees at Galveston by water and land tomorrow night. . . . If the Yankees fight well it will be a desperate affair & our loss may be terrible, but if we succeed entirely of which I think there are reasonable hopes it will be a brilliant affair. Galveston will certainly suffer great injury, and may be entirely destroyed. I don't care for this if the enemy can be captured.

WILLIAM PITT BALLINGER,
December 30, 1862

Although Galveston had been abandoned to the enemy without any serious resistance, the feeling persisted throughout the state that this had been a terrible mistake. Colonel Debray had proposed a plan to reoccupy the island as early as November 6, 1862, only a month after Renshaw's forces raised the United States flag at the Customhouse.[1] This plan had been rejected because General Hebert apparently believed that its execution would require more men and arms than were available. Governor Francis Lubbock, however, was not so easily deterred and urged Debray to come up with another plan to present to the new commander (Magruder), who had just arrived in Texas:

Colonel, can we not do something at Galveston? If you could devise a plan whereby you could drive those fellows from the wharves of the city and occupy the place, with the sanction of General Magruder, it would make you a name and do much to raise the spirits of our people. I will most cheerfully co-operate with you in such an undertaking, and will accompany you on any expedition that you may get up for such a purpose. I think, if it is possible, we should repossess the place.[2]

Since Debray was occupied with supervising defensive preparations at Virginia Point, the problem of just how to "repossess the place" was left to be solved by Consulting Engineer Caleb G. Forshey. Forshey, who had been an instructor at a military school for boys on the island before the war, had given considerable thought to the best way of attacking the Union forces in Galveston Harbor. He had probably designed hypothetical attacks against the island as a part of the military education he designed for his students.

This time, however, the attack he designed would be more than a classroom exercise.

Professor Forshey discussed the situation with Magruder during the general's long journey to Houston to assume command and suggested that if a land attack were supported by two or three boats coming down the bay, "it is more than probable that the enemy would evacuate the entire bay." Such an attack should also be made at night, Forshey recommended, to maximize its chance of success.[3] Someone in the staff accompanying Magruder dared to ask the obvious question, "Is it feasible?" to which Forshey instantly replied, "General, I think the best plan is to resolve to retake it, and then canvass the difficulties."[4] Magruder agreed with Professor Forshey's aggressive analysis and arrived in Houston with the firm commitment to redeem his reputation by recapturing Galveston Island.

Forshey's proposed night attack by land and sea appealed to Magruder's dramatic instincts. It was also consistent with a separate recommendation that the general had received from an entirely different source. On his way from Richmond to Houston, Magruder had stopped on the Sabine River, where he had met Captain Armand R. Wier of Cook's Regiment of Heavy Artillery. Wier, who was commanding a fort on the Sabine, had expressed strong support for Magruder's announced intention to reoccupy the Texas coast. More importantly, he had volunteered to take his artillery and man a steamboat on the Sabine for the purpose of clearing the enemy from the mouth of that river.[5] As an old artillery officer himself, Magruder was impressed with the captain's commitment and bravery and determined to find an appropriate place to put him to use.

The genius of "Prince John" Magruder had always been his ability to pull together seemingly unrelated resources and triumph over a more powerful foe. Unlike his assignments on the peninsula in Virginia, however, at Galveston the general's forces must do more than march around in circles and scare an enemy with theatrical tricks. This time his players had to attack and defeat an enemy force that had gunboats with far heavier guns than anything in Magruder's little arsenal. It would take the performance of his life for Magruder and his players to succeed.

The starting point for a successful attack at Galveston was to come up with a good plan. Magruder decided within days of reaching Houston to combine elements of Forshey's plan (night attacks by land and water) with Wier's proposal (artillery units on steamboats). Implementing such a plan would be difficult, and Magruder knew it. Even if Magruder had possessed military resources in abundance, which he certainly did not, to launch this kind of a combined attack at night was to risk disaster. As a historian reviewing this battle plan later observed, "None but a Magruder would have attempted such a hazardous undertaking; it was contrary to all the maxims of scientific warfare. But the battle plan was no more bold or unconventional than Prince John himself."[6]

There were two obvious problems in implementing Magruder's battle plan: first, he had almost no properly armed infantry forces, and second, he had no naval vessels capable of assaulting Union gunboats. As soon as he arrived in Texas, therefore, Magruder began combing the area to locate any and all available forces. Between December 1 and December 27, 1862, Magruder wrote no less than eleven separate letters seeking men and weapons from Texas and Confederate authorities.[7]

In addition to seeking help from higher authorities, Magruder did everything he could to help himself. Skillfully manipulating the military bureaucracy, the general first claimed that he had ordered the Valverde Battery (which included the guns seized from the Union forces at the Battle of Valverde) to report to him in Houston. Then, asserting he could not determine precisely where its associated infantry unit—the Sibley Brigade—was supposed to go because of conflicting orders, Magruder moved the whole brigade to the coast pending further orders.[8] Combining this force with volunteers and state militia, Magruder had narrowly obtained the troops he needed for his land assault.

Planning the naval assault posed problems that were completely beyond Magruder's expertise. Fortunately, however, Leon Smith, whom the general had known in California, was more than ready to take charge of this side of the plan. Smith (see Figure 8) had been a seaman since the age of thirteen. He had spent many years running mail routes between San Francisco and Panama, and with the Morgan line had traveled extensively between New York and Galveston.[9] Magruder was not deterred from relying on Smith by the fact that it was widely believed, and Smith apparently claimed, that he was the half-brother of Caleb Blood Smith, who served in President Lincoln's cabinet as Secretary of the Interior.[10]

Becoming a volunteer aide on Magruder's staff, with the honorary rank of "major" or "commodore," depending on the occasion, Leon Smith supervised all of the naval preparations for the coming attack. At Houston, he began work on two steamers that had been in the Galveston to Houston trade before the war. Such steamers were a common feature of Galveston's wharf scene (see Figure 9) and would be the key to Magruder's battle plan.

Magruder's plan, inspired by A. R. Wier's comments, was to have his ar-

FIGURE 8. *Photograph of Leon Smith.*
Courtesy of Rosenberg Library, Galveston, Texas.

tillery companies mount a thirty-two–pounder rifled gun on the *Bayou City*
and to put two twenty-four–pounder howitzers on the *Neptune*. The general
then directed Leon Smith, in a typical Magruder touch, to put large amounts
of cotton on board the decks of both ships "to give the appearance of protection," but told Smith not to wait to fasten the cotton if it would cost much
time.[11] Smith's assignment in the coming engagement was to take these two
"cottonclads" with about three hundred volunteers and make an attack on

FIGURE 9. *Photograph of Morgan's Wharf and steamer traffic, 1861.*
Courtesy of Rosenberg Library, Galveston, Texas.

the Union fleet while Magruder and his land forces made a diversionary attack on Kuhn's Wharf (where the enemy's infantry forces were located)
from the shore.

The artillery to be mounted on the steamers in this attack was delayed in
reaching Smith, giving him the time he needed to completely secure the
cotton bales, two or three deep, on his two gunboats. The cotton was arranged
in such a fashion that it protected the boilers and machinery of the ships, the
cabins, and the hurricane decks (where the sharpshooters were to be located). In addition, Smith mounted grappling hooks, suspended in the air
on both sides of the vessels, that could be released to fall on an enemy ship
and hold it fast while it was boarded.

Although the attack was originally planned for the night of December 27,

1862, Smith's improvised gunboats were not ready for action until New Year's Eve.[12] This timing worked out well since Magruder had been advised by his chief engineer that the tides would be particularly conducive to an attack during that night.[13]

In planning his attack, Magruder was well informed as to the nature and placement of enemy forces. Scouts were sent into the city almost every night to survey and report on enemy activity. The general himself led a scouting party on horseback one night that examined the Union infantry defenses and potential avenues of attack.[14] These scouting expeditions were not without their casualties, but not due to any conflict with the enemy. While riding back across the railroad bridge to the mainland one night, a member of one of Magruder's scouting parties fell down and accidentally fired his gun. The inadvertent shot hit another member of the party, breaking his right arm and shoulder blade.[15]

On the day before the battle, Magruder sent some of his Galveston civilian volunteers into the city to determine the exact position of all the Union ships, as well as report on the condition of the defenses being constructed by the infantry forces on Kuhn's Wharf. He even had the local scouts draw detailed maps of the city, showing the principal houses and wharves that could be used as shelter by the attacking forces.[16] Finally, Magruder's planning was complete.

When the battle plan was revealed to the Confederate forces that would be involved in the land attack, both the officers and men were pleased to finally be taking an aggressive action against the enemy. They were well aware of the risks that were associated with the unconventional attack. As one pessimistic, but romantic, soldier in Cook's artillery regiment wrote to his wife on the day before the battle was to take place, "I will write again as soon as I return from the island — if I live. If I should be one of the unlucky ones that should fall on the battlefield — which probably will be the case — you will treasure this last epistle from the Idol of your heart."[17]

When it came to gathering information about the operation and armament of the Union ships, Magruder had a real stroke of luck. The coxswain of the *Owasco*, a man named Monroe, had deserted, probably because he had been punished by Union naval authorities for being drunk and fighting. Monroe claimed that this incident had involved a matter of principle, however, and said that he wanted to lead a ship in the coming fight to get even with his former shipmates. Magruder sent the man on to Leon Smith, urging that he be used as an informant to the maximum extent possible, but noting that he should be kept away from guns and liquor for obvious reasons. Magruder's instructions on the man's reliability were simple and to the point: "He will not play false. If he does he dies."[18]

In Houston, Smith's naval expedition experienced difficulty in raising the three hundred volunteers that were required to serve on the cottonclads as sharpshooters and boarding parties. Not even posters with patriotic messages and a parade with a brass band raised the needed men. When the Sibley Brigade was approached about filling this requirement, Tom Green agreed to do so if he was placed in charge of the expedition. General Magruder initially declined this stipulation, but when time grew short, he worked out an arrangement whereby Green was placed in charge of all of the infantry forces on the ships and Leon Smith was given command of the naval expedition as a whole.[19]

Arthur Bagby and his regiment were to be assigned to one ship and Green and his men to the other. Bagby and Green were anxious to participate in the coming fight, in no small part because they hoped it might undo some of the damage that had been done to their reputations during the aborted New Mexico campaign.

At Harrisburg, the Fifth and Seventh Texas regiments and a few companies of Davidson's Battalion were drawn up into line. Colonel Green stood before the men and delivered a speech that, at least to modern ears, seems unlikely to have been designed to generate a very enthusiastic response:

> Soldiers, you are called upon to volunteer in a dangerous expedition. I have never deceived you; I will not deceive you now. I regard this as the most dangerous enterprise that men ever engaged in. I shall go, but do not know that I shall ever return. I do not know that any who go with me will, and want no man to volunteer who is not willing to die for his country and die now.[20]

Remarkably enough, when volunteers were requested to step two paces forward after this speech, the whole line stepped forward, and the officers had to choose which of the many volunteers would go with them on the cottonclads. Thus, from these Texas cavalry units, most of whom had never been to sea, were chosen the approximately three hundred men who would go down in history as the "Horse Marines" or "Horsemen of the Sea" because of their gallant service as sharpshooters and boarding parties on the cottonclad steamboats.[21] These volunteer sharpshooters were then armed either with the Enfield rifles that Magruder had brought with him from Virginia or double-barrel shotguns.

At Harrisburg, the Confederate cottonclads comprising the expedition were made ready, and the volunteers from Sibley's Brigade were taken on board. The *Bayou City* was still under the command of Captain Henry S. Lubbock, the governor's brother. In addition to Tom Green, commanding the sharpshooters on board, Captain A. R. Wier, who had been the first volunteer for the expedition, manned the large rifled gun that had been mounted on this ship.

The *Neptune* was under the command of Captain William H. Sangster. Its guns were placed in charge of Captain Harby (formerly of the U.S. Revenue Cutter *Dodge*) and Lieutenant Harvey Clark. Colonel Bagby, of the Seventh Texas, was in charge of the sharpshooters on this vessel. Joseph Faust, a teenage soldier from New Braunfels, was not impressed by the appearance of the cottonclads and described the *Neptune*, on which he served with Bagby, as nothing more than an "old dilapidated thing." [22] The *John F. Carr, Lucy Gwinn,* and *Royal Yacht* also went along as tenders or reserves, but played no part in the fighting. [23]

When all was in readiness on the evening of the thirty-first of December, the ships proceeded down the bayou to Morgan's Point, where this Confederate "fleet" was greeted by a messenger from General Magruder. The courier relayed Magruder's instructions to proceed to the upper part of Galveston Bay and wait until the sound of artillery announced that the land attack had commenced, then and only then to immediately engage the Union vessels in the harbor. [24] The courier then handed Smith the following personal message from Magruder:

> To Major Smith in command of the Gunboat Expedition, and Colonel Green, in command of the land forces on board:
> I am off, and will make the attack as agreed, whether you come up or not. The Rangers of the Prairie send greetings to the Rangers of the Sea. [25]

Having given the traditional curtain speech to his players, Prince John was now ready for his play to begin.

The Battle of Kuhn's Wharf

General: It gives me great pleasure to mingle my congratulations with the
many thousands that you have received. You, sir, have introduced a new era in
Texas by driving from our soil a ruthless enemy. . . . Your advent was scarcely
known in Texas when we were awaked from our reverie to the realities of
your splendid victory. Its planning and execution reflect additional
glory on your former fame, as well as on the arms of Texas.
SAM HOUSTON,
January 7, 1863

At dusk on December 31, 1862, General Magruder arrived at Virginia Point,
the designated rendezvous point for the troops who were to participate in
the land attack that night. The bridge from the mainland to the island, approximately two miles long, had been planked over with wood to facilitate
the movement of the troops and the artillery. When all was in readiness, the
signal was given and the men began moving across the bridge to the island,
being as quiet as possible. A slight delay developed, however, when the mules
refused to go on the bridge. With some encouragement from their officers,
the men quickly unharnessed the mules and pulled the remaining artillery
across themselves.[1]

After all of the men and guns were across the bridge, the column of troops
and artillery was formed at Pyron's Camp, several miles from the town. With
so many guns and men, the column was lengthy and moved very slowly. The
island being flat and devoid of much vegetation, it was feared that this large
land force might be spotted by the Federal naval forces. This fear seemed to
be confirmed when it was observed, at about 1:00 A.M., that signal lights
were being displayed on the Union gunboats.

It was later learned that these lights had nothing to do with the land
forces. What had actually occurred was that the Confederate naval force had
arrived early and had been observed by the *Harriet Lane* before retreating
out of sight. It was this naval activity, rather than the movements of the land
forces, that had resulted in the signal lights. Actually, the activity by Smith's
naval forces had inadvertently served to distract the attention of the Union

gunboats away from the shore and allowed Magruder and his artillery to make their approach almost completely unnoticed.[2]

The signals by the Federal fleet caused the Confederates to reevaluate their route of approach. The moon was still shining brightly, and it was feared that a direct march toward the city would further alert the Union forces of the attack that was coming. Accordingly, although it would result in a substantial delay, Magruder determined to take a circuitous back way to reach the waterfront where the battle was to commence.[3] The forces going to the eastern end of the island were sent ahead first since they had the greatest distance to travel.

Dividing his forces along roads with which he was not very familiar must have made Magruder uncomfortable. He was undoubtedly reminded of the day six months before when going down the wrong road leading to Malvern Hill had cost him valuable time and ultimately the confidence and respect of Robert E. Lee.

By this time, Magruder was in a very excited and nervous condition. He galloped up to a group of soldiers and demanded in a harsh tone of voice to know what the men thought they were doing. When the men indignantly replied that they were the advance guard, placed there by his own order, the general apologetically told them to "proceed cautiously" and hurried off to see to the disposition of the rest of his forces.[4] These men may well have had difficulty comprehending Magruder's questions. Because he had a pronounced lisp, Magruder sometimes had trouble making himself understood. A doctor in Richmond used to entertain at parties by imitating how Magruder would simultaneously lisp and swear while giving orders. Mary Chesnut wrote in her diary that she had found the doctor's "chawge fuwiously" skit to be extremely comical.[5]

Since the troops heading for the center part of the Confederate line were unfamiliar with the back roads on which they were traveling, they were ordered to meet at the Ursuline Convent, a well-known landmark at which the troops could make final preparations and leave their horses. General Magruder had sent word ahead to the Sisters warning them of what was to come and offering them safe transport off the island. The Sisters refused to go, however, saying that they would instead open their doors to serve as a hospital for the wounded of both sides. During the battle, the Federal gunboats apparently at one point directed their fire at the convent, mistaking it in the dim light for a Confederate fortification. Legend has it that at General Magruder's suggestion, the convent hoisted a student's yellow petticoat as a warning flag and thereby averted significant damage to the structure.[6]

Magruder's plan was to distribute his artillery along Galveston's water-front for a substantial distance so that it could focus on the wharf on which the Massachusetts troops were located without giving the Union gunboats a single target at which to return fire. In all, he had six siege pieces (one of which weighed 5,400 pounds), fourteen field pieces, and a railroad ram (about which, more will be said later). Getting these guns to the right place was a difficult job. Some of them had to be transported up to nine miles under the cover of darkness and over very poor roads.[7]

The east end of Galveston Island curved around to the north in a fish-hook shape in 1863, and the fort near the end of that hook (Fort Point) was a critical place in Magruder's plan. The three guns to be placed here under Captain Sidney T. Fontaine were supposed to draw the attention of the Union gunboats away from the cottonclad steamers approaching from the other direction. The fort at Fort Point gave much less protection to its defenders than might ordinarily be expected from a fort. It had been designed to protect a force firing out in the direction of the Gulf, not backward in the direction of the harbor. Realizing that this fort provided almost no cover for his artillery, Magruder sent six companies of infantry under the command of the experienced Colonel Pyron along to add to this important battery's security.[8]

The remaining guns were to be distributed along the waterfront for a distance of about two-and-one-half miles. Moving as quietly as possible, the infantry and artillery units settled into their assigned positions. The suspense must have been almost painful to Magruder as he waited for word that all of his forces were in place. Finally, shortly after 4:00 A.M., the word came. Undoubtedly with visions of Washington at Yorktown ringing in his head, Magruder personally fired the first gun to signal the start of the attack, enthusiastically declaring: "Now, boys, I have done my best as a private, I will go and attend to that of General."[9]

The battery of light artillery from which Magruder fired the first gun was under the direct command of Captain Thomas Gonzales. Born in Spain, Captain Gonzales organized a battery of 150 men that performed valuable service for Magruder in Texas and Louisiana. The Gonzales Light Battery extended along the waterfront from the Hendley Building on the west to the Hutchings Wharf to the east. The section of this battery located at the eastern end of the line was later termed the "Iron Battery." When the action was over, this battery reported that it had fired at least 317 rounds.[10]

Within minutes after Magruder fired the first gun, the entire Confederate line opened up with artillery and rifle fire aimed both at the Union gunboats and the Massachusetts troops on the wharf. Helping to operate the guns was John R. Baylor (former Confederate Governor of Arizona), who fought in the Battle of Galveston as a private. Magruder's official report praised Baylor for "serving the guns during the hottest of the fire, and with his coat off working to place them in position during the night."[11] The Union gunboats were not slow to return fire with their own shells either, followed by discharges of even more deadly grape and canister.

Magruder knew from his reconnaissance that Colonel Burrell's position on Kuhn's Wharf (see Figure 10) could not be taken by a frontal assault. His battle plan called for Colonel Joseph Cook to lead about 500 men (including a portion of Dick Dowling's Davis Guards, who would later gain fame at Sabine Pass) into the water on either side of the wharf. After wading out through the shallow water, and covered by a protective fire from sharpshooters at the ends of the wharves on either side of Kuhn's Wharf, these forces were supposed to scale the ladders that they carried, mount the wharf behind Burrell's defenses, and capture the Union position from the rear.[12]

It was probably a good plan in concept, but went badly awry when the ladders proved to be too short to reach the top of the wharf. The troops involved in this assault consisted of Pyron's Regiment, Griffin's Battalion, and Companies "A" and "B" of Elmore's Regiment. Colonel Cook wrote after the battle that his men "all acted well, and braver men I never desire to behold, wading into the water up to their hips under a galling fire of grape and canister and musketry, they found no chance to get at the enemy, the ladders being too short for the high barricade. It was indeed a desperate affair." Cook wanted to include the names of some of these brave men in his official report, but it was too dark for him to see or recognize them.[13]

Wet and disheartened, Cook's assault force was forced to retreat under fire from the Union troops on the wharf, who fired with deadly effect from above and behind them. A substantial number of Confederate troops were killed or wounded in this ill-fated wading attack. It is a lasting tribute to their bravery that the Confederate troops who retreated with Cook back out of the water did not give up the fight. Some of them went up on the roofs or into the upper stories of buildings on the Strand and returned the favor by firing down at the Union troops on Kuhn's Wharf.[14]

After the ladders did not work out as planned, the Confederates tried another flanking maneuver by attempting to move a piece of artillery to the end of one of the wharves that paralleled Kuhn's Wharf. This also was unsuccessful. The gun fired only one shot, of no effect, before concentrated fire from Burrell's troops prevented it from being reloaded or serviced.[15]

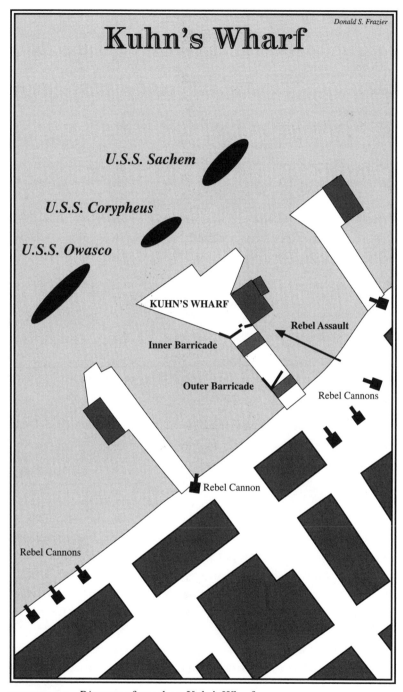

Kuhn's Wharf

Donald S. Frazier

U.S.S. Sachem

U.S.S. Corypheus

U.S.S. Owasco

KUHN'S WHARF

Rebel Assault

Inner Barricade

Outer Barricade

Rebel Cannons

Rebel Cannon

Rebel Cannons

FIGURE 10. *Diagram of attack on Kuhn's Wharf.*
Prepared by Donald S. Frazier.

One of the earliest casualties of the battle, Lieutenant Sidney Sherman (son of General Sidney Sherman, Galveston's first Civil War commander), was mortally wounded while tending his gun soon after the battle began. He was taken to the hospital at the Ursuline Convent. While being carried there, Sherman is reported to have instructed his comrades to "Tell my father and mother that I fell beside my gun, and that I die happy in behalf of my country."[16] The young soldier died in the arms of Mother St. Pierre about an hour after arriving at the convent.

During the initial phase of the conflict, some of the men from Sibley's Brigade who had not been chosen to serve on the cottonclads were ordered to take cover behind the Customhouse (see Figure 11) to avoid heavy shelling from the Union gunboats. Theophilus Noel, a scout and runner who was "packed like sardines" with hundreds of other Confederates behind this building, recalled:

> We were rushed in behind the Custom House, a brick building which had been erected only a short time before the commencement of hostilities, and were ordered to be still. By this time the balls and shot and shell from the Federal fleet was playing havoc with the brick and stone buildings that were then on the island, and mortar and dust and brickbats and pieces of shells were about as thick as anyone ever saw weasels in a barnyard, and there we were in a very dilapidated if not scared condition.[17]

Noel also recalled that to ease the tension, one of the men behind this building called out in a loud (and apparently profane) voice:

> Boys be ——— ——— still, for if them ——— ——— Yankees hear us and find out where we are they will bring out that ——— gun they have got that shoots around corners.[18]

The nervous laughter elicited by this comment had barely subsided when a large shell struck nearby and put an abrupt end to further conversation. Noel observed that one shot fired by a Federal gunboat came down Tremont Street, just skimming the face of the earth, and after rolling and bouncing its way through the town to the Gulf it ricocheted and "the last I saw of it it was on its way to Tampico, Mexico."[19] Three shots went entirely through the Customhouse while Noel and his comrades took shelter behind it.[20] Repairs to the building necessitated by this bombardment can still be seen to this day.

As Magruder planned his battle strategy, he must have been intrigued by the presence of a railroad line in the immediate vicinity of the place where

FIGURE 11. *Nineteenth-century photograph of the U.S. Customhouse at 20th and Postoffice. Courtesy of Rosenberg Library, Galveston, Texas.*

he intended to fight the battle. At Savage's Station, six months earlier, the general had used an armored, rail-mounted gun for the first time in history, but with little effect. Still fascinated with the concept of an armored, mobile battery (in essence, the predecessor of the tank), Magruder once again contrived to mount a large naval gun on a railway flat car and had it hauled into the city. This time, however, the gun was protected by cotton bales rather than iron armor.

Magruder's cottonclad gun was carried over the railroad bridge to a switch track in the vicinity of 32nd Street that was within a few hundred yards of the shore. Although it was indeed used in the battle, the rail-mounted gun was too far away from the action and, as at Savage's Station, does not appear to have had much impact.[21] The Confederates in Galveston were apparently impressed enough with Magruder's mobile gun concept that they were not deterred by its initial failures. At the end of the war they were constructing a "turret-car" (never completed) to serve once again as a "battery on wheels."[22]

As daylight approached on New Year's Day, the Union gunboats had begun to effectively use their heavier guns to drive back the Confederate land forces and their small field pieces (see Figure 12). At a distance of not more than three hundred yards from the Confederate batteries, the Union gunboats' fire was, as Magruder conceded in his official report, "deadly."[23]

Many of the Confederate artillerymen who participated in this unequal contest never forgot the noise and furor. Joseph E. Wallis wrote after the battle that he had heard another survivor declare that "all of them that want to fight Gunboats can do it, but he will be d——d if he will do it again."[24] Another survivor who had escaped death under the awful fire from the Union gunboats reasoned long after the war that on the basis of this experience he was glad he had not been in any other battles, "for if I had been I might have lost my life."[25]

The noise from the firing of so many guns in such close proximity reverberated throughout the city and was so disquieting that dogs in the city started howling in sympathy. Civilians were roused from their beds and scrambled to safety on the beach, where they anxiously huddled behind sand dunes until the battle was over.[26] The sound of the battle was heard for many miles. A former slave named Jacob Branch recalled, when interviewed as part of a government project in the 1930's, that although he was not sure exactly what was going on, he could clearly hear the sounds of battle miles away in the countryside:

> One morning Alex and me got up at the crack of dawn to milk. All at once came a shock that shook the earth. The big fish jumped clean out of the bay, and turtles and alligators ran out of their banks. They plumb ruined Galveston! We ran into the house, and all the dishes and things jumped out of the shelf. . . . The soldiers put powder under people's houses and blew up Galveston.[27]

Even the Massachusetts troops, who were lying down for protection at the end of Kuhn's Wharf, observed that the "crashing of walls and falling timbers, and a constant rain of bricks, mortar and roofing, as the shot and shell plunged through buildings, added to the crash of many hundreds of window panes, assisted to make the night hideous."[28] One Confederate soldier watching the proceedings had a different impression, calling the spectacle "the most terribly sublime scene I ever witnessed."[29]

As dawn broke and the Union gunboats could more easily see their targets, the Confederate artillery and infantry forces were being badly battered. With Magruder's consent, the experienced General Scurry did a creditable job of supervising the withdrawal of as many guns as possible to more secure positions behind buildings. As Magruder gave the order to begin withdrawing his artillery forces, he must have felt deeply discouraged. His grand assault on Kuhn's Wharf had turned out to be nothing but a repeat (on a

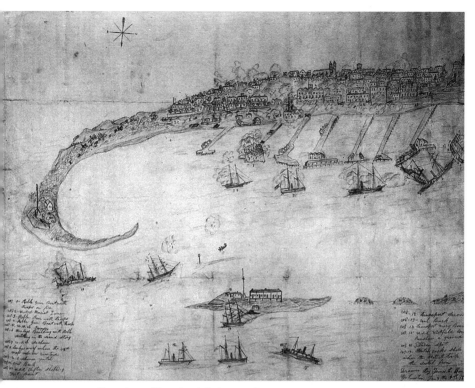

FIGURE 12. *Drawing of Battle of Galveston by contemporary eyewitness. Courtesy of Rosenberg Library, Galveston, Texas.*

smaller scale) of the disaster at Malvern Hill. With a heavy heart, and anticipating a possible counterattack, the general also ordered out a cavalry detail to round up some stragglers, authorizing them to use the bayonet if necessary to get the men to return to their duties.

At Magruder's headquarters, local volunteer Henry Trueheart observed that "every man's countenance looked as long as a hoe handle."[30] Major Albert Lea and another member of the general's staff had been assigned the job of monitoring the battle from the top of a large residence (possibly the house now known as "Ashton Villa") near headquarters. Although these observers probably had the best view of the battle of anyone in Galveston, the smoke and dim light made it difficult for them to accurately see all of the details. Accordingly, when the *Harriet Lane* and the *Bayou City* collided, as described in the next chapter, Lea reported to Magruder that it was likely that the *Lane* had disabled or captured the Confederate ship. Shortly after receiving this erroneous report, the despondent Magruder was overjoyed to receive a message from General Scurry confirming the true extent of the

Confederate victory.[31] Within minutes, what looked like a Confederate disaster had instead become a triumph.

William P. Doran, an unusually candid war correspondent for the *Galveston News* who wrote under the code name "Sioux," observed from his vantage point near the Customhouse that when an orderly retreat was first ordered, a number of Confederate troops with blanched faces abandoned their positions on the Strand and ran away crying "We're whipped! We're whipped! I don't want the Yanks to take me to New Orleans!" Doran also noted that after the battle had successfully concluded in the Confederates' favor many of these same men ran past him on their way back to the Strand, throwing their hats into the air and proudly exclaiming, "We've whipped 'em!"[32]

There was no such elation at the end of Kuhn's Wharf. Colonel Isaac Burrell, who was in command of the Forty-Second Massachusetts Regiment, had objected from the very start to the placement of his command in what he viewed as an exposed position on this wharf. His objection had been overruled by Commander Renshaw, who confidently assured him that Union ships would be stationed so that they could defend and pick up his regiment within minutes if problems developed. When Colonel Burrell attempted to send a boat out during the attack to obtain this promised assistance, the boat sank because it was so riddled with bullet holes.[33]

At the first shot from the Confederates, Colonel Burrell had prudently ordered all his men to lie down behind the barricade that had been constructed that day. To conserve his garrison's small quantity of suitable ammunition, the colonel also restrained his men from firing unless, as in the case of the Confederate attempts to flank his position, it was absolutely necessary. Burrell had foreseen that the Confederates would probably direct their fire at the storehouse, and deliberately kept his men out of that building as much as possible. After a shell exploded in the storehouse, a fire started in the tents that were being stored there. The burning tents were dumped into the water through a back door, and the fire was eventually extinguished.[34]

When Colonel Burrell saw white flags of truce flying from the Federal fleet, he also displayed one on Kuhn's Wharf. Possibly because the smoke and haze obscured this flag from view, the Confederates continued to fire for ten or fifteen minutes after this truce flag was first displayed. After the battle, a controversy developed about this firing. In an unusual gesture, Colonel Burrell wrote an unofficial statement for the Confederate authorities in which he praised General Scurry, who ultimately accepted his surrender, for his "gentlemanly conduct and uniform kindness." Burrell also offered his personal opinion that Scurry had neither known about nor authorized any violation of the white flag.[35]

Although Colonel Burrell requested that a three-hour truce be granted so that he could consult with naval forces and consider his options, this request was peremptorily refused by General Scurry. It was later reported that Scurry told Burrell: "If you can stand the fire of my battery that length of time, you can have [three hours to consider surrender], but not otherwise."[36]

With the departure of the Union naval forces (described in the next chapter), and no chance for a truce, Burrell was left with no alternative but to surrender. He offered his sword to General Scurry, who, as a tribute to Burrell's brave defense of his position, refused to accept it.[37] About 9:00 A.M. the Massachusetts troops stacked their arms and marched off, thus ending the battle at Kuhn's Wharf.

Despite the fact that he had been forced to surrender, the military preparations that Colonel Burrell had ordered with respect to his defensive position on Kuhn's Wharf had served his forces well during the battle. Every precaution that Burrell had taken turned out to have been necessary. In addition to the Confederate artillery aimed at them from the vicinity of the Strand, Confederate sharpshooters had fired at them from the tops of buildings and wharves on both sides, wading troops had fired upward at them from beneath the wharf, and they had been forced to contend with errant shot and shells coming from their own gunboats behind them.

Despite this heavy fire directed at their position from almost every possible direction, the Massachusetts troops suffered amazingly few casualties on Kuhn's Wharf. Only one man was mortally wounded and few others were even seriously wounded. Some of the men improvised their own unique means of protection. For example, to escape injury during the battle, the chaplain for the Massachusetts regiment crawled into an iron caldron. Because of this unusual choice of personal armor, he was thereafter affectionately referred to by the men as "Old Ironclad."[38] Another member of the regiment, trying to add humor to the situation, apparently shouted during the worst of the firing, "For God's sake, get where the sergeants are and we will be safe!"[39]

Cottonclad Victory

Gen. J. B. Magruder: I am much gratified at the receipt of your letter
[containing] details of your brilliant exploit in the capture of Galveston
and the vessels in the harbor. The boldness of the conception and the daring
and skill of its execution were crowned by results substantial as well as
splendid. Your success has been a blow to the enemy's hopes.
JEFFERSON DAVIS,
January 28, 1863

Although Magruder's original battle plan had called for him to launch his attack at approximately midnight, the artillery was late getting into position and consequently the first gun was not fired until between 4:00 and 5:00 A.M. Almost five hours earlier, at a few minutes after midnight, Leon Smith and his cottonclads had arrived in sight of the Federal fleet. When they did not hear the land forces fire any sort of signal, Smith and the other leaders of the naval expedition gathered on the *Bayou City* to consider their options.

Upon reexamination of their orders, they concluded that Magruder had clearly intended that it was the land forces that were to initiate the battle. Therefore, it was agreed that the cottonclad armada would retreat up the bay until there was some definite indication that the land forces had begun their attack. The night was hazy and the ships actually retreated farther up the bay than Leon Smith had originally intended.[1] While the cottonclads were waiting for the signal, one of the anxious sharpshooters asked Smith whether he thought the cotton bales on deck would provide much protection against the Federal artillery. His honest (if not encouraging) reply was: "None whatever, not even against grape shot, our only chance is to get along side before they hit us."[2]

When lookouts on the Confederate ships finally spotted the flash of the guns from shore and heard the Union gunships return fire, Major Smith gave the order to attack. The cottonclads slowly turned around and packed hot-burning fuel such as pine knots into their furnaces to ensure as much speed as possible.[3] It was almost dawn before the *Neptune* and the *Bayou*

City reached the edge of the Federal fleet and made a mad dash at the nearest ship, which, as luck would have it, turned out to be the *Harriet Lane.*

As the *Bayou City* made its appearance, Captain Wier opened fire with his thirty-two-pounder rifled gun. In his excitement, the first shot that Wier fired was mistakenly directed at an old schooner (the *Governor Runnels*) that was not even an active part of the Federal fleet.[4] Realizing his error as the cottonclads got closer, Wier then corrected his aim and fired two more shots at the right target.

As he was preparing to fire a fourth shot, a nearby spectator asked the captain to give the enemy a New Year's present for him. In answer to this request Wier called out, "Well here goes your New Year's present!" as he fired the next shot. Unfortunately, the gun did not deliver the promised present. Instead, it exploded, killing Captain Wier and wounding several other men who had been tending the gun.[5] Eight months following the battle, the Confederates determined that this explosion had probably occurred because Wier and his men were using cartridges that were too large for the gun they were firing.[6]

The ebbing tide was strong, and the two Confederate steamers, heavily loaded with men, guns, and cotton, were difficult to navigate. The plan was for the cottonclads to strike the *Harriet Lane* on opposite sides, thus maximizing the chance that at least one of the Confederate ships would be able to send over a boarding party. The *Bayou City*'s first attempt to ram the *Lane*, however, was a complete failure, striking only a glancing blow that took off part of the Confederate ship's wheelhouse. Slowly turning around, it again steered for the larger and more heavily armed Union ship.[7]

Meanwhile, the *Neptune* set a course for the wheelhouse on the other side of the *Lane*. By this time, the *Lane* had gotten up steam and was moving. This movement caused the *Neptune* to strike the Union ship's side, missing the wheelhouse by about ten feet. The *Neptune*'s bow was seriously damaged by this collision, causing it to take on water. In addition, as it passed around under the stern of the *Lane*, several shots by the Federal gunners penetrated the *Neptune*'s hull, causing it to begin to sink. Because he was an experienced pilot, Captain Sangster was able to run the *Neptune* up on the flats, where it sank in only eight feet of water, leaving the sharpshooters on board above the waterline and free to continue firing at the Union gunboats.[8]

Although its initial ramming attempt had proven to be counterproductive, the *Neptune* had succeeded in occupying the attention of the *Lane* while the *Bayou City* took careful aim and rammed it a second time with as much momentum as it could muster. The Confederate ship struck the *Lane* under the end of its port water wheel, causing the Union vessel to careen over and ending any further movement.[9] Either the collision with the *Bayou City* or a lucky shot from the *Neptune* also carried away the *Lane*'s cathead (a beam near the bow of the ship to which the anchor was fastened), causing the anchor to inadvertently deploy. This left the Union vessel a sitting duck.[10]

As soon as the ships became locked together, the Confederate boarding party proceeded across to the deck of the enemy ship (see Figures 13 and 14). Because he was an experienced mariner, and therefore used to moving between ships, Leon Smith was the first man to cut away the nets intended to repel boarders and reach the deck of the *Harriet Lane*. The Confederate boarding party made short work of the officers on deck (most, if not all, of whom had already been injured), and the remainder of the crew soon surrendered. Nearly every officer on the ship was killed or wounded, most by virtue of the heavy fire delivered by sharpshooters on the two cottonclads before the boarding party had even arrived. The Union officers who were killed or mortally wounded included Captain Jonathan Wainwright and second in command Lieutenant Edward Lea.[11]

When the *Bayou City* struck the *Harriet Lane* so forcefully, portions of the *Lane*'s wheel brace had actually run through the deck of the Confederate ship, locking the two vessels tightly together. This caused problems when the *Owasco* came steaming toward them, firing wildly in an attempt to drive off the Confederate boarders. Thinking quickly, Leon Smith ordered the Union prisoners to be brought up on deck and placed at the front as a human shield to discourage the *Owasco* from firing.[12]

When the *Owasco* was only two or three hundred yards away, an attempt was made by the Confederate boarding party to turn the *Lane*'s guns on the approaching Union gunboat. This proved impractical because the deck of the ship was leaning at such an angle that the guns could not be properly aimed. The Confederate sharpshooters instead poured a heavy fire at the Federal ship with their rifles and shotguns. The *Owasco*'s captain became concerned that he might run aground in the narrow channel or injure the Federal prisoners, and decided to retreat. After the failure of this rescue attempt, a white flag was raised on the *Harriet Lane* and it formally surrendered.[13]

Captain Lubbock requested permission to take one of the *Lane*'s boats and see if he could obtain the surrender of the rest of the Union fleet. Commodore Smith readily agreed. Lubbock took with him Josiah Hannum, the senior surviving Union officer on board the *Lane*. Flying a flag of truce, Lubbock approached the *Owasco* and asked who had charge of the fleet.

FIGURE 13. *Sketch of Civil War vintage by George Grover of the capture of the U.S.S.* Harriet Lane. *Courtesy of Rosenberg Library, Galveston, Texas.*

When told that it was Captain Richard Law on board the nearby *Clifton,* Lubbock promptly went to that ship and boarded it. Captain Law met him on the gangway and demanded to know his business. Lubbock asked to discuss his business privately in the captain's stateroom, and this request was granted.

In this more congenial setting, Captain Lubbock boldly proclaimed that he was there to demand the surrender of the whole fleet in the name of his commander, Commodore Leon Smith. When asked the basis for this remarkable demand, Lubbock responded that the Confederates had captured the *Lane* and had killed most of the crew (a statement that although untrue was apparently corroborated by Acting Master Hannum of the Union ship), and that Hannum was the senior living officer.

What Lubbock was hinting was that the Rebels were about to use the *Harriet Lane* and its powerful guns against the rest of the Union fleet. Lubbock knew, of course, that this was impossible due to the condition of the interlocked vessels. Law, however, did not know this and asked what terms Lubbock was prepared to give. Thinking well on his feet, Lubbock proposed

FIGURE 14. *Detail of* Harriet Lane *capture from Grover sketch.*
Courtesy of Rosenberg Library, Galveston, Texas.

that the Union naval forces take one vessel to remove all of the crews from
the harbor and that all of the rest of the ships and public property be turned
over to the Confederates. Law, who had apparently mistaken Captain Lubbock for the Confederate governor by the same last name, asked for three
hours to go over and discuss these terms with Commander Renshaw, and a
truce for the specified period was granted.[14]

Law took a small boat and went to find Commander Renshaw, who was
otherwise occupied. When the Confederate ships had first been sighted at
around midnight, and elected to retreat up the bay, Commander Renshaw
and his flagship, the *Westfield,* had apparently moved toward them to investigate. In the dark and the fog, and at the worst possible time, the ferryboat
had run aground on Pelican Spit for the second time. The ship could not be
hauled free, but instead simply lay there, alone and helpless, during the attack on Kuhn's Wharf and the capture of the *Harriet Lane.* It is no wonder
that when Law finally reached Renshaw and told him of the Confederate
surrender demand, Renshaw was in no mood to entertain it. Law was told

sharply that no surrender would ever be made and was instead directed to take his vessels and immediately leave the harbor.

At about 8:00 A.M., Commander Renshaw ordered the *Saxon* and the *Mary Boardman* to come near his ship and take on board its crew. He had reluctantly decided that the *Westfield* must be destroyed to prevent its capture and use by the enemy. It can only be imagined what thoughts went through Commander Renshaw's mind as he made this fateful decision. Perhaps he thought about the explosion of the Confederate ironclad *Louisiana*, which had narrowly missed destroying him and other officers on board the now-captured *Harriet Lane*. Perhaps instead he thought about the explosion of the *S. C. Jones*, whose premature destruction he had used as the basis for urging dismissal from the service for two junior officers. Almost certainly Renshaw was beginning to consider how he would explain this debacle to Admiral Farragut, who had recently demanded that if attacked Renshaw and his fleet must "make a defense that will do credit to the Navy as well as yourselves." [15]

Whatever Renshaw's thoughts on this occasion, they were destined to go unrecorded. He determined to use an improvised explosive charge, ironically called a "slow match" due to its delaying feature, to dispose of the *Westfield*. Its decks were covered with turpentine, powder trails were laid to the open magazine full of powder, and the safety valves of the boilers were chained down to maximize the destruction that would be caused by the planned explosion. [16]

There was only one problem. Renshaw's "slow match" turned out to be either too slow, or too fast, depending on which account is accepted. One account of what followed is that at about 8:45 A.M. the commander set the fire and was descending the ladder to his boat when the charge prematurely blew up, killing Renshaw and the crew of the small boat that was to carry him off. [17] Another explanation of the disaster is that Renshaw and the crew of his small boat originally pulled off from the *Westfield* to a safe distance, but the charge did not explode by the time anticipated. When Renshaw returned to the vessel to see if the fuse had gone out, the charge then blew up, taking his boat and crew with it. [18]

Quartermaster Charles Burrell, the colonel's brother, who was on the deck of the *Saxon* at the time, claimed to have witnessed the explosive destruction of the *Westfield* so closely that he had seen Commodore Renshaw "rapidly ascending, and then coming down in small pieces," a fate that one of the embittered Massachusetts troops later declared to have been a "fit ending of a traitor's life." [19]

Prior to the explosion of the *Westfield,* while Law had been off consulting with Commodore Renshaw, Captain Lubbock had taken the opportunity to go over to Kuhn's Wharf, where he was helped up from his boat by a tall man who introduced himself as Colonel Burrell of the Massachusetts forces. Lubbock explained that his proposed surrender terms did not extend to the land forces, and offered to go with the Union officer to discuss the matter with General Scurry. They were met at the end of the wharf by Scurry and his staff, to whom Lubbock introduced his new acquaintance. While that group discussed the subject of Burrell's surrender, Lubbock rode off on a borrowed horse to visit with General Magruder.[20]

Magruder's headquarters during the battle had been situated at the home of E. B. Nichols, who was serving as one of the many volunteer aides on the general's staff. Lubbock found Magruder having breakfast at this residence on Broadway and told him the details of the success enjoyed by his "Rangers of the Sea." The understandably excited Magruder embraced Lubbock and proclaimed himself anxious to view the captured *Harriet Lane.* Lubbock and his boat then took the general to tour his new acquisition. The officers and staff members were very impressed with the *Lane* and its rich furnishings. Even though the deck was still covered with blood, one of Magruder's staff observed that it was a "splendid craft, fitted up in the finest style," on which "every place where they could mount anything with brass they have done so."[21]

As the deadline for expiration of the truce approached, Colonel Tom Green and Captain Lubbock were sent to get the Union response to their surrender demand. Always ready with a bluff, Magruder had instructed Lubbock to tell the Federal commander that the Confederates had two more ships just like the cottonclads coming down the bay and a large land force in reserve, and that there was simply no option other than accepting the terms that had been previously offered.[22] When Lubbock's party reached the *Owasco* and boarded it, they were surprised to feel that ship begin steaming toward the entrance to the harbor, still flying the flag of truce. Lubbock complained to the captain, who explained that he was only following the orders he had received from Commander Law. At about this point, shortly after 8:00 A.M., the *Westfield* blew up.[23]

Lubbock and Green were taken to the *Clifton* (which was also under steam), where they confronted Commander Law with his clear violation of the truce. Law responded that he was only following Renshaw's orders and offered to take the Confederate representatives to discuss the situation with that officer. None of the Union or Confederate representatives then present knew at the time that such a discussion had been rendered impossible by the explosion that they had recently witnessed in the distance. Following Renshaw's example, Law advised the commander of one of the smaller Union schooners to spike his guns and burn his vessel in preparation for a hasty departure, but the smaller ship's commander declined to do so, a decision for which he was later promoted.[24]

As the *Clifton* neared the entrance to Galveston Harbor, Green and Lubbock angrily demanded to be let off and were permitted to return to shore in their boat. Under these strange circumstances, the portions of the Union fleet that had not been captured or blown up steamed out of Galveston Harbor while flying the white flag of truce. Commander Law, to whom command of the fleet had fallen with Renshaw's death, was frightened that the Confederates would use the captured *Harriet Lane* against his ships. He took what was left of the mortar flotilla and headed immediately back to New Orleans to report the bad news.[25]

Captain Lubbock taunted long after the war that "I felt then, as I do now, that it was not a manly act to leave the harbor with the flag of truce flying."[26] Thus, in an ironic finish to what had already turned out to be one of the most unusual battles of the war, the Union fleet that had steamed into Galveston Harbor under a flag of truce less than three months earlier, departed in this same, unorthodox fashion.

When General Magruder finally realized that the enemy fleet was escaping under a flag of truce, he ordered the Confederate batteries to ignore the truce flags and resume firing, but by that time the Union ships were too far out of range. One of the more zealous Confederate artillery companies fired a large gun mounted on the *Harriet Lane* at the escaping ships. The stern of the captured vessel being in the way because of the angle at which the ship was leaning, the gunners fired a round of grape shot first — to make a hole in the stern — and then unsuccessfully fired shots through the hole that they had just created.[27]

As what was left of the Union fleet steamed toward the Gulf of Mexico, Leon Smith could not stand by and watch them go unchallenged. With a group of volunteers, he boarded the *John F. Carr* and headed after the departing ships. Although it was a dramatic gesture, the small ship Smith had chosen was too slow to catch any of the enemy vessels and ended up being almost overcome by breaking waves. On the way back into the bay, however, Smith captured three small Union ships (the *Cavallo*, *Elias Pike*, and *Lecompte*) and substantial cargoes of supplies.[28]

This ended the Battle of Galveston. The Confederates had reoccupied the city and emerged with a decisive victory that was greater than any they could possibly have anticipated. In addition to the three small supply ships captured by Leon Smith at the end, Magruder's forces had captured the *Harriet Lane* and her crew (109 prisoners), indirectly caused the destruction of the *Westfield* and the Federal naval commander, and had captured all of the Union land forces (approximately 260 men) with their supplies. This had certainly not come without cost, but considering the heavy fire that they endured, Confederate casualties were relatively light. General Magruder's official report later stated that he lost a total of 26 killed and 117 wounded.[29]

News of the Confederate victory traveled swiftly. Newspaperman Ferdinand Flake sent colorful status reports from Galveston to Houston by telegraph while the battle was in progress, making it one of the few Civil War battles to have been the subject of what was essentially "live" news coverage. Newspapers all over Texas and the South used these wire reports, quickly preparing extra editions with headlines proclaiming the "glorious news" of the "Recapture of Galveston from the Yanks!"[30]

Aided by such dramatic news coverage, General Magruder became the hero of the hour and received congratulatory messages from across the Confederacy. President Jefferson Davis congratulated Magruder on his "brilliant exploit."[31] Confederate Governor Francis R. Lubbock, whose brother Henry was the captain of the cottonclad *Bayou City* that had rammed the *Harriet Lane* and turned the tide of the battle, hailed the Battle of Galveston with family pride as the "most dashing affair of the war."[32]

Both the Texas legislature and the Confederate Congress passed special resolutions praising Magruder and his forces for their "brilliant" victory.[33] The news eventually reached all the way to the Confederate troops in the field in Virginia, where J. E. B. Stuart joked around the campfire that Magruder was guilty of the rape of Harriet Lane.[34] Prince John relished the attention he received from the press and the jubilant citizens. In Houston, he was given a parade and a ball, at which he made a speech and was presented with a sword.[35]

It is not surprising that from the United States Navy's viewpoint, the Battle of Galveston was considered to be one of the great debacles of the war. Union Admiral David Farragut, who was in charge of the West Gulf Blockading Squadron, of which the naval forces at Galveston were a part, referred to the battle as the "most unfortunate" and "most shameful" incident in the entire history of the Navy.[36] He wrote shortly after the battle that the "disaster at Galveston has thrown us back and done more injury to the Navy than all the events of the war."[37] Assistant Secretary of the Navy Gustavus

Fox agreed, noting that the defeat at Galveston "was the most disgraceful affair that has occurred to the Navy during its whole history."[38]

Although agreeing that the battle was an unmitigated Federal disaster, the Northern press preferred to focus on the "noble and gallant defense" that had been unsuccessfully made by the officers of the *Harriet Lane.* To emphasize the extent of this gallant defense, the *New York Tribune* erroneously reported that all but 10 or 20 of the 130 men in the crew of that vessel had been killed by the Rebels.[39]

As with every disastrous defeat, the search for scapegoats by the losing side began almost immediately. Admiral Farragut confessed to the Secretary of the Navy that it was difficult to conceive of a "more pusillanimous surrender" than that which had occurred in the case of the *Harriet Lane.*[40] Navy Secretary Welles was mortified by the events of January 1, 1863, and wrote ominously in his diary that "someone is blamable for this neglect."[41] Within two weeks, a Court of Inquiry was convened in New Orleans to find that "someone."

Since Commander Renshaw was not around to receive the blame, Commander Law was court-martialed for the incident. Law was charged with not doing his utmost to recapture or destroy the *Harriet Lane,* and also with leaving his blockading station without permission. He was eventually found guilty of both of these charges and sentenced to be dismissed from the Naval Service, a sentence that was later lightened to a three-year suspension from rank and duty.[42]

From the U.S. Army's perspective it was difficult to find a deserving scapegoat other than the U.S. Navy. Colonel Burrell and his men had performed their duties with courage, and could not easily be blamed for the debacle at Galveston. General Banks, however, was concerned that there might potentially be some blame attached to his having sent such a small force of Massachusetts troops to Galveston and determined to shift it to a more convenient target.

As part of an elaborate effort to conceal its real objective, the Banks Expedition had arrived in New Orleans accompanied by General A. J. Hamilton, who had been named Military Governor of Texas by President Lincoln. When Hamilton learned that the destination of the expedition was New Orleans, and not Texas as he had been led to believe, he and the men with him (whom Banks denounced as commercial mercenaries) complained bitterly. Using these complaints as his excuse, Banks explained to the Secretary of War that in addition to the Navy's false assurances of safety, Hamilton's "impatience and the violence of those about him led me sooner to send a detachment of troops to Galveston than I should otherwise have done, and is immediately the cause of the small loss the army has sustained there."[43]

Even more than two years after the Confederate recapture of Galveston, General Banks was still smarting from the loss of the island. Saying that Galveston, as a military position, was second in importance on the Gulf Coast only to New Orleans and Mobile, Banks wrote to the Secretary of War in April 1865 that the loss of Galveston was "the most unfortunate affair that occurred in [the Department of the Gulf] during my command."[44]

After the Battle

Soldiers of the Army of Galveston:
The New Year dawned upon an achievement whose glory is
unsurpassed. That glory is yours. You have recaptured an island 2 miles
from the mainland. You have repossessed yourselves of your beautiful "Island
City," and made its hostile garrison, entrenched behind inaccessible barricades,
surrender to you at discretion. . . . Your general is proud to command you;
your State and country will honor you as long as patriotism and
heroism are cherished among men.

GENERAL JOHN BANKHEAD MAGRUDER,
Address to the Army of Galveston, January 14, 1863

After the surrender, General Magruder, wearing what the Union troops described as a "gorgeous" uniform, visited the wharf that he had encountered such resistance in capturing. The storehouse at the end of Kuhn's Wharf had so many holes that it looked like a sieve. Impressed by the severity of this damage, General Magruder expressed surprise at the small number of Union casualties and correctly predicted to Colonel Burrell that he would never again be subject to such a heavy fire and suffer so small a loss.[1] Magruder uncharacteristically declined the swig of whiskey offered to him by the surgeon of the Union regiment and told Colonel Burrell (inaccurately as it later turned out) not to worry since he would probably soon be paroled.

Although Magruder did not take the offered celebratory drink, the same could not be said about his extensive official and unofficial staff, which the Union troops described as consisting of numerous "colonels" and "majors" who "seemed to be thick as bees." Magruder's "staff" began the New Year by sampling a case of fine liquors that had been the private property of the Union officers in such a fashion that it was "never seen afterwards."[2] This inattention to property rights was by no means confined to the officers. Some of the Confederate soldiers took advantage of the chaos accompanying the battle to break into homes and stores in the city and plunder their contents.[3]

The captured Union troops were amazed at the appearance and lack of discipline of the Confederate soldiers. Private George Fiske expressed his surprise at the fact that the Confederates did not have ranks, but instead seemed to fight "everyone on his own hook, like a party of indians." He was also critical of their clothing, noting that there were almost no uniforms, and that the soldiers were dressed in all colors and descriptions of homemade clothes.[4] Another Union soldier recorded that the "uniforms" of his captors were so poor that "if you could gather all the rag pickers and beggars that are in New England they could scarcely compare with the Texas soldiers."[5]

After the battle, the Confederate surgeon who was in charge of the hospital at the Ursuline Convent was assisted in treating wounded combatants by the Union surgeons from the captured naval vessels and the Massachusetts infantry regiment. He was in dire need of such assistance because one of his own assistant surgeons had been killed during the battle while moving between wounded men.[6]

One Confederate soldier who received treatment at the convent for a face wound described the scene at the improvised hospital at a veteran's reunion many years later:

> The sisters had turned their convent into a hospital ward and had the wounded laid out in rows on blankets — more than eighty of them — when I went in, boys in blue and boys in gray. They treated them all alike — didn't make any difference to them — they were suffering brothers. They had even picked up a few Negroes that had got shot somehow and had them laid out there, too. The doctors had more than they could do, and mighty little help except the sisters. One of them held the basin under my face while the doctor was dressing my wound, and she wasn't excited a bit — just as cool as if she had been used to such sights and such work all her life.[7]

For their gallant and unselfish service during and after the Battle of Galveston, Mother St. Pierre and the Ursuline Sisters of Galveston are officially recognized on the Nuns of the Battlefield Monument in Washington, D.C.[8]

Other incidents of compassion following the battle were not so formally recorded. There is probably not a more heart-stirring story in the whole Civil War than the story of the reunion of the Lea family at the conclusion of the Battle of Galveston. Edward Lea was the young first officer of the *Harriet Lane* who had been mortally wounded when that ship was stormed by Leon Smith and his boarding party from the *Bayou City*.[9]

Edward's father, Colonel Albert Miller Lea, a classmate of General Magruder's at West Point, served as a volunteer on the general's staff during the battle. In the last letter he had written to his son before the war, Albert Lea had advised his son to join the Confederate cause, noting prophetically that "if you decide to fight for the Old Flag, it is not likely that we will meet again except face to face on the battlefield."

Because of his enthusiasm and dedication to the Union cause, Edward Lea had become one of Admiral David Dixon Porter's favorite young officers. On one occasion, while Porter was using the *Harriet Lane* as his flagship, Lea confided to the older officer that his father had warned that "if he should ever meet me in battle he would shoot me like a dog." When Porter asked the young man whether he ever regretted his decision to stay with the U.S. flag, Edward Lea replied proudly and firmly that he did not, saying, "I would die before I would desert it, and do not desire the love of my family if I can only possess it by turning traitor to my country." [10]

After the fighting had stopped at the Battle of Galveston, Albert Lea revealed to General Magruder for the first time that his son had been serving on one of the Union vessels involved in the battle. Saying, "My God! Why didn't you tell me this?" Magruder immediately gave his old friend permission to go look for his son. As he had predicted before the war, Albert Lea arrived on the deck of the captured *Harriet Lane* to discover his son lying on the deck, dying of multiple wounds. A member of Colonel Lea's family described the events that followed:

> They carried him, his cap and uniform, riddled through, to the hold below, and there he looked up and recognized the face of his father, bending over him. With a smile upon his lips, he asked for "Mother and the children." Then, "Father, I wish I could have given [orders to move the vessel] sooner." The father knew the end must come soon, but felt it had best come away from the noise and confusion of tramping feet, muffled groans, and Rebel yells. And so he left his dying boy to go in search of the litter and ambulance that he alone could find. When he returned his boy's brave fight was over. When asked by his surgeon friend, "Lieutenant, have you any last message?" all the love and trust of the boy at home again in the mountains of Tennessee showed in the words, "No, my father is here." [11]

Edward Lea died before his father could obtain transportation for him to the improvised hospital at the Ursuline Convent. What made this event even more tragic is that, unknown to either of the Leas, on January 1, 1863, the same day that Edward died, Admiral Farragut signed an order directing the young man to leave the *Harriet Lane* and report to him in New Orleans to take command of his own ship and the entire mortar flotilla.[12]

Also killed during the boarding of the *Harriet Lane* was its captain, Jonathan Mayhew Wainwright. Major Philip Tucker, who served on General Magruder's informal staff, was one of the most active organizers and members of the Masonic lodge in Galveston. Learning that Wainwright had been a Mason, Major Tucker insisted on a formal funeral service for him with full Masonic honors. General Magruder initially resisted the idea of burying Wainwright with Masonic honors, saying that it was unprecedented to go to such trouble for a dead enemy. Tucker then reminded him that Lieutenant Colonel William P. Rogers of Texas had received such a funeral by Union authorities after his death during the attack on Battery Robinett at Corinth, Mississippi.

Appealing to Magruder's well-known vanity, Tucker commented that he had heard it "said that you are never outdone in courtesy by a friend or enemy." Agreeing "not by a d——d sight," Magruder finally relented and granted Tucker's request. He ordered not only his own men, but also all of the Union prisoners, turned out the next day to attend the joint funeral for Wainwright and Lea.[13]

On the day following the battle, Edward Lea was buried in the same grave with his commanding officer, Captain Wainwright. Albert Lea read the funeral service over his son's hastily prepared grave in a burial plot in the Episcopal Cemetery donated by Mayor George Grover. Albert Lea's closing words to the Confederate troops and Union prisoners attending the funeral were:

> Allow one so sorely tried in this his willing sacrifice to beseech you to believe that while we defend our rights with our strong arms and honest hearts, those we meet in battle may also have hearts as brave and honest as our own. We have buried two brave and honest gentlemen. Peace to their ashes; tread lightly over their graves. Amen.[14]

Edward Lea's poignant last words—"My father is here"—were appropriately inscribed, along with an anchor and spyglass, on his grave marker.

The Northern newspapers, particularly the New York papers, carried dramatic and sensational accounts of the capture of the *Harriet Lane*. By the time the story reached New York, Leon Smith had become the "notorious Smith," who had shot down Commander Wainwright in cold blood after he had already surrendered. This scandalous charge by the *New York Herald* later came to Smith's attention in Havana, where he had stopped for a rest after running the blockade. In December 1864, Smith wrote a letter to the *Herald* condemning its "wanton desire to defame my character and to pervert well established facts of history." Smith denied killing Wainwright after his surrender, claiming that the Federal officer had been killed twenty minutes earlier "gallantly defending himself with his revolver and cutlass." [15]

A Trap Fails to Close

[Magruder] put on naturally all those grand and
imposing devices which deceive the military opponent.

GENERAL DANIEL H. HILL

On the morning after the Battle of Galveston, the Union steamship *Cambria* arrived off the bar, carrying Colonel (later Brigadier General and Texas Governor) Edmund J. Davis and reinforcements for what Davis believed to be the occupying Union forces.[1] The wily Magruder knew that word of his capture of the city had not yet spread and had set a trap to lure the Federals into port. He continued to fly the United States flag at the Customhouse and on the captured *Harriet Lane*. He also moved the iron buoys marking the channel to ensure that any unsuspecting Union vessel that entered the port would run aground.[2]

After signaling for a pilot for some time, the *Cambria* lowered a boat and a small group of men rowed into the port. This party was captured when they stopped to ask directions at one of the small barks that had been seized by the Confederates the day before.[3] In command of the boat was Thomas Smith, a deserter from the Confederate forces at Galveston who had acquired a reputation as a thief and arsonist prior to the war. He had obtained his nickname, "Nicaragua," when he participated with William Walker and other soldiers of fortune in a series of attempts to gain control of that country and its rich natural resources.[4] Upon being questioned by Magruder, Nicaragua Smith admitted that the *Cambria* was expecting a pilot and had no idea that Galveston was back in Confederate hands.

Magruder's attempt to lure the Union vessel into his clutches was almost spoiled when the fort at Fort Point opened fire on a sailboat that was erroneously believed to be going out to warn the enemy ship. Fortunately for Magruder, the *Cambria* was not scared off by this display. Night was coming on and the Confederates determined to wait until the next day to spring their trap. Then, not having any operative steamships that could go out into the Gulf after the *Cambria*, Magruder equipped a small group of sailing vessels with guns and sent them out toward the Union ship.

Unfortunately for Magruder's plan, the wind proved to be so light that only one of these vessels — a small pilot schooner — could make its way out to the *Cambria*.[5] Alone in this schooner was Captain John W. Payne, who had volunteered for the mission. Payne tried to motion to the *Cambria* to follow him in, hoping to lure the ship in close enough that the other Confederate vessels could make their move. He got too close to the Union ship, however, and was recognized by some of the Texas refugees on board. They turned their guns on him, and Payne was ordered to come aboard.

As Edmund Davis explained after the war, Captain Payne had none of Magruder's native talent to deceive, and narrowly escaped death when the Confederate plan was discovered:

> [Payne] was then cross-examined and soon becoming confused, confessed what had happened and what his purpose was. The men very naturally were much incensed and wanted to hang him at once & he had in fact forfeited his life according to the law usually applied to such cases. . . . I interfered and stopped the proceedings & took him to New Orleans where he was paroled soon after. Payne was a very brave man and seemed honest too. He remarked when I was questioning him that his mother had taught him not to lie and therefore acknowledged the facts.[6]

When Payne admitted the true situation in Galveston, Colonel Davis decided with very little prodding to go elsewhere. There was some discussion about whether to take Payne's boat with them, but Davis resolved the dispute in favor of letting the boat go. He reasoned that if the *Cambria* took the boat with it, the Confederates watching from shore would know immediately that their deception had failed and would send the *Harriet Lane* out after them. Releasing the boat, therefore, Davis took his ship, along with Captain Payne, and headed for New Orleans.

At New Orleans, Payne was questioned extensively by Admiral Farragut. Farragut was relieved to learn that the prisoners from the *Harriet Lane* had not been massacred, as had been falsely reported. After being confined for three days, Payne was then paroled. The captain told friends in Galveston that he was never treated so well in his life as he was during the next six weeks after being released to the care of the ladies of New Orleans.[7]

Captain Payne's fate was very different than the fate of Nicaragua Smith. Smith was tried as a deserter on January 7, 1863, was not surprisingly found guilty, and was executed the next day on the parade ground by a firing squad of ten men. When asked if he had any last request, Smith responded with an obscene reference to the Confederacy and a demand that his adversaries bury him face down. As one reporter later noted, "whatever his faults may have been, cowardice was certainly not one of them."[8]

Magruder's trap did not work out as planned. Instead of luring in and capturing another Union vessel, he had furnished Admiral Farragut with a witness about conditions in Galveston who apparently lacked the capacity for effective evasion and deception. Undeterred by this failure, on January 5, 1863, Magruder issued a proclamation announcing that since the enemy's blockading forces had departed, the blockade of Galveston was now over and the port was "open for trade."[9] As a matter of international law, the general was probably correct. The Confederate government in Richmond certainly wanted to believe he was, and also sent notices (that they knew no rational person would heed) to all of the foreign consuls announcing the end of the blockade in Galveston.[10]

The point became moot when a new fleet of Union warships arrived within the week and again restored the blockade. Immediately upon learning of the disaster at Galveston, Admiral Farragut had ordered Commodore Henry Bell to proceed there with the *Brooklyn* and retake the place if feasible. This was important not only to avenge an ignominious defeat, but also because Farragut felt he "must try and recover the *Harriet Lane,* as she would be a most formidable cruiser if she gets out, on account of her speed and battery."[11]

The thought of the *Lane* as a Confederate cruiser made Farragut shudder. Within a week after its capture, he changed all of the fleet's signals on the assumption that the *Lane*'s signal book had fallen into enemy hands.[12] On January 5, 1863, he warned James Alden, who had initiated the blockade at Galveston in July 1861, that "if the *Lane* gets out, she will be as bad as the *Alabama.*"[13] The admiral's admonition is remarkable in light of the next turn of events at Galveston.

Still Another Disaster off Galveston

It becomes my painful duty to report still another disaster off Galveston. . . . After the abandonment of Galveston Harbor, I sent down Commodore Bell with the Brooklyn and six boats, as fast as I could get them off, to retake the place, but it appears that they had not all arrived [when] a sail was discovered in the offing, and the Commodore ordered the Hatteras to chase, which terminated in the capture of that vessel by a bark-rigged steamer, supposed to be the Alabama or 290.

REAR ADMIRAL DAVID G. FARRAGUT,
Report of January 15, 1863

When Commodore Henry Bell arrived at Galveston on the seventh of January, 1863, he was a man with a definite mission. He had every intention of recapturing the city and the *Harriet Lane* as Farragut wished. Like Farragut, Bell had tremendous respect for the *Lane,* considering it "capable of doing nearly as much injury to our commerce on the ocean as any vessels the rebels have afloat." He knew that none of his ships could individually match the *Lane* in speed or armament, but hoped that with a greater number of ships he might still gain the advantage.[1]

All went well for the Union fleet at first. Their long-range guns made life miserable for Confederate defenders on the beach. Magruder had realized immediately after the battle that another fight was coming soon, and had directed his engineers to supervise troops and borrowed slaves in the construction of earthworks and fortifications as rapidly as possible. While waiting for the other Union warships to arrive, Bell contented himself with driving off these working parties with the *Brooklyn*'s rifled guns. The other ships that joined him made a sort of contest out of this firing, with the *New London* winning the prize for shooting down the Rebel flag at one fort.

Although the Confederates occasionally brought field artillery over to the beach and fired at the new blockading vessels, the gunboats simply moved back out of their relatively short range to avoid damage. It must have seemed a virtual certainty to the Union sailors that they would soon recapture the city. As the paymaster on one of the ships confidently predicted to his father:

Galveston is a doomed town; the disgrace attending the capture of the *Harriet Lane* must be wiped out, and vengeance upon its butchers and captors will be awful. On Monday we shall attempt to pass the forts at the mouth of the harbor. May God preserve us in the terrific conflict and crown our efforts with success.[2]

This Union sailor was not the only one convinced that the Northern naval forces were about to make a serious effort to recapture Galveston. A Confederate soldier at Virginia Point reported to his brother at about the same time that "We expect to have hot work in G[alveston] before long — if we had two weeks more undisturbed we could give them a warm welcome."[3] The Confederate forces at Galveston were to get the two-week reprieve wished for by this soldier, but from a totally unexpected source.

On the afternoon of January 11, 1863, a strange sail was spotted in the distance. Assuming that it was only another blockade runner, Commodore Bell sent the *Hatteras* to chase it at about 3:00 P.M. As darkness was falling, the *Hatteras* caught up with the sail, which turned out to be attached to a bark-rigged steamer. Captain Blake of the *Hatteras* hailed the strange vessel and asked its identity. In answer, the other ship replied that it was a British ship (either the *Petrel*, the *Vixen*, or the *Spitfire*, depending upon which account is consulted). Blake decided to send a boat to investigate. The boat had hardly left the *Hatteras* when a shout came from the other ship of "We are the Confederate steamer *Alabama*," which was accompanied by a broadside.[4]

To understand the horror with which this announcement must have been received by the Union sailors serving on the *Hatteras*, it is necessary to briefly review the unusual career of the C.S.S. *Alabama*. Known originally as the *Enrica* or the "*290*" (because of its hull number at the shipyard), the ship was launched at the Laird Shipyards in Liverpool, England, in May 1862. The United States ministers in Britain had done their best to prevent its purchase by Confederate agents, but had failed in this effort.

Eager to take possession of their new ship, the ship's Confederate agent owners took it out for what was ostensibly to be a trial or test run, and never returned to the shipyard. After avoiding a Federal vessel that was supposed to intercept it, the ship set a course for the Azores, where it received its armament, was renamed the *Alabama*, and took on board an experienced commander — Captain Raphael Semmes.

Within a few months, Semmes and his vessel had become the terror of Northern shipping in the North Atlantic, capturing and destroying twenty prizes within the *Alabama*'s first two months of operation as a cruiser. Northern newspapers reported the exploits of this ship and its commander in a sensational, inflammatory fashion and branded Semmes a bloodthirsty pirate. As the number of its captures grew, the reputation of the Confederate cruiser spread far and wide in the North.

Running short on coal and provisions, the *Alabama* was eventually forced in the fall of 1862 to head south to the Caribbean, where it received pre-arranged shipments of supplies and made some minor repairs. After capturing a few other small ships, Semmes heard rumors, that appeared to be confirmed by false stories planted by the U.S. Army in Northern newspapers, that the Banks Expedition was headed for Texas. He knew that a large military expedition like this would of necessity be supplied by many transports heavily loaded with arms, food, and other provisions. As Semmes considered the possibilities, these ships presented tempting targets.

Captain Semmes knew that any expedition headed for Texas would have Galveston (which had been under Union control since October) as a primary base of operations. He also speculated that because of the difficulty in getting loaded transports across the relatively shallow sand bar at the entrance into Galveston Harbor, many of these transports might be anchored outside of the bar. If he timed matters just right, the *Alabama* could appear off of Galveston one night, sink or set fire to a number of these vessels, and then escape before the Federal ships could mount an effective pursuit.[5] With this plan, and without any knowledge that Magruder and the Confederates had recaptured the city on New Year's Day, the *Alabama* set sail for Galveston and arrived off the island shortly after noon on January 11, 1863.

When the *Alabama* approached Galveston, it was probably the closest to a Confederate port that this famous cruiser would ever get. Semmes had not intended to get close enough to the shore for his ship to be seen during daylight. But the island's flat topography was deceptive; before the captain knew what was happening, the island was in sight and the *Alabama* had been spotted by the Union fleet. Determined to make the best of a bad situation, Semmes decided to keep his sails rigged (and not get up steam) in order to present the appearance of an easy capture. He hoped by this deception to lure the ship sent to chase him — the *Hatteras* — away from the rest of the Union fleet. His plan succeeded, and shortly before dark, Semmes stopped and gave battle to his unfortunate pursuer.

Although brief, the sea battle between the *Alabama* and the *Hatteras* was one of the most famous encounters between two ships of the entire war. The fighting only lasted about thirteen minutes. The *Hatteras,* which was nothing more than an excursion boat that had been equipped with light guns, was no match for the powerful *Alabama*. In a few minutes the Union ship was on fire in two places and was "riddled like a sieve." Water was entering the unfortunate *Hatteras* from so many different places that it soon began to sink rapidly. The *Alabama* took the crew of the sinking ship on board and headed for Jamaica, where it landed the prisoners and repaired the slight damage it had suffered during the engagement.[6]

Bell and his fleet at Galveston tried to investigate when they heard the distant firing of the guns, but their search did not turn up anything during the night of January 11, 1863. At 11:00 A.M. the next morning, however, they discovered two masts standing straight out of the water with a United States naval pennant flying "playfully and unconscious." From a mark on its upper deck they were able to identify the sunken ship as the *Hatteras*. Later that day they recovered six survivors of the wreck, who were the men on the boat that had been lowered from the *Hatteras* just before the fight began. These men confirmed that the enemy ship had indeed been the dreaded *Alabama*.[7]

It was several weeks after this brief but decisive battle before the Confederate troops in Galveston learned what had really happened out at sea. Like the Union sailors, they had seen flashes and heard the firing of guns far out at sea, but it was at first thought that these were only indications that another blockade runner had been captured or sunk. Magruder began to suspect the truth when a variety of unusual articles began to drift ashore, including barrels of pork, pickles, onions, and other provisions that could only have originated from a Union naval vessel. When two large hatchways drifted in, both of which had been splintered by shot, the nature of the incident seemed to be confirmed.[8]

The sinking of one of his ships by the *Alabama* put the planned attack on Galveston in an entirely new light for Commodore Bell. Now, in addition to worrying about the captured *Harriet Lane* inside Galveston Harbor, he had to worry about the *Alabama* (or other similar Rebel cruisers that were rumored to exist) that might be lurking in the Gulf of Mexico behind him. At 4:00 P.M. on January 12, 1863, Bell called together the commanders of all of his ships and held a council of war to discuss the continued feasibility of an attack on Galveston.

The other commanders were all willing to participate in the attack, but Bell finally concluded that it should not be made. The loss of the *Hatteras*, in his view, made it "injudicious to hazard the vessels without a better prospect of success." He wrote in his diary about his extreme reluctance to give up the plan to attack Galveston:

It is with a bitter and lasting pang of grief I give it up, as the blockade of the port with the *Harriet Lane* ready for sea is a very difficult task for so small a fleet as is in the Gulf. There will be censure, inconsiderate censure, but I can't help it.[9]

Thus, although Galveston probably could and should have been retaken by the Union shortly after Magruder's victory, these plans were thwarted by the almost coincidental intervention of the *Alabama*. The *Alabama*'s unexpected appearance and attack, coming so closely on the heels of the ignominious defeat on New Year's Day, so unhinged Union plans to recapture Galveston that they were delayed until Magruder's improvements to the city's fortifications rendered them impractical.

Farragut himself estimated that the delay in attacking Galveston caused by the *Alabama* had enabled the Confederates to fortify their positions to such an extent that it would now require at least double the originally estimated loss of life to recapture it.[10] By January 20, 1863, Farragut had received reports that led him to conclude that the greatly enhanced Confederate fortifications made any plan to retake the city far too dangerous.[11]

An Entrenched Camp

*I hereby announce that the city of Galveston and vicinity, an
entrenched camp, surrounded on all sides by my lines, will be subject to the
rules and regulations established or to be established for the security and welfare
of such camp, and persons will be punished according to military law for
infractions of the same. All persons . . . remaining in the city or on
the island . . . will be looked upon as followers of the camp.*

BRIGADIER GENERAL HENRY E. MCCULLOCH,
August 28, 1863

The new year of 1863 had begun in triumphant fashion for the Confederates
when Galveston was recaptured from the Federals in glorious style. Less
than two weeks later, an attempt to invade the city had again been thwarted
by the fortuitous appearance of the *Alabama*. But the threat to Galveston's
security was far from finished.

Commodore Bell continued to shell the troops engaged in building or
strengthening fortifications on the island. When some of these shells missed
their targets and hit near the city, Bell was chastised not only by the foreign
consuls (who could predictably be relied upon to protest whenever there
was firing), but also by some of the Union surgeons who were still tending
to battle casualties in the city. As a result of these complaints, the commodore then agreed not to shell the Ursuline Convent if it was marked with a
yellow flag.[1]

On January 21, 1863, Bell was angered by the change in location of some
buoys that he believed had been unfairly moved by the Confederates under
a flag of truce. He therefore issued a proclamation giving twenty-four hours
to "innocent and helpless persons" to withdraw from the city prior to commencing a bombardment.[2] But the city had endured these types of threats
before. As the Confederates accurately sensed, Bell had no real desire or in-
tent to bombard the city, and after a few anxious days, life returned to normal, or as normal as it could be in a city under the guns of an enemy fleet.

On January 29, 1863, to test the island's enhanced defenses, the *Brooklyn*,
escorted by the *Owasco* and two other ships, went within a short distance of

shore and began to shell the batteries on which the Confederates were working. A few of the shells came close to the city and civilians scrambled for
cover in the graveyard.[3] The Union ships did little damage, but were able to
confirm that at least one of the Confederate forts now had a gun with a range
more than sufficient to reach them.[4] By the beginning of February, Bell had
determined, as he informed Farragut, that "the defenses and natural obstacles of Galveston are too strong for the gunboats to overcome them."[5]

Galveston was saved during this period by the fact that using the forced
labor of thousands of slaves, as well as his own troops, Magruder and his engineers had supervised the erection of an elaborate chain of earthworks and
wooden fortifications (see Figure 15). This work was both difficult and dangerous. Interment records document that from February to April, 1863, at
least sixty-two black men were buried in Galveston. Although their cause of
death was listed simply as "not known," many soldiers suspected that these
deaths were due to overwork, neglect, and a virtual epidemic of lice.[6] One
soldier in Galveston warned his family in Falls County that if their slaves
were ordered to come to the island, they should also send a "good and atten-
tive overseer . . . as a great many of them die here, and mainly for want of
good attention."[7]

As might be expected of any defenses associated with Magruder, the
Confederate fortifications he ordered constructed in Galveston were frequently not as imposing as they appeared to the Union Navy. In order to
fool the blockaders into thinking that he had more working guns than he actually possessed, Magruder tried a variation of the tricks he had played on
McClellan in Virginia. To deceive any spies that might be watching, it was
announced that the Confederates had designed a foundry and were now
making their own cannon. Large piles of scrap railroad iron were transported to the site of this alleged "foundry," along with wood supposedly to
be used in constructing gun carriages. A careful observer, however, would
have noticed that the pile of wood went down rapidly while the pile of iron
was almost untouched.

What was actually happening in the "foundry" was that twenty German
craftsmen were making at least two hundred highly polished wooden cannons that were virtually indistinguishable from the real thing at a distance.
These "deaf and dumb" cannon were placed in batteries on foggy mornings.
The "Quaker guns," as they came to be called, were usually sufficiently close
copies of the original to deceive the enemy at a distance.[8]

Occasionally, however, circumstances conspired to destroy the illusion.
After a particularly strong storm, for example, one of these "cannon" was

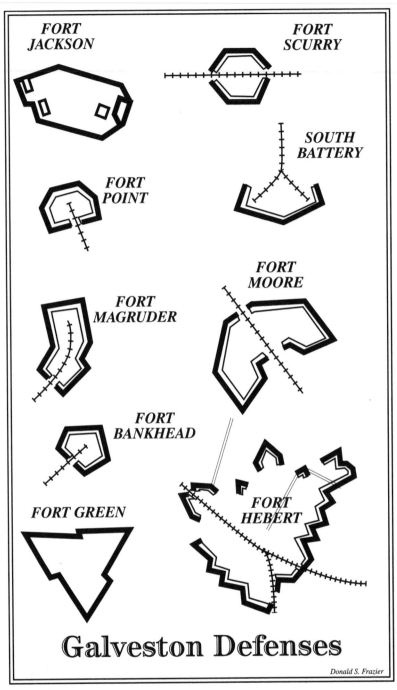

FORT JACKSON

FORT SCURRY

SOUTH BATTERY

FORT POINT

FORT MOORE

FORT MAGRUDER

FORT BANKHEAD

FORT GREEN

FORT HEBERT

Galveston Defenses

Donald S. Frazier

FIGURE 15. *Diagram of fortifications in the vicinity of Galveston Island. Prepared by Donald S. Frazier.*

found by the Union Navy to be floating in the water. It also did not help that a single Confederate soldier was occasionally observed picking up and moving one of these guns without assistance.[9] The crew of one of the Union warships was so amused by this Confederate practice that they hauled one of these painted logs onto their ship with the intention of carrying it home as a souvenir.[10]

Magruder's artillery tricks did not stop with wooden cannons. The various Confederate batteries on the island were all ultimately connected by railroad tracks. The Confederate engineers then placed guns (real ones this time) on gravel carts so they could be moved from fort to fort on the railroad tracks. By firing the same gun from different forts each day the defenders convinced the Union Navy that the island's defenses had many more guns than they ever did.[11] After two false starts, Magruder had finally found a practical application for his gun mounted on a railroad car. Galveston civilians, aware of both the importance and inadequacy of their artillery defenses, nicknamed one of the cannons surveying the Gulf the "forlorn hope."[12]

In addition to frantically constructing batteries and defenses, the Confederates spent the days following their victory on New Year's Day attending to some of the ships and supplies that they had captured. Their first objective was to salvage as many guns as possible. Magruder was delighted to learn that the explosion of the *Westfield* had not destroyed all of its guns. Five cannons were recovered from the wreckage, with two of them found to be intact with gun carriages on the floor of the bay not thirty feet from the wreck.[13] The iron shafts of the *Westfield* were also salvaged from the wreck, using timbers and the rising tide to lift them to the surface. They were then machined under very crude conditions into cannons.[14]

The captured *Harriet Lane* was the next order of business. There was no doubt that this had been a formidable vessel in the United States Navy. The problem was determining if and how it could be used effectively in Confederate service. The Navy Department in Richmond appointed Lieutenant Joseph N. Barney to command the vessel and make a report on its condition. As Barney soon discovered, however, his appointment conflicted with the wishes of General Magruder, who thought that Leon Smith should have the honor of commanding the vessel that he had captured.[15]

In the long run, however, the question of who should command the ship did not matter. The truth was that the *Harriet Lane* was not particularly useful in regular Confederate service. Although the U.S. Navy was terrified that the ship might be converted into a cruiser like the *Alabama*, the vessel's limitations made this impractical. To begin with, the *Lane* had only moderate speed for a cruiser, moving at a top speed under steam alone of about three to five knots.

In addition to lacking sufficient speed and power, the *Lane* was a voracious consumer of coal. Its capacity was about 135 to 140 tons of coal, which would last no more than six days at its consumption rate of about one ton per hour. A Confederate cruiser that had to pick up massive amounts of coal more than once per week would have trouble satisfying its requirements due to a lack of funds, not to mention the difficulty of continually having to evade the blockade. Finally, it was going to be a very tricky project just to get the ship past the blockade and out of Galveston.

Lieutenant Barney estimated that if the ship were fully loaded with coal, its weight would make it draw too much water to get over the sand bars and obstructions at the mouth of Galveston Harbor. This added weight would also reduce its speed to the point that it would have a difficult time avoiding the blockading ships. Barney believed that with some effort he could probably find a suitable crew, but warned that the ship "had been robbed of everything movable." [16] In fact, the souvenir hunters had gone over the captured ships so thoroughly after the Battle of Galveston that someone had even stolen two pistols and a shotgun belonging to Captain Lubbock of the Confederate boarding party. [17]

In the end, the Confederate Navy concluded that the *Lane* was more trouble than it was worth and turned the vessel back over to General Magruder. [18] Before doing so, however, the Navy removed some of its larger guns and sent them to Louisiana for use on the ironclad *Missouri*. [19] Magruder and his staff began to think seriously about converting the *Lane*, stripped of its large guns, and unwanted by the Navy, into a blockade runner. The theory was that the *Lane* could be run into a neutral port, where its cargo and possibly the ship itself could be sold for money that would then be used to purchase badly needed military supplies. [20]

Issues involving disposal of captured property did not always relate to such weighty matters as guns and ships. At one point shortly after the battle, Governor Lubbock wrote to General Magruder and requested that the seed potatoes left behind by the Massachusetts troops be used to develop a new crop for the state. Even more bizarre was a controversy that eventually developed between Colonel Debray and the provost marshal's office over the distribution of captured hats.

When General Magruder determined to recapture Galveston, Henry Trueheart (the county's tax assessor and collector) joined Magruder's forces as a volunteer scout and guide and served in that capacity during the battle.[21] Trueheart proved so capable that after the battle General Magruder appointed him assistant provost marshal with the unofficial rank of captain. At first, this arrangement worked out well and Trueheart was extremely effective.

To combat the "pernicious effect" of drunkenness, for example, Trueheart issued a strong notice threatening to banish from the island any person who was detected "in the introduction, sale or distribution of vinous or spiritous liquors without a proper permit."[22] He also vigorously enforced the conscription laws, ordering the guards to shoot any persons who tried to run to avoid being enrolled for military duty.[23] All went well until June 1863, when a strange dispute over hats led to Trueheart's resignation.

In dividing the spoils of battle, a large number of captured Union Army hats had been distributed to the Confederate soldiers who occupied Galveston after its recapture. Since the war had severely restricted commercial activity of many types, it is perhaps not surprising that a brisk market in these hats apparently materialized when the men began to sell and trade their hats to other soldiers and civilians. This practice angered Colonel Debray exceedingly. He ordered Trueheart to send out guards to seize all of the hats, wherever they might be found.

It appears that tax collectors in 1863 had more scruples than they are commonly believed to have today, because Trueheart flatly refused to seize the hats if they were in the possession of civilians. Debray viewed this as insubordination, placed Trueheart under arrest, and confined him to the city limits. To avoid this unjust punishment, Trueheart resigned his unofficial position and left for Virginia, where he later joined a Confederate cavalry regiment.[24]

Dr. John W. Lockhart found that his assignment to issue clothing to the soldiers in early 1863, unlike Trueheart's unpleasant experience in retrieving hats, was an agreeable task. Because of the plentiful captured supplies, he was able to issue shirts, pants, and "drawers" to all of the men who wanted them. As he wrote to his wife, he found the soldiers' reaction to this free clothing interesting and educational:

I am amused at the different countenances and expressions when one would apparently draw a better article than another. Some selected with as much care as if the fate of nations depended on it, others did not seem to care and took the first they came to. Camp is a great place to learn human nature.[25]

After holding the position informally for several months, Colonel Xavier Blanchard Debray was officially appointed to the command of Galveston Island in February of 1863.[26] This was not an easy command. In addition to worrying about such matters as the illicit trade in hats, and the ever present threat of invasion, Debray had to deal with a host of local disputes. One such dispute, surprisingly enough, involved scheduling the flow of railroad and cattle traffic.

The butchers of the city, who had already demanded and received the Union Navy's respect, claimed the inalienable right to drive their cattle across the railroad bridge to and from the mainland. The railroad company, understandably enough, wished to have free and unrestricted access to the bridge built for its use. In a decision worthy of Solomon, Debray decreed that the cattle would be allowed free passage across the bridge only for two hours in the morning and a short period in the evening, providing that they went across in "droves not exceeding twenty each."[27]

In addition to directing livestock traffic, Debray's job description also included entertaining foreign visitors. Colonel Arthur James Fremantle, an English army officer who visited Debray at his residence on May 3, 1863, recalled the frontier atmosphere that prevailed in Galveston at that time:

> We sat down to dinner at 2 P.M., but were soon interrupted by an indignant drayman, who came to complain of a military outrage. It appeared that immediately after I had left the [railroad] cars, a semi-drunken Texan of Pyron's regiment had desired this drayman to stop, and upon the latter declining to do so, the Texan fired five shots at him from his six-shooter, and the last shot killed the drayman's horse. Captain Foster [of Debray's staff] (who is a Louisianan and very sarcastic about Texas) said that the regiment would probably hang the soldier for being such a *disgraceful bad shot.*[28]

As the war dragged on through 1863, and the threatened second invasion of Galveston did not materialize, the Confederate troops on the island became increasingly bored with army life. One soldier wrote to his wife that "I am tired of soldiering I assure you, it is far from being the vocation I should select for a constant occupation."[29]

With time on their hands, the troops eagerly sought any and all forms of entertainment. The available diversions were sometimes shocking to men who either came from strict religious backgrounds or small towns. One soldier in the Arizona Brigade complained to his family that his camp in Galveston "was the wickedest place I ever saw. It is useless for me to try to describe what sort of wickedness is practiced here."[30]

Certain types of diversions for which Galveston had been famous were seriously inhibited by the war. Shortly after the Battle of Galveston, for example, a group of soldiers (including at least two officers) heard that an "assignation house" was operating on the beach. Borrowing General Magruder's hack, the men hurried to the site of this enterprise, only to be informed by the proprietor that there were no women in residence. Disappointed by this news, the party insisted on searching the house to verify the owner's story. To console themselves when their quarry proved elusive, the searchers helped themselves to some brandy they found in one of the otherwise unoccupied rooms.[31]

Drunkenness and crime among the occupying forces were problems that afflicted Galveston throughout the war. Despite official prohibition of the practice, abuse of alcohol (including crudely manufactured products) became so severe that by October 1863, the official cause of death for one Irish soldier was listed simply as "Bad Whiskey."[32] In fact, lawlessness grew so rampant in Galveston, particularly in the later stages of the war, that the civilian population sent a formal petition to General Magruder requesting him to replace the provost guard with a new military force hand-picked for the task of protecting the civilian population from the soldiers.

While serious offenders were sometimes forced to wear a ball and chain, the frustration and boredom experienced by the large number of soldiers who served in Galveston primarily found its outlet either in fights or the commission of petty thefts. Punishments for these offenses were creative. Thus, for example, in the fall of 1863, when a private in an artillery regiment was found to have stolen and fenced a variety of items of clothing and jewelry, he was sentenced to wear a "barrel shirt" for one hour each day for ten days (excluding Sunday). The barrel was marked "Thief" in large letters on both the front and rear to identify the nature of his crime.

While wearing this strange contraption, the prisoner was marched up and down Market Street where he would draw the most attention. To make certain that he would draw the attention of onlookers, thus adding to the unfortunate soldier's shame, the prisoner was accompanied by a guard with fife and drum playing the tune "Yankee Doodle." After this strange (but probably effective) sentence was completed, the presumably shamed private was then placed in solitary confinement on bread and water for an additional ten days to contemplate his offense.[33]

The civilians who returned to the city after its recapture at the beginning of the year did not find Galveston to be the paradise many of them remembered. Most of the basic necessities had by this time become scarce. As just one illustration, the lack of firewood for fuel began to be a serious problem in the summer of 1863. To add even further to the misery of the island's inhabitants, a severe drought set in and soldiers and civilians alike suffered from thirst.[34]

The soldiers were not thirsty because they needed water to wash down the excellent rations with which they were being provided. On the contrary, the quality of the food (particularly the cornmeal) became increasingly worse as the year wore on. The rations being issued on a daily basis consisted almost entirely of beef, molasses, and cornmeal. By the first of August, Colonel Debray estimated that more than 15 percent of his men were sick due to problems associated with bad food.[35] Even the officers were writing formal complaints about the sour, dirty, and weevil-eaten meal.[36]

Matters all came to a head on August 11 and 12, 1863, when a mutiny broke out among the men under Debray's command. On the first day, the Third Regiment of Texas Infantry refused to drill or obey its officers. Not one to endure what he regarded as insubordination, Debray waited until this regiment later went to dress-parade, and then directed his still obedient cavalry regiment to line up on either flank of the men with loaded carbines. In front of the disobedient regiment he also stationed artillery pieces loaded with canister. He then made the offending soldiers stack their arms and march to their tents, where they were confined under an armed guard.[37]

Debray was convinced that this show of force had made his point and went to bed that night convinced that he had reinforced his authority. On the next morning, however, several companies of Cook's Regiment of Heavy Artillery refused to drill or leave their batteries. With both the infantry and now the artillery refusing his orders, the situation looked ugly. The colonel feared that violence might break out at any moment.

Fortunately, Acting Brigadier General Philip N. Luckett, a more practical and sensible officer, appeared on the scene and acted as peacemaker. He learned by talking to the men that their main problem was not that they were disloyal, but that they simply did not see any good reason to drill four hours a day in the August heat while being provided rations that were so grossly insufficient and unwholesome. Anyone who has experienced the heat of a hot August day in Galveston can appreciate the justice of the soldiers' complaint. Luckett issued an order suspending drills until the food improved. He also appointed a board to "study" the problem.[38] This commonsense accommodation seemed to placate the men and things went back to normal.

Almost as soon as the immediate threat to Galveston seemed to have passed, General Magruder began diverting troops to other parts of Texas and other theaters of the war. By the middle of 1863, there were not enough troops to fill up the imposing fortifications that had been constructed at Galveston. The militia units that were raised were essentially useless because there were no guns with which to arm them. Colonel Debray reported on August 1, 1863, that he had less than a third of the men necessary to defend the city properly. In fact, Debray was so worried about his small force being overwhelmed in a surprise attack at night that he withdrew them to the town and left the forts essentially unprotected after dark.[39] This problem only intensified as Federal invasions elsewhere in Texas drew off more troops from Galveston.

As quoted in the introduction to this chapter, on August 28, 1863, General Henry McCulloch (temporary commander of Texas) issued an order declaring Galveston an "entrenched camp" and designating all the citizens that remained in the city "camp followers." Probably inspired by the mutinies that had occurred earlier in the month, he prohibited any act or word that might have the effect of demoralizing the troops. He suggested that all civilians leave the island because of the "difficulties of procuring provisions, wood and water, and the dangers of an attack."[40] The citizens of Galveston began to get the not so subtle hint that they were no longer welcome in their own city.

As the end of 1863 approached, Magruder became increasingly concerned about the concentration of troops in Arkansas and Louisiana, not because he opposed defending those points but because it exposed the areas he had successfully protected in Texas to what he viewed as an unacceptable risk of capture. As the general warned in a letter to the Chief of Staff for the Trans-Mississippi Department, "should the enemy succeed in forcing the Sabine, or Galveston, or the Brazos, he will soon take possession of the [farm and ranch country], and will virtually be master of Texas." The result of the department's wholesale diversion of troops to other states, he cautioned, was to force him "to leave vital points on the coast almost destitute of the means of defense."[41]

News of Confederate defeats at Vicksburg and Gettysburg in July finally made its way to Galveston, causing shock and low spirits among the island's residents. To deal with the loss of the Mississippi River to Union control, and the resulting lessening of communications with Richmond, General E. Kirby Smith called a meeting of the governors west of that river to develop a plan of action. Galvestonians were very interested in the details of this plan. Everyone on the island had his own idea of what should be done to defend Texas against potential invasion.

One of the most novel ideas was advanced by attorney William Pitt Ballinger. He wrote a paper in August 1863 calling for the construction of a number of entrenched defensive positions around the state, in itself not a very controversial proposition. What made Ballinger's proposal unique was that he planned to occupy these fortifications primarily with slaves, who would be made part of the Confederate Army and issued muskets. This part of the proposal, although controversial, Ballinger viewed as "vital to us." Although Ballinger circulated his proposal for comments, and tried to get a copy to General Smith, there is no evidence that it was ever treated very seriously in Confederate military circles.[42]

On August 10, 1863, most of the men in the Forty-Second Massachusetts Regiment finally arrived back in their home state. The enlisted men who had been taken prisoner at the Battle of Galveston had been paroled and reached New Orleans at the end of February. The regiment's officers, however, were still in Confederate prisons and would not return to Massachusetts for another year.

On arriving in Boston, the regiment was marched to Faneuil Hall, where it was addressed by the mayor. While conceding that its history was "peculiar and unlike most of the regiments which have gone from Massachusetts," the mayor nevertheless insisted that the men were owed thanks for all they had done and all they had attempted to do. As he rationalized the situation, "It has not been your fate to command success, but we know that you have deserved it."[43]

Back in Texas, Galvestonians wanted to believe that their armies still had a chance of securing Confederate independence despite the terrible losses they had suffered at Gettysburg and Vicksburg in July 1863. This optimism intensified when, in September 1863, Confederate forces won another decisive victory on the Texas Gulf Coast at the Battle of Sabine Pass.[44]

General Magruder knew that his recapture of Galveston would not prevent the Union from making another attempt to invade Texas at some other place. Therefore, beginning in the spring of 1863, he assigned the same engineers who had worked on Galveston's defenses to supervise construction of new fortifications at the entrance to Sabine Pass. Some old guns in bad condition had been repaired at Galveston's foundry and were carefully placed into position behind earthen and wood fortifications along with guns reassigned from other less important locations.

On the afternoon of September 8, 1863, a fleet of Union gunboats attempted to steam past these fortifications with an infantry force of about five thousand troops. Facing them at Fort Griffin, as the crude fortifications at Sabine Pass were called, were Dick Dowling (a Houston saloon keeper) and forty-two Irish dock workers from Houston and Galveston known as the "Davis Guards." While the heavy Union gunboats were firing at the Confederate fort, Commodore Leon Smith arrived on the scene and stood on the rampart, waving the flag and cheering the men on.

The fire from Dowling's Confederate battery of about six guns was astonishingly quick and accurate. In less than an hour they had damaged and captured two gunboats (one of which was the *Clifton,* which had participated in the fighting at Galveston). They also had killed or captured over three hundred men, turning back the Yankee expedition and saving Texas once again from invasion. To desperate Texans looking for a sign that their cause might still succeed, the outcome of the conflict at Sabine Pass seemed nothing short of miraculous. Never short on praise after a success, Magruder was quick to pronounce this contest "the most extraordinary feat of the war."[45]

The threat to Texas was far from ended. In November 1863, General Banks launched another attack at the southern coast of Texas, this time landing at Brazos Santiago and working his way up the coast toward Galveston. Pulling together as many troops as he dared behind the Brazos and San Bernard rivers, Magruder managed to check the Federal advance until the invading forces were withdrawn and sent back to General Banks to participate in the unsuccessful Red River Campaign of 1864.[46]

As Christmas of 1863 approached, the people of Galveston considered themselves fortunate. Although danger still threatened to their south, their Island City was back in Confederate hands, and Union forces had been repeatedly turned back from Texas shores. An October storm had done more damage to Galveston's fortifications than the Yankees did during the entire year.[47]

As the holiday season approached, the thoughts of the Confederate soldiers guarding Galveston Island drew increasingly homeward. One private notified the local newspaper from his camp at Fort Point that his company intended to hang up their stockings in the hope that generous readers would send them either tobacco or the seed to grow it. In a burst of holiday bravado, he vowed that "we mean to defend this place till h[e]ll freezes over, and then fight the Yankees on the ice."[48] The severity of the coming winter would probably make this soldier regret his bold choice of words.

Treated like a Conquered City

From the outbreak of the civil war, Galveston was looked upon as a city that was doomed, and after its recapture, the 1st of January, it was treated more as a conquered city than one that was loyal to the Confederacy. The military gentlemen who were place[d] in command of its defenses, and to whom was entrusted its protection and security, seem to have acted on the principle that the citizens who remained upon the island and city had no rights that they were bound to recognize or respect. They were treated more like aliens than friends.

CHARLES W. HAYES, 1879

In many ways, the events that made news in Galveston in 1864 were not that different from the events that make news today: weather, scandals involving those in authority, and a series of bizarre deaths and crimes. With military attention focused on campaigns and battles in other places, the civilian and military inhabitants of the city concentrated on making the most of their lives in the confines of an occupied city. It was not an easy task.

The year started out with one of the coldest winters on record. The western part of Galveston Bay was covered with ice to a depth of as much as an inch-and-a-half in thickness. Snow fell and accumulated on the ground to a depth of one inch, an almost unheard of event in Galveston. The cold weather continued throughout the winter months, with one storm from the North following another. The weather caused much suffering for soldiers and civilians who were without sufficient firewood to keep warm or cook their meals. This problem became so acute that orders were issued allowing vacant houses and unused wharves to be torn apart and used as fuel.[1]

Unfortunately for the city's inhabitants, the cold weather did not deter criminal behavior. Burglaries and petty thefts were so common that the local paper reported in January that chickens and pigs "disappear nightly from their pens, and in most cases the whole contents are stolen."[2] Some of the thefts were not confined to poultry or livestock.

On the evening of March 18, 1864, Lieutenant Linsey of the Confederate Signal Corps left his office in the Pix Building on Postoffice Street. He was seized by two men who threw him to the street and robbed him of $1,500 in

Confederate money. During the struggle, one of the men produced a pistol and pointed it at Linsey's chest. Fortunately for Linsey, the gun misfired on its initial discharge. Unfortunately for Linsey, the gun did fire properly on the second attempt, with the bullet grazing his leg.[3] Another member of the Signal Corps, Peter Willis, was also attacked and shot in the street not long following the Linsey incident.

With so many soldiers quartered in the city, clashes between civilians and soldiers were inevitable. Some of these were relatively insignificant and easily handled. In August, for example, frequent complaints led the military authorities to issue an order forbidding "flagrant insults" to ladies riding or bathing on the beach.[4]

Other confrontations, however, were not so easily and successfully resolved. A man named Baker, an English resident of the city, was awakened by a noise one night to discover a soldier in the act of stealing one of his chickens. Having been the victim of one too many such thefts, Baker fired his gun, killing the thief. The authorities took Mr. Baker to jail, where he was to await trial. Later, however, a deputy acting without authority took the prisoner out of the jail and led him to the company of which his victim had been a member. There, the thief's two brothers, aided by other members of the company, stabbed Baker to death and then hung his body in front of his residence as an example.[5] Needless to say, this type of occurrence did not improve relations between the civilian and military residents of the city.

Not all of the deaths in Galveston during 1864 resulted from murders. One of the bigger local news stories of the year occurred in July when a father accidently killed his own daughter under very strange circumstances. A man named Prosch was shooting at a chicken in his yard. History does not record whether the chicken in question was his own or a neighbor's. In any event, Prosch was successful in shooting the chicken. The unlucky shot passed through the chicken, however, and went through the door of a privy, where it killed the man's nine-year-old daughter.[6] The town was greatly shocked by this unusual and tragic event.

As summer approached, the population of the island actually increased, as citizens returned from the Houston area to spend the summer months where they could receive the benefit of the sea breeze. To keep order, General James Morrison Hawes directed that the civilian inhabitants again register their families with military authorities and stay off the streets at night. A correspondent for a Houston newspaper complained that Galveston should be called the "City of Registry" because of its excessive military red tape. The curfew, however, served its intended purpose. The same correspondent reported that Galveston was, without doubt, the most quiet city in the Confederacy.[7]

As times got tougher, the garrison in Galveston grew increasingly tired of grand promises and cheery predictions from their commanders, particularly when it seemed that these officers were not sharing their privations. Even the heroes of the Battle of Galveston were not exempt from this criticism. One night in March, some ladies saw fit to give General Magruder and his staff a dinner, followed by a ball. Word of this event spread quickly among the soldiers, who resented the holding of such a frivolous activity at a time when many of them were suffering from bad rations and disease. It probably did not add to the gaiety of Magruder's evening when approximately five hundred of these angry men showed up outside of the house where the ball was being held demanding to see the general.

Magruder decided to meet with the men, probably because they were carrying arms and had two pieces of artillery to emphasize the sincerity and urgency of their request. While a messenger was being sent out the back door to gather troops to quash this mutiny, the angry demonstrators told their commander "that it was no time for feasting fiddling and dancing — that they themselves were on sufferance — their families at home on sufferance and the country bleeding at every pore."

The general then made the men all kinds of promises, including a pledge that they would receive better food, if they would only disperse. Eventually, it was agreed that the men would disperse if Magruder and his officers would leave the party. This compromise turned out to be only another Magruder deception. Later in the evening, the general rallied the ladies and continued the adjourned party until late that night.[8]

On April 15, 1864, General James M. Hawes assumed command of Galveston and its defenses.[9] Hawes was a forty-year-old Kentuckian who had graduated from West Point in 1845. He had seen substantial action in the Mexican War and had served with distinction in the 1857 action against the Mormons under Albert Sidney Johnston. When the Civil War broke out, Hawes had been highly praised by Johnston, eventually becoming a brigadier general in March 1862. He served as a commander of cavalry and then was placed in charge of a brigade that included several Kentucky units.

When General Braxton Bragg was placed in command of the Army of Tennessee, he expressed a lack of confidence in Hawes and worked to get him transferred. Hawes was then transferred to the Army of the Trans-Mississippi (the military department that included Texas), where he would spend the rest of the war.[10] When Hawes showed no real ability to handle troops in this army either, he was assigned to the command of Galveston, apparently under the mistaken belief that an administrative position might be more suited to his talents. As events in Galveston would prove, however, Hawes was not the right man for this difficult job.

Hawes arrived in Galveston to find his new command in a terrible mess. Desertions were common and crime of every description was rampant. The civilian population was in an uproar and army morale was low.[11] Shortly before General Hawes' arrival, one soldier had written home to his wife that "the troops are so dissatisfied with everything that an angel could not please them."[12] As later events would show, Hawes was certainly no angel, but he was smart enough to know that something had to be done quickly.

In looking through the files at his new command, Hawes came across a copy of the order that General McCulloch had issued in August of the previous year declaring Galveston an entrenched camp. He decided that to show his authority and gain control of this unruly situation he would reissue the order and put some teeth in it. Accordingly, he published, as part of his Special Order No. 4, a statement that Galveston and its defenses were an "entrenched camp" and again designated all of the civilian inhabitants "camp followers" subject to the rules of war. To take what amounted to an inventory of these people, Hawes ordered all of the civilians to register in person with the provost marshal.[13]

Hawes was completely unprepared for the storm of protest that was generated by his order. Galveston's mayor and Board of Aldermen met within a week and unanimously adopted a resolution condemning the new commander's action. Protesting Hawes' attempt to revive the "odious and obsolete" order of the previous year, the resolution accused the general of unnecessarily insulting the ladies of the city by calling them "camp followers" and directing them to register their names and occupations. The resolution went on to proclaim that the insult by Hawes was something that might have been expected from Benjamin "Beast" Butler, the hated Union commander of occupied New Orleans, but never from Confederate rule.[14]

General Hawes was greatly angered by this resolution, which was published in all the local newspapers. He wrote to General Magruder and requested authority to arrest the mayor and city officials and expel them from the island.[15] Magruder did not support this extreme reaction, but instead modified the offending order to placate the citizens so that women and children were registered privately by officers who came to their residences. Because of his tough and uncompromising attitude, the civilian population turned against General Hawes, whom they referred to as the "Beast Butler of Galveston."

Friction between Hawes and the people of Galveston soon mounted, resulting in what became known as the "bread riot" of 1864. When a scarcity of provisions forced the general to order the Confederate commissary to cease selling flour to the families of soldiers in May, a group of women conducted demonstrations both at the general's residence and his office at the Customhouse. Never a man of great patience, Hawes soon grew tired of these demonstrations and responded by arresting the women. Although he released all but seven or eight women on the same day that they were arrested, the remaining "ringleaders" were put on trains and sent to Houston with instructions not to return.[16]

In June of 1864, another controversy arose between Hawes and city officials over a runaway slave. The city authorities refused to release the slave to his purported owner because of some unpaid fees. The military authorities ordered the slave released to his owner and, when he was not released, arrested the city officials, took the jail keys from them by force, and freed the slave to his owner. Believing that they had been mistreated, the city officials then secured a court order declaring the military's action (which had been expressly approved by General Hawes) to have been unlawful.[17]

As required by the court's order, General Hawes then directed the slave to be returned to the sheriff. Scorning the court's decision, he justified the military's original action by declaring that "treason of the darkest dye" existed in Galveston and that the safety of the citizens depended upon "preserving the highest military discipline and efficiency." Hawes noted that Galveston is "the only Seaport which has ever been recaptured from the enemy," and that it is "differently situated from any other command in the Confederacy." The general's statement left no doubt that he viewed military necessity as sufficient authority to outweigh any civil authority or rights of civilians.[18]

The discipline problems that Hawes experienced were not confined to his dealings with civilians. Although it is hard to imagine in light of the severity of previous complaints, the rations available to be issued to troops had grown increasingly worse. This time, however, it was the beef, rather than the meal, that affected morale. On one Sunday morning, the beef issued to a regiment was of such poor quality that it was completely inedible. To demonstrate their disgust, the men put the meat on a stick and marched it around the city, accompanied by muffled drums and with arms reversed.

They then held a mock funeral service for the beef and buried it with military honors in Galveston's main public square. One of the more poetic marchers had composed the following inscription, which was attached to the offending meat prior to its burial:

Died in the Butcher Pen at Galveston on Saturday Night March 5, 1864. An Ancient Gentleman Cow, in the 129th year of his age. Disease: Poverty.[19]

Many soldiers wrote home complaining of their boredom, exposed condition in bad weather, and the poor quality of the rations. As one soldier assigned to duty at Virginia Point recorded in his diary in February 1864:

The beeves that we eat here are so poor that they can scarcely stand. It is an outrage that confederate soldiers should be compelled to live upon what we live upon. The citizens are made to pay a tenth of all they make, for the purpose of feeding the army. Where it all goes to, I cannot tell. None of it comes to this army. . . . I am afraid our country will never prosper, when there [is] so much fraud and perfidy practiced upon the private soldier by the functionaries of the government. I am the last one to mutinize or desert; but if there are any justifiable causes for such things, it is here in our army.[20]

Being located at Virginia Point also had certain advantages for the soldier with time on his hands. The same soldier who complained so bitterly about the quality of his rations in the diary excerpt above was able to supplement his diet by gathering oysters and frying them with the objectionable beef and ever-present corn bread.[21] Other than poor rations, the main problem faced by troops in the Galveston area was boredom. At one point in 1864 one of the colonels advertised in a Houston newspaper for fifteen musicians and a competent leader to form a band to entertain his regiment.[22]

Faced with the prospect of killing and death, the soldiers who served in Galveston gave considerable thought to religious matters. The letters and diaries of these soldiers frequently record attendance at revivals and church services. Harvey Medford, a Confederate soldier stationed at Galveston in 1864, noted in his diary that he had attended Sunday services at the Catholic, Episcopal, and Methodist churches—all in the same day.[23] Medford also recorded that a number of backsliders continued in their evil ways despite numerous apparent conversions and expressions of religious zeal:

A great many soldiers are professing religion and joining the churches. Our regiment is the most wicked of any I have ever seen. If hell were disgorged of all its base contents, I think such another set could not be found.[24]

This religious fervor found fresh converts as a new disaster struck in September. The year that had started with a winter of unparalleled fury ended with a serious epidemic of yellow fever that lasted from September until almost the end of November. During this one epidemic, over one hundred soldiers died of yellow fever.[25] In Galveston, as was true elsewhere in the Confederacy, many more soldiers died of disease than ever died in battle.

The yellow fever epidemic of 1864 was no respecter of rank. General Hawes was disabled by the disease, and Colonel Ashbel Smith, a Galveston physician, had to temporarily take command while the general recovered.[26] His recent transfer back to Galveston had enabled Smith to again study yellow fever, a subject upon which he would later write a number of treatises and scientific articles. In an October 1864 letter, Colonel Smith complained about the army's ineffectual treatment of this disease:

The army surgeons have appeared to much disadvantage, doubting and denying the existence of the disease, while persons are dying of black vomit [yellow fever] in rapid succession and numerous cases are occurring with characteristic symptoms, all within a radius of 75 yards. My regiment was moved out of the city at my own request on the day following the first alarm — it was impossible for me to mistake so distinctly characteristic a disease — but they carried the disease with them. Their barracks had been in the very focus of the pestilence.[27]

There were so many cases of yellow fever during the 1864 outbreak that the Tremont House Hotel had to be turned into a hospital to house all of the suffering soldiers.[28]

Despite the weather, the epidemics, and the generally terrible conditions in the city, work continued on the defenses of the island throughout 1864. As soon as winter had released its icy grip to the extent that such work could proceed, the Confederates continued their program of obstructing the entrances to Galveston Bay. This work was not only difficult, but also dangerous.

In an operation carrying "torpedoes" (mines) to be placed at the entrance to the harbor, one of the devices exploded, mangling a soldier's lower body and setting his clothes on fire. He crawled into the water, putting out the fire and probably saving his life, but the damage was already done. He had been so severely burned and wounded that eventually his leg had to be amputated. Other soldiers working on Galveston's defenses were more fortunate. A local newspaper reported that several men had uncovered thousands of Spanish doubloons (presumably buried by pirates) while arranging the earthen defenses of one fort.[29]

Although many aspects of the defenses of Galveston improved during 1864, others deteriorated badly. By the beginning of May, for example, General Hawes was forced to report to his superior that the *Bayou City* — the ship that had won the Battle of Galveston — was in a "sinking condition and may go down at any time." Hawes advised that the ship was in such bad shape that it was unsafe even to put a guard on it. It simply "could not be used in any emergency," because no gun could be fired from its deck without doing severe damage.[30]

By the end of the year, the Union blockading squadron had noticed the absence of effective Confederate naval protection in the harbor and had decided to take advantage of it. On the night of December 26, 1864, Acting Ensign N. A. Blume of the U.S.S. *Virginia* got permission to make another night raid into Galveston Harbor. Taking a small cutter, Blume waited until about 1:00 A.M. and approached the schooner *Belle,* only four hundred yards from the Confederate guards on board the *Lecompte.* Slipping quietly aboard the schooner with his boarding party, Blume and his men captured the crew (five prisoners) and, unlike the capture of the *Royal Yacht* in 1861, managed to take the schooner out of the harbor with them. They reached the fleet with their prize, and its cargo of ninety bales of cotton, at daylight.[31]

Thus, the year 1864 drew to a close with yet another daring night raid into Galveston Harbor. In a strange twist of fate, the most significant military events in Galveston during the Civil War all seemed to occur at night. In 1861, James Jouett and his crew had made the first dramatic invasion of Galveston Harbor, burning the *Royal Yacht* and capturing its crew. At the beginning of 1863, a little over one year later, General Magruder took advantage of darkness to launch his successful raid on the *Harriet Lane* and the rest of the Union fleet. Finally, at the end of 1864, another such raid occurred and the Union spirited away the *Belle,* perhaps symbolizing that this war was at long last drawing to a close.

Running the Blockade

*As late as the spring of 1865 there were a number of schooners engaged in
running the blockade out of Galveston to Mexican and Cuban ports. In fact,
when cotton had reached a fabulous price, almost any kind of craft that would
float was loaded with that staple and, taking advantage of the winter northers,
boldly put to sea, some of them never again to be heard from.*

BEN C. STUART,

July 16, 1911

After Mobile and New Orleans were captured, Galveston became one of the
only major Southern ports still in Confederate hands. It therefore became an
increasingly prominent port for vessels engaged in the lucrative (if somewhat risky) practice of running the blockade. Although histories of the Civil
War typically devote more attention to the ships that ran the blockade on the
East Coast, statistics show that there were significantly more attempts to
run the blockade on the Gulf Coast than in the Carolinas.

As documented by drawings of the blockaders made by Galveston resident
George Grover (see Figure 16), the Union ships on blockade duty included
a wide variety of ships and supply vessels. By April of 1864, the commander
of the Union blockading fleet at Galveston was forced to report that the coast
in his vicinity was "becoming a principal field of operations for blockade
runners."[1] A year later, as the number of uncaptured Confederate ports continued to shrink, a soldier in Galveston recorded that "vast quantities" of
goods were now coming in by the blockade, with nine steamers lying at the
wharf and a new ship coming in or going out every night.[2]

Wild rumors began to circulate among the Union blockading vessels at
Galveston and elsewhere about a new fleet of Confederate vessels specially
designed and constructed to eliminate the blockade. One such rumor at the
beginning of 1864 warned of a group of ships known as the "China fleet,"
supposedly constructed in England for the Chinese government, but subse-
quently purchased by Confederate agents. With this "Chinese fleet," the rumor had it, the Rebels intended to sweep away the blockade from in front of

FIGURE 16. *Sketch made by George Grover of blockading Union ships at Galveston in October 1864. Courtesy of Rosenberg Library, Galveston, Texas.*

their ports.[3] This threat did not materialize, however, and the blockade stayed in effect (and even tightened) during the rest of the war.

Although steamers were generally preferred as blockade runners because of their reliable speed, the engines and coal that they had to carry added significantly to their weight. When importing heavy material like iron or machinery, it was often necessary to use a sailing vessel to be certain that the ship could get over the sand bar at the entrance to Galveston Harbor or one of the shallow draft landing places for cargo in the area. This was the case with the *Rob Roy* in December 1863, which brought in a cargo including about twenty-five tons of iron.[4]

Incoming cargoes on a blockade runner consisted generally of war materials or luxury goods. After the arrival of a ship, the stores of Galveston would open for a few days until they sold out of contraband materials. Then the stores would close until the arrival of the cargo from the next ship.[5]

The outgoing cargo on a blockade runner was invariably cotton, pressed as tightly and stacked as densely as possible. The rewards for engaging in this illicit activity were substantial; the profit from one successful trip was sometimes sufficient to pay the cost of a vessel.[6] For example, the *Zephine*, which came to Galveston in late 1864, was purchased for $100,000 in gold and was said to have returned a profit on its first voyage of over $300,000 in gold.[7]

Many of the men who became influential in Galveston after the war owed the core of their fortunes to the profits they made running the blockade.[8] Not all of these men were wealthy merchants who shipped out huge quantities of cotton. One captain ran the blockade in 1862 carrying only five bales of cotton, explaining to his wife that by limiting his cargo, if he got out safe he would be happy, but if not it would be as much as he could afford to lose.[9]

Ships that had previously seen duty as pilot boats or simple transports were now lured by the high potential rewards into attempting to run the blockade. For example, in the spring of 1863, the *Royal Yacht* (without Commodore Chubb) saw action as a blockade runner under the command of Thomas Saunders (her former mate). The luck of this vessel had not improved. On April 15, 1863, after a six-and-a-half-hour chase and the firing of fourteen shots, the Union bark *William G. Anderson* captured this unfortunate vessel and its military career ended. Saunders thus had the dubious distinction of having been captured twice aboard the same ship in less than two years.[10]

Even the captured *Harriet Lane* was refitted as a blockade runner and slipped out of Galveston one night.[11] The circumstances under which this escape occurred were very mysterious. After considerable debate, General Magruder had assumed responsibility on his own authority to negotiate an arrangement with Thomas W. House, a merchant from Houston, whereby House would supply the cotton to be the *Lane*'s cargo in return for a substantial share of the proceeds from its delivery to a neutral port.[12]

While these negotiations with House were being conducted by the Confederates, a second set of clandestine negotiations was being held with Union Admiral Farragut. Farragut was still positively obsessed with desire to recapture the *Lane* and redeem the Navy's honor. This had become something of a personal crusade for the admiral. He had written to Secretary Welles that "I must try and recover the *Harriet Lane*, as she would be a most formidable cruiser if she gets out."[13] When an unnamed individual offered to run the ship out of Galveston and deliver it to the blockaders, Farragut was more than willing to listen.

The deal that was offered to Farragut was simple. The individual proposed to fill the vessel with cotton and run it out to the Union fleet. He would then show a light and turn the ship over to the blockaders. In return, Farragut would guarantee that this individual could then sell the cargo of cotton and keep the proceeds. Such a scheme clearly thwarted the entire purpose of the blockade and was personally distasteful to the admiral. He was a desperate man, however, and on April 5, 1864, sent a letter agreeing to the terms outlined.[14] He then wrote to Captain John Marchand, who was in charge of the blockading fleet at Galveston, to tell him of the unusual arrangements that had been made.

Marchand must have thought that the admiral had gone mad when he received the byzantine details of the ship-for-cotton transaction. The instructions from Farragut directed that when Marchand was approached by a certain man and a woman, he was then to send a messenger to deliver certain letters to the French consul under a flag of truce. While delivering these letters the Union messenger would be approached by another man, at which point the messenger would inform the man about the presence of the woman on board. This third man was then supposed to come out to the ship and make final arrangements with the woman to deliver the *Lane* into Federal hands.[15]

Marchand wrote back to the admiral saying that he would do what he could, but noted that this confusing transaction stood very little chance of success since, delivery to the French consul or not, the Confederates did not allow his truce boats close enough to shore for any messages to be delivered to inhabitants of the city.[16] Whether the scheme could have worked or not turned out to be immaterial. On the night of April 30, 1864, the *Harriet Lane* and several other vessels took advantage of a dense rain squall and ran the blockade by using a channel that was thought by the blockaders to be too shallow to be used by ships of any size.

One Union ship, the *Katahdin,* heard the blockade runners leaving and went after them. The *Katahdin* did not even signal the other Union ships of its departure, assuming that what it was pursuing were only small sailboats. When morning came, Lieutenant Commander John Irwin realized his mistake and tried to make the capture that would make or break his career. In an effort to gain speed, he used all of his soft coal, firewood, and lumber, and even burned some pork and tar. It was to no avail. Irwin was forced to report his "bitter mortification" at failing to capture the *Lane* or any of the other blockade runners.[17]

The news of the escape of the *Harriet Lane* was a great blow to Admiral Farragut. Not only was that ship now loose to become what he believed would be another cruiser like the *Alabama,* but he had been made to look like a fool by a fraudulent scheme. Farragut vowed that he would "have no more such arrangements." He also chastised Lieutenant Commander Irwin of the *Katahdin* for not giving the other blockaders some alarm and obtaining their assistance. If the faster steamship *Lackawanna* had been brought into the chase, as it should have been, Farragut believed it to be evident that the escaping ships "would, in all probability, have been captured, and the blockade would have escaped further rebuke of the Navy Department."[18]

The predicted rebuke was not slow in coming. Secretary Welles could hardly conceal his disgust when he observed that "it can not but be looked upon as a miserable business when six good steamers, professing to blockade a harbor, suffer four vessels to run out in one night."[19] The *Harriet Lane* succeeded in reaching Havana, where it was given a British registry and was renamed the *Lavinia.*[20]

Blockade running gradually became almost a science. The vessels leaving Galveston were redesigned to meet the specialized needs of this trade. These accommodations included removing projections so that the ships extended as little above the water as possible. To provide camouflage, the visible portions of the ships were painted either the color of seawater or a lead color.[21]

To maximize his chances, the captain of one of these custom-designed blockade runners would go up into the lookout on the top of the Hendley

Building at dusk on what was preferably a stormy or overcast day. The surgeon on one of the blockading Union vessels off Galveston described the strategy that was then followed:

When a blockade runner got in and unloaded, her cargo of cotton was always ready, and instantly loaded, ready for a start. Then came a period of waiting for a favorable chance to run out — that meaning a stormy, dark night, when the low hulls of the vessels, painted a dirty white, were quite invisible a hundred yards away. At the last moment before dark, the bearings of each man-of-war outside would be carefully taken, and steam got up. This part we could see from our stations, and always had plenty of warning of a coming attempt. As soon as it was dark they would creep slowly down the channel, over the bar, and then, with every possible pound of steam and the greatest speed, would make a dash for our line. All we could hear would be the beat of paddles upon the water — but sound in darkness is so deceptive that no one can tell from which direction it comes, and as nothing could be seen, we usually kept perfectly still and let them go. Indeed, at the speed with which they were going, even if we had seen them, only a shot could have overhauled them — our clumsy blockaders, never.[22]

As this account emphasizes, only a small percentage of the ships that attempted to run the blockade at Galveston were ever captured or destroyed. Shipping records confirm that during 1864, approximately 87 percent of all of the steamers that attempted to run the blockade on the Gulf Coast were successful.[23]

There were a few blockade running attempts, however, that ended up being spectacular failures. These usually occurred when the vessels ran aground on the treacherous shoals and spits that guarded the entrance to Galveston Harbor. The *Will-o'-the-Wisp*, for example, tried to enter the harbor while being chased by two Union blockaders. The blockaders lost contact with their target, but the *Wisp* ran aground a few miles south of the city. Several days later, a Union boat expedition burned what was left of the wreck.[24] Even the *Denbigh,* which was one of the most successful blockade runners of the entire war, ended up running aground near the entrance to Galveston Harbor in May 1865 and was destroyed by a Federal boarding party.[25]

Some of the most famous blockade runners made calls at Galveston, particularly near the end of the war when fewer Confederate ports were available as options. Thomas Taylor, for example, who probably ran the blockade successfully more times than any other man, came in with his ship, the *Banshee* (II), in 1865. As happened to many other ships approaching Galveston from Havana, the island was so flat that the *Banshee* was in among the blockading fleet before it realized it was so close to shore. Carefully and slowly, to avoid being recognized, Taylor and his crew backed out to sea and spent the next day planning their strategy.

As night approached, the *Banshee* crept slowly up the coast until the Union fleet was just visible. The plan was to come closer during the night, wait until daylight was breaking, and then make a mad dash for the harbor. Taylor had come to the unsettling conclusion that his pilot was "no good whatever," but saw this bold plan as his only chance.

As daylight came, Taylor found his ship to be located even farther from the harbor entrance than he had anticipated. Even worse, there was a blockading ship very close to his bow. Nevertheless, the decision was made to make a desperate run for the harbor through a narrow swash channel. Taylor describes the dramatic events that followed:

> [T]he fleet had opened fire upon us, and shells were bursting merrily around as we took the fire of each ship we passed. Fortunately there was a narrow shoal between us, which prevented them from approaching within about half a mile of us; luckily also for us they were in rough water on the windward side of the shoal and could not lay their guns with precision. And to this we owed our escape, as, although our funnels were riddled with shell splinters, we received no damage and had only one man wounded. But the worst was to come; we saw the white water already ahead, and we knew our only chance was to bump through it, being well aware that if she stuck fast we should lose the ship and all our lives.[26]

Taylor survived the trip into Galveston, but was not impressed with the city. He found it to be "a most forsaken place," and noted that the only bright side to the picture was that he had several excellent dinners with General Magruder, who provided "cheery entertainment" because all of his staff seemed to have some musical talent.[27]

Galveston even had a blockade runner that was more or less a community favorite or mascot. The trim side-wheel steamer *Susanna*, which made a number of trips to and from the island, was commanded by Captain Charles W. Austin, formerly of the Morgan steamship line. The *Susanna* had room for a cargo of up to 1,200 bales of cotton. On one of its outbound trips in 1864, many residents stayed up all night waiting to hear word of its successful escape. During one inbound trip late in the war, the ship made its attempt at daybreak under a heavy barrage from a number of Union gunboats. Despite severe damage to its funnel, and a shattered bow, the *Susanna* limped into Galveston Harbor, where it was greeted by the cheers of hundreds of soldiers and civilians who lined the shore to applaud the vessel's success.[28]

The "Closing Act of the Rebellion"

*Come what may, we will . . . be true to our colors and to the interests of
the great State of Texas. We are not whipped, and no matter what events
may transpire elsewhere, recollect that we will never be whipped.*

MAJOR GENERAL JOHN BANKHEAD MAGRUDER,
Address to the People of Texas, May 4, 1865

As the military campaigning season of 1865 commenced, and Union troops
were freed up from other commands to concentrate on the remaining military targets, it began to appear increasingly likely that Galveston would be
the starting point of a Union invasion of Texas. General John G. Walker, who
had temporarily replaced Magruder in command of the District of Texas,
New Mexico, and Arizona, warned Governor Pendleton Murrah, the last
Confederate Governor of Texas:

> It is my firm conviction that an effort will be made, and I fear very soon,
> by the enemy to invade this state. Galveston, I feel certain, will be the
> point of attack, and should be reinforced by several thousand men before
> there could be any reasonable hope of holding it against such an attack as
> is soon threatened.[1]

The likelihood of increased Union attention to recapturing Galveston
seemed to be confirmed when, on the night of February 7, 1865, yet another
Union boat expedition from the blockading fleet entered Galveston Harbor
and returned with twenty prisoners and two schooners loaded with cotton.[2]
This expedition, at least the third such successful small-boat invasion of the
war, showed that with shallow draft boats and plenty of men, it was just a
matter of time until Galveston would be in Union hands again.

Despite many patriotic speeches by their officers, Confederate soldiers
on the island sensed that the end was near. Desertions to the Federal fleet
became increasingly frequent, some in groups of as many as seven men at a
time.[3] Not all attempts at desertion were successful. One of these failed attempts resulted in Galveston's second (and last) military execution of the war.

Private Antone Richers of Dege's Battery was sentenced in early 1865 to be shot for attempting to desert.[4] A contemporary newspaper account describes the tragic events that accompanied his execution on March 3, 1865:

A sharp rattle of musketry, and the prisoner fell dead, several balls having passed through his breast. . . . The saddest part of the story remains to be told. The friends of [the prisoner] had sent Rev. Father Ansteadt on the day before the execution, by hand car, to Houston, as bearer of documents addressed to General Walker, showing that [Richers] was not of sound mind, and setting forth other reasons why he ought to be respited. The telegraph line between [Galveston] and Houston broke down the evening before the execution, and remained down [until] fifteen minutes after the execution. No intelligence from General Walker could therefore reach [Galveston]. But as soon as the telegraph operated, a dispatch was received from General Walker, dated the night before, containing *an order for the respite of Anton [Richers]*. It was too late — the man was dead.[5]

On April 14, 1865, General Hawes was relieved of command in Galveston and was replaced by Colonel Ashbel Smith.[6] Smith was well known in Galveston and was a popular choice. If anyone could hold the disintegrating Confederate forces on the island together, it would be this man. Born in Connecticut, Smith studied medicine at Yale and arrived in Texas in 1837 (at the age of thirty-two). He developed an excellent reputation and was not only made surgeon general of the Texas Army, but also held a number of important diplomatic posts for the new Republic of Texas.[7]

When the Civil War broke out, Smith had been elected captain of a company organized in Harris and Galveston counties that ultimately became part of the Second Texas Infantry Regiment.[8] The Second Texas fought with great distinction at Shiloh, and Smith was promoted to lieutenant colonel when William P. Rogers was killed leading a charge at Corinth, Mississippi.

Smith and most of his regiment had been surrendered at Vicksburg in July 1863 and managed to find their way back to Texas after being paroled. When they were finally exchanged in October 1863, the portion of the regiment that was still willing and able to serve the Confederacy straggled into camp at Houston. By this time, the regiment had been transferred to General Magruder's department. At first, the regiment was assigned to the defenses at Velasco, which was in Brazoria County not far from the southern end of Galveston Island. In August 1864, after a tour of duty on the Caney River, the regiment rejoined Colonel Smith in the garrison at Galveston. It would never leave Texas again.

Although Smith had an unusual leadership style, he was respected and admired by the troops he commanded. When one of his subordinates refused to obey an order, calling it foolish, Colonel Smith gave the man his card and offered to settle the dispute with a pistol duel. The impudent officer then backed down because he knew that Smith had the reputation of being an excellent shot.[9]

While he insisted on absolute obedience to orders, Colonel Smith was a practical officer and very protective of his men. For example, he frequently looked the other way or even made excuses for his regiment when they found it necessary to supplement their rations with local, informally requisitioned provisions. As one regimental history notes: "Many a hog was shot in 'self-defense,' while trying to attack one of the regiment, and its carcass partitioned for the mess."[10]

A voracious reader, the colonel was frequently observed by his men reading one of the Greek or Latin classics, even in the midst of an artillery bombardment during the siege of Vicksburg. He was awkward with horses, and the noise caused by the rattling of his sword, canteen, and spurs while riding led the men to call him "Old Jingle."[11] Despite increasingly bad news from the East about the outcome of the war, Smith (a strong supporter of the institution of slavery) remained convinced until very late in the conflict that a Confederate victory was both possible and inevitable.

By this late stage of the war, the best troops had been sent to other areas, and the troops available to Smith in the vicinity of Galveston usually either were locally recruited or suffered from some deficiency that made them undesirable elsewhere. For example, the Inspector General's reports for 1865 criticized the Second Texas Cavalry for disobeying a series of orders in Louisiana. The report also noted that this regiment had "tended to injure the country in which they were serving fully as much as if it had been occupied by an equal number of the enemy."[12]

On May 14, 1865, two to three hundred of Smith's command in Galveston decided to desert the army *en masse*. But they had not reckoned on the determination or resourcefulness of their commander. Warned of the escape attempt by other, loyal troops, Colonel Smith met the would-be deserters just after dusk with an armed guard at the mouth of the railroad bridge from Galveston Island to the mainland. He warned them that he would oppose their desertion with every means at his disposal and tried to calm their fears about capture by an overwhelming Union force. The men sheepishly returned to their commands and were back at their duties the next morning, with the exception of certain ringleaders whom Smith arrested as examples.[13]

The last blockade runner from Havana to Galveston entered the harbor at 3:00 A.M. on May 24, 1865. Its reception certainly did nothing to improve Galveston's reputation as a tourist destination for the blockade running trade. As the side-wheel steamer *Lark* steamed past the fort at Fort Point, its crew noted with surprise that the earthworks at that point were unoccupied. Proceeding on into the deserted harbor, the vessel tied up at the Central Wharf. It had barely been secured before a mob of several hundred people descended on the ship and began to steal everything that was even remotely valuable.

When the captain of the *Lark* attempted to save what was left of his cargo by moving his vessel away from the dock, the looters seized every small boat that was available and rowed out to continue their work. The looting continued until well into the afternoon. The "authorities" were well aware of what was going on. A guard of twelve men was sent to the *Lark*, but they merely joined with the mob in plundering the helpless ship.[14]

The understandably aggravated captain of the unfortunate *Lark*, vowing that he would either take his ship out or blow it up, took what was left of his vessel and ran the blockade back to Havana as soon as possible.[15] More than forty-six years after the incident, local Galveston historian Ben Stuart could still vividly recall seeing the spectacle of "stout old women staggering through the streets heavily burdened with sets of artillery harness and other plunder taken from the vessel."[16]

When news of Robert E. Lee's surrender at Appomattox Courthouse on April 9, 1865, first reached Galveston, it was denounced as Yankee lies and propaganda. When it became clear that the surrender was an accomplished fact, General E. Kirby Smith, commander of the Army of the Trans-Mississippi, issued a statement conceding its occurrence but urging his own army to continue to fight:

> The crisis of our revolution is at hand. Great disasters have overtaken us. The Army of Northern Virginia and our Commander-in-Chief are prisoners of war. . . . You possess the means of long-resisting invasion. You have hopes of succor from abroad — protract the struggle and you will surely receive the aid of nations who already deeply sympathize with you. Stand by your colors — maintain your discipline.[17]

Smith's words were eloquent, but his message rang hollow in the ears of men who had spent more than four years at war. Even General Magruder had lost hope. A week later he reported candidly to General Smith that

"Blockade running to the port of Galveston may be considered almost at an end. If the port itself be not taken the enemy will so cover the Gulf with cruisers as to make its continuance almost impossible."[18]

While Magruder realized privately that the war was coming to a close, Prince John nevertheless maintained to the end a confident public appearance designed to keep up the morale of his troops. As late as May 4, 1865, almost a month after Lee's surrender, he issued a proclamation to the "People and Army of Texas" condemning the reports of disaster from the East as "entirely untrue" and urging the citizens to "encourage by your patriotic example your noble Texan soldiers in performing their duty!"[19] But it was too late in a long and bloody war for such flowery rhetoric to have much effect. The very fact that Magruder felt it necessary to resort to this type of appeal was sufficient proof to his soldiers that matters were dire indeed.

To demonstrate his confidence in the failing cause to the troops in Galveston, Magruder conducted a formal inspection of its defenses on May 11, 1865. Declaring that "no terms will ever do short of independence," Magruder said that he was prepared to die rather than "submit to a foe so base, so grasping, and so devoid of all that constitutes a respectable people."[20] An observer of these proceedings noted that the troops listened to Magruder with respect and silence, but without any manifestation of enthusiasm.[21]

Eventually even Magruder recognized that these speeches were no longer persuasive. As May wore on, the tone of his exhortations changed. Instead of confidently predicting victory over the Northern oppressors, Magruder urged the men to stay at their posts in order to allow the government's representatives to negotiate the best settlement terms possible.[22] Preparing for the expected invasion, he made contingency plans to spike the guns at Galveston and abandon the island for a second time.

As an incentive to his men to assist with these final tasks, Magruder promised to write on their discharges that they had stayed and done their duty to the last.[23] This message did not have its intended effect. The soldiers realized now that the end of the war was only a matter of weeks, perhaps days, away. They began looting public property, rationalizing this theft by claiming that the Confederate government owed them large sums for back pay. Matters got so bad that a large group of soldiers looted some government warehouses and then commandeered a railroad train to take them and their booty to the mainland. One historian has speculated that this may have been the last troop train of the war to act under some semblance of Confederate control.[24]

The situation got so out of control that the children of Galveston were stealing military supplies of powder and cartridges, which they then exploded in the streets to amuse themselves. At least twenty young people were injured in explosions of this type. Two powder magazines were completely blown up by what the newspaper referred to as a gang of "terrible boys."[25]

When it became apparent that he could no longer hold together any serious force of troops, Magruder decided to unilaterally attempt to negotiate an honorable surrender. He telegraphed General E. Kirby Smith repeatedly requesting his presence in Houston to attend to what he euphemistically described as "important business."[26] When the general did not appear as requested, Magruder decided that the matter could be delayed no longer.

Colonel Ashbel Smith at Galveston was instructed to initiate general surrender discussions with the commander of the Federal fleet, which he did on the twenty-second of May.[27] Three days later, after receiving confidential oral instructions from Magruder as to surrender terms, Colonel Smith and William Pitt Ballinger went out under a flag of truce and were taken to New Orleans to negotiate with Union commanders.[28] While his representatives were away, Magruder reached an informal understanding with the commander of the Federal blockading fleet, Captain Benjamin F. Sands, that in return for not invading the city the Confederates would not change the garrison at Galveston.[29]

The unstable situation in Galveston was now rapidly turning chaotic. On the morning of May 23, 1865, a young soldier on horseback arrived from Houston and summarized the Confederate Army's morale there in the plainest of terms: "The whole thing is busted up. . . . The soldiers have laid down arms and want to go home, war is over."[30] It was clear to all that the authority that had maintained law and order in the city during the war was now disintegrating. As the paymaster on board the blockading steamer *Florida* reported to his wife:

> Refugees who come off [from Galveston] represent that all is disorder & confusion in & about the place. Robbery & plunder by those who acknowledge no law but might is the order of the day & neither life or property are safe. They are urging our naval forces to go in and take possession that they may have their protection.[31]

By the time Smith and Ballinger reached New Orleans, the terms of the surrender of the Trans-Mississippi region had already been worked out through other channels. On May 26, 1865, a representative for General E. Kirby Smith had signed a military convention with a representative for Union General E. R. S. Canby by which all of the men of the Army of the

Trans-Mississippi were to be paroled and all of the public property to be turned over to the United States.[32]

This General Canby with whom the surrender was negotiated was the same officer who had commanded the Union troops that opposed the Sibley Brigade's New Mexico campaign. Canby instructed Brigadier General E. J. Davis to take the military convention to Galveston and obtain the signature of General Smith above his own.[33] Davis must have looked forward to returning to Galveston under these triumphant conditions, having almost been captured there on the *Cambria* in January 1863.

Arriving in New Orleans, Ballinger and Smith were surprised to read in the local newspaper that their principal mission had already been accomplished. They nevertheless took the opportunity to meet with Union Generals Canby and Phil Sheridan to inform them of the chaotic military situation in Texas and suggest ways in which the now certain transition to Union military occupation might be made smoother.[34]

As a lawyer, Ballinger was uncomfortable with the fact that the military convention approved by Canby appeared to contemplate obtaining each soldier's signature on a parole and the turnover of all military supplies. Satisfying either of these conditions was a practical impossibility. Ballinger and Colonel Smith advised General Canby that "at the time we left Texas a large portion of the Confederate troops had actually disbanded themselves and gone to their homes, and before intelligence of the convention of surrender shall be received the remainder may also be dispersed." They also admitted that almost all of the "movable public property" had already moved into the homes of the citizens and former soldiers and was irretrievably lost.[35]

On June 2, 1865, the surrender of the Army of the Trans-Mississippi, the last major armed force in the Confederacy to surrender, was signed on board the U.S.S. *Fort Jackson*. The *Jackson* was then stationed off of the sand bar located outside of the entrance to Galveston Harbor. General Edmund Kirby Smith personally visited the Union blockading fleet and signed a ratification of the surrender terms that had already been negotiated by his agents in New Orleans. Witnessing the signing of the surrender for the Union was Brigadier General (and future Texas Reconstruction Governor) Edmund J. Davis, who had known Kirby Smith before the war in Florida.[36]

General Magruder was also present to witness Smith's signature for the Confederate side. Davis recalled after the war that during this last meeting Smith and Magruder were "much alarmed, and thought severe measures would be taken against them." Davis tried to reassure them and offered to take them to New Orleans and "see them safe." Some of the staff officers accepted his invitation, but Magruder chose to stay. It seemed to Davis that Magruder was in some doubt as to which side (Union or Confederate) he had more to fear from.[37] He later resolved this fear by going to Mexico. Before going, Magruder is rumored to have gathered his staff together and said something on the order of "Boys, the jig's up. Help yourself to any supplies you can carry home."[38]

On the morning of June 5, 1865, Captain Benjamin Sands of the United States Navy entered Galveston Harbor with the *Cornubia*, followed by the *Preston*. These were the last two Union ships to enter a Confederate port. Sands went ashore and, at the Customhouse, formally took possession of Galveston on behalf of the Union forces.[39] As with the first Union occupation of the city in 1862, Federal authority was again asserted by flying the United States flag at the Customhouse for about half an hour.

Before raising the flag, Captain Sands delivered a few conciliatory remarks. He indicated that he had been assured of the peaceable intentions of the city's inhabitants and had therefore come ashore with only a few officers. The captain assured the anxious crowd that he had worn a side arm only as a sign of respect for the mayor.[40]

As a contemporary news account describes, the crowd assembled here in 1865 to witness the formal surrender of Galveston was not the same boisterous and excited group that had so joyously called for war when Sam Houston addressed the crowd at the Tremont House Hotel in 1861:

No demonstration whatever was made by the assembled citizens, either by actions or words, but all was profound silence, with the exception that one voice was heard to call for three cheers, but to this there was no response whatever, but the same deep silence continued.[41]

Captain Sands wrote after the war that it was "pleasant duty" to see the United States flag raised over the Customhouse in Galveston since that flag "now was flying over every foot of our territory, this being the closing act of the great rebellion."[42] In a final irony, of which Sands was apparently unaware at the time, the Customhouse over which he raised his flag as the last symbolic gesture was a highly appropriate place for the war to come to a close. Its location had been chosen by an army engineer who had supervised construction at Fort Sumter. And the ironwork used in the building had been created under the watchful eyes of Major Robert Anderson, whose surrender at Fort Sumter in 1861 had marked the beginning of the war.[43]

Epilogue

There has never been an armed force which in purity of motives,
intensity of courage and heroism has equaled the army and navy of
the Confederate States of America, 1861–1865.
INSCRIPTION ON "DIGNIFIED RESIGNATION"
Monument erected in Galveston, 1912

The Union occupation of Galveston at the conclusion of the war in June 1865 brought many changes to the city. Merchants and former inhabitants rushed back to the island, many to find their homes and businesses pillaged and destroyed. Eventually, the return of trade would bring new prosperity, and by 1870, Galveston would become the largest city in Texas. But in June 1865, Galveston was an occupied city, and the devastation that had been inflicted by more than four years of war made such a recovery seem unlikely and far away indeed.

The large number of Union troops in the city caused a number of personal adjustments. The Seventy-Sixth Illinois Regiment decided to make their camp adjacent to William Pitt Ballinger's residence and satisfied their water needs from his cistern. Ballinger complained in his diary that the Union troops "distracted the ladies by their depredations," and lamented that, like the Confederate troops before them, they "go into our chickens every night."[1]

On June 18, 1865, General Gordon Granger arrived in Galveston and began to set up the army administration that would govern Texas until Reconstruction governments were established. From his headquarters on the Strand, on June 19, 1865, General Granger issued General Order No. 3, which officially informed the people of Texas that slavery had been terminated by virtue of President Lincoln's issuance of the Emancipation Proclamation.[2]

Although June 19 is now celebrated in Texas as a holiday (known as "Juneteenth" in commemoration of the date of Granger's order), there was no real legal importance to Granger's order on that date. Lincoln's Emancipation Proclamation had been issued in September 1862. That proclamation provided that all slaves were to be freed effective January 1, 1863, the same day on which the Battle of Galveston took place.

As it turned out, General Granger's order was largely symbolic as far as it concerned racial relations. Although it did confirm that the Emancipation Proclamation was in effect in Texas, it also stated in a patronizing tone that the "freedmen" were advised to stay at home and work for their former masters for wages. Black men and women were still many years away from being treated with equality. Less than two weeks after Granger's order, for example, the mayor of Galveston fined and jailed one of the former slaves for having given a ball without his permission. Although the Union authorities arrested the mayor for this act, it was done more for jurisdictional reasons than any genuine sense of moral outrage.[3]

Revisionist personal history soon became the rage among former Confederate officers. It was amazing how many men determined, when it came time to write their applications for pardons, that they had been secret Union sympathizers and supporters from the beginning. In August 1865, William Pitt Ballinger took a number of these applications and went to Washington, D.C., to seek pardons for himself and a number of his clients. Ballinger received what he believed to be the first pardon granted to a Texan. While in Washington, he met with President Andrew Johnson and argued the case for even more pardons in Texas. The president received him courteously, and Ballinger was soon able to report to his clients the successful completion of his mission.[4]

If Galvestonians were ever inclined to forget the part that they had played in America's great internal conflict, there were plenty of postwar reminders. A number of important Confederate politicians and general officers visited or settled in Galveston after the war. In 1874, General (and Texas Senator to the Confederate Congress) Louis T. Wigfall came to the island after returning to the United States from exile in England. Wigfall had been one of the most influential of the prosecession antebellum leaders who became known as "fire-eaters" because of their vigorous defense of slavery and states' rights. He died in Galveston on February 18, 1874.[5]

Two years later, in 1876, former Confederate General Braxton Bragg, who was employed as a railroad surveyor at the time, also died in the Island City within just a few paces of the Customhouse, where the city had finally surrendered.[6]

Galveston's postwar visitors were not limited to dying Confederate dignitaries. In 1880, Ulysses S. Grant came to the city with much fanfare and publicity following a world tour. Meeting him for a banquet at the Tremont

House Hotel was former General Phil Sheridan, who used the occasion to apologize for a highly publicized comment he had made in 1866 that suggested he would prefer to live in hell than Texas.[7]

The descendants of Galveston's Civil War adversaries also returned and received public recognition from time to time. The daughter of Captain Jonathan Wainwright, Marie, became a famous actress who opened Galveston's Grand Opera House at the beginning of 1895. Jonathan Wainwright's grandson (who was also named Jonathan Mayhew Wainwright after his brave grandfather) made a name for himself during World War II by bravely defending Bataan and Corregidor until forced to surrender them to the Japanese. The Union descendants were not all confined to the Wainwright family either. One of Lieutenant James Jouett's youngest cousins was stationed on the island in 1929 as a member of the Army Air Corps.[8]

Even the ships that had been so much a part of the Civil War story of Galveston had a way of returning and stimulating interest in the island's wartime story. In 1872, the *Harriet Lane*, greatly altered in appearance and rechristened the *Elliot Ritchie*, visited Galveston as a lumber freighter and appropriately discharged its cargo at Kuhn's Wharf.

Hundreds of curious citizens (including many veterans of the battle in which the ship had been captured) toured its decks, recalling the day nine years earlier when it had been captured only a few hundred yards away. Twelve years later, in 1884, the *Harriet Lane* would be lost in a storm off the coast of Argentina. But a series of new Coast Guard ships, proudly bearing the same name, took over for their famous predecessor and have performed valuable service for the United States ever since.[9]

Even the *Santee*, from which the first invasion of Galveston Harbor had been launched in 1861, was towed back to Galveston in 1913. By that time, of course, it was an old hulk that was falling to pieces and was headed back to the North to be salvaged. But at Galveston, it was repaired and fastened together so that it could make the rest of its final voyage back to Boston.[10]

The Confederate heroes of the Battle of Galveston gradually disappeared one by one as the years following the end of the war went by. Two of these men had not lived to see the end of the war. Tom Green was killed at Blair's Landing, Louisiana, in 1864 contesting another threatened Union invasion of Texas along the Red River. A little more than two weeks later, William Scurry was mortally wounded at the Battle of Jenkins' Ferry in Arkansas.

The commander of the cottonclad fleet, "Commodore" Leon Smith, who General Magruder stated had earned himself an "imperishable name upon the page of history," quietly drifted from the scene after the war. By 1869, Smith and his family had settled in the Alaska Territory. As Christmas approached that year, Smith probably recalled the same date seven years earlier when he had spent the day putting the finishing touches on as odd an assortment of warships as the Civil War produced. As fate would have it, he would not live to celebrate the seventh anniversary of the battle.

Smith lived in a dangerous area of the frontier in Alaska. There, he had the misfortune to run afoul of a Stick Indian named "Scutd-doo," who was seeking revenge for the murder of one of his companions. On the morning of December 26, 1869, this Indian chose Leon Smith to be the instrument of his retribution. True to his performance at Galveston, the commodore was apparently brave and tenacious to the end.

Witnesses rushed to the scene after they heard shot after shot being fired near the trading post. Smith was found, mortally wounded, with seventeen separate bullet wounds. Amazingly, the tough old sea captain lingered for thirteen more hours before he died. At the murder trial for Smith's Indian assailant, the man explained that he had killed a "Tyhee," a person of great importance, and would explain to Smith in the next world why he had been murdered.[11]

Unlike his friend Leon Smith, Prince John Magruder—the man of most importance in the Civil War story of Galveston—did not have the theatrical end he deserved. As E. J. Davis had correctly observed at the Army of the Trans-Mississippi surrender ceremony, Magruder was justifiably apprehensive about his treatment by United States authorities after the war. To buy time, he elected to go to Mexico, where he held several administrative offices under Emperor Maximilian. When that regime came to a sudden and bloody end, Magruder returned to the United States, where he lectured to make ends meet and lived in relative poverty. The "Prince" had become a pauper.

On one occasion in 1869, Magruder managed to scrape together the means to visit Boston as part of a traveling lecture tour. There, he ran into Isaac Burrell, his former adversary, at a social function. Burrell was still smarting from criticism about his capture at Galveston and asked Magruder for a written vindication of his actions. The cordial Magruder put pen to paper and assured his former prisoner that "no military man of whatever rank or experience could have made better arrangements and displayed more ability and courage than you and your troops did in the face of the most trying and embarrassing situations that I have ever seen officers and men placed in."[12]

Two years later, in 1871, Magruder died in Houston, probably of a lingering heart condition. With absolutely no fanfare, one of the most creative military men of his time was given a pauper's burial in Houston.

Galveston did not forget Magruder, however. Years later his body was moved to Galveston, where it was buried only a short distance from the simple monument to Union naval officer Edward Lea and what would eventually become the site of the Battle of Galveston monument. Over Magruder's grave was erected a large spire with chiseled portraits of his battles on the sides. Such a gesture would undoubtedly have appealed to Magruder. The Prince and his players had left the stage, but their drama would never be forgotten.

NOTES

The following abbreviations are used in these notes:

CAH   The Eugene C. Barker Texas History Collection of the Center for American History, University of Texas at Austin
CWTI   *Civil War Times Illustrated*
GDN   *The Galveston Daily News, The Galveston News,* or *Galveston News*
GTHC   The Galveston and Texas History Center of the Rosenberg Library, Galveston, Texas
MS   Manuscript
OR   U.S. War Department, *The War of the Rebellion: A Compilation of the Official Records of the Union and Confederate Armies,* Series 1 unless otherwise noted
ORN   U.S. Naval War Records Office, *Official Records of the Union and Confederate Navies in the War of the Rebellion,* Series 1 unless otherwise noted
SHSP   *Southern Historical Society Papers* (Richmond; reprinted, Wilmington, N.C.: Broadfoot Publishing Company and Morningside Bookshop, 1990–1991)
SWHQ   *Southwestern Historical Quarterly*
TS   Typescript

INTRODUCTION

1. Barbara J. Rozek, "Galveston Slavery," *Houston Review: History and Culture of the Gulf Coast* 15, no. 2 (1993): 76.

2. Earl W. Fornell, *The Galveston Era: The Texas Crescent on the Eve of Secession* (Austin: University of Texas Press, 1961), 23–24.

3. Fornell, *The Galveston Era,* 115–125; Rozek, "Galveston Slavery," 76–82; Arthur J. L. Fremantle, *The Fremantle Diary Being the Journal of Arthur James Lyon Fremantle, Coldstream Guards, On His Three Months in the Southern States,* ed. Walter Lord (Boston: Little Brown and Co., 1954), 58; Randolph B. Campbell, *An Empire for Slavery: The Peculiar Institution in Texas, 1821–1865* (Baton Rouge: Louisiana State University Press, 1989), 11–13, 52–53, 55–56, 125–126.

4. Fornell, *The Galveston Era,* 25, 35, 61.

5. Ibid., 36–37, 145, 153–154.

6. Willard and D. Richardson, *The Texas Almanac for 1861, with Statistics, Historical and Biographical Sketches, &c, Relating to Texas* (Galveston: Galveston News, 1861), 237–238.

7. Sam Acheson, *35,000 Days in Texas: A History of the Dallas News and Its Forbears* (New York: Macmillan Company, 1938), 53; Mark Grimsley, "Inside a Beleaguered City: A Commander and Actor—Prince John Magruder," *CWTI* 21 (September 1982): 35.

8. Colonel I. S. Burrell to Major George B. Drake, New Orleans, July 27, 1864, quoted in Charles P. Bosson, *History of the Forty-Second Regiment, Infantry, Massachusetts Volunteers, 1862, 1863, 1864* (Boston: Mills, Knight & Co., 1886), 137.

9. N. P. Banks to the Secretary of War, New York City, April 6, 1865, *OR,* vol. 26, pt. 1:7.

10. Ludwell H. Johnson, *Red River Campaign: Politics and Cotton in the Civil War* (Kent, Ohio: Kent State University Press, 1993), 278–279.

1. THE WAR IS POSTPONED

1. Bruce S. Allardice, *More Generals in Gray* (Baton Rouge: Louisiana State University Press, 1995), 252.

2. Jesse A. Ziegler, "General E. B. Nichols, Early Merchant, Helped Magruder Retake City from Federals," *GDN,* February 3, 1935; Annie Charlotte Terrill, "Life of Ebenezer B. Nichols," San Antonio, Texas, June 1935, TS, Texas State Archives, Austin.

3. Ernest W. Winkler, ed., *Journal of the Secession Convention of Texas* (Austin: Austin Printing Company, 1912), 54–59 (hereafter cited as *Secession Convention*).

4. Ibid., 28.

5. Ibid., 81–82.

6. Margaret Swett Henson, *Samuel May Williams: Early Texas Entrepreneur* (College Station: Texas A&M University Press, 1976), xi–xii, 78.

7. *Secession Convention,* 317–318.

8. Ibid., 320.

9. Ibid., 350.

10. Ibid., 337.

11. Committee on Public Safety to Colonel John S. Ford, February 5, 1861, quoted in *Secession Convention,* 321–324.

12. Fornell, *The Galveston Era,* 283–284.

13. *Secession Convention,* 337.

14. Alwyn Barr, "Texas' Confederate Field Artillery," *Texas Military History* 1 (August 1961): 1.

15. Order No. 5, Headquarters Fort Brown, Texas, February 21, 1861, *OR,* 1:537.

16. Colonel John S. Ford to J. C. Robertson, Chairman of the Committee on Public Safety, Brownsville, February 22, 1861, quoted in *Secession Convention,* 325.

17. E. B. Nichols, Commissioner, to Captain B. H. Hill, Brownsville, February 22, 1861, *OR,* 1:538.

18. Captain B. H. Hill to E. B. Nichols, Fort Brown, February 22, 1861, *OR,* 1: 539–540.

19. *Secession Convention,* 340.

20. Robert Hodges to Father, Brazos Santiago, February 22, 1861, quoted in Maury Darst, "Robert Hodges, Jr.: Confederate Soldier," *East Texas Historical Journal* 9 (March 1971): 22.

21. *Secession Convention,* 343–345.

22. Ibid., 345; Dudley G. Wooten, *A Comprehensive History of Texas: 1685 to 1897* (Dallas: William G. Scarff, 1898), 2:520–521.

23. Reports of Wm. Hoffman, C. A. Wale, and Larkin Smith, *OR,* 1:517–522.

24. *Secession Convention,* 345–346.

25. E. B. Nichols to Committee on Public Safety, Brazos Santiago, March 5, 1861, MS, Sidney Sherman Papers, GTHC.

26. E. B. Nichols to Colonel J. S. Ford, quoted in *Secession Convention*, 348–349.

27. Colonel John S. Ford to John C. Robertson, Brownsville, March 20, 1861, quoted in *Secession Convention*, 403.

28. Arthur T. Lynn to Lord John Russell, Galveston, March 14, 1861, MS, British Consular Records, GTHC.

2. A SAFE CONDITION

1. John C. Robertson to George Williamson, Galveston, February 14, 1861, quoted in *Secession Convention*, 308–309.

2. Thomas O. Moore to Jefferson Davis, New Orleans, April 16, 1861, *OR*, 53:671; *Secession Convention*, 309–310.

3. John C. Robertson to O. M. Roberts, March 8, 1861, quoted in *Secession Convention*, 389–391.

4. *Secession Convention*, 181–182.

5. S. Sherman to J. C. Robertson, Galveston, March 6, 1861, quoted in *Secession Convention*, 395; Ben C. Stuart, "First Revenue Cutter in Texas Waters Was Sent to Hunt Down Privateers," *GDN*, June 16, 1918.

6. Captain William J. [F.] Rogers to O. M. Roberts, Galveston, March 13, 1861, quoted in *Secession Convention*, 182.

7. John C. Robertson to A. M. Gentry, Galveston, February 24, 1861, quoted in *Secession Convention*, 392; original in Sidney Sherman Papers, GTHC.

8. Sidney Sherman to J. C. Robertson, Galveston, March 6, 1861, quoted in *Secession Convention*, 395.

9. James J. Diamond et al. to Gen. Sidney Sherman, Galveston, February 26, 1861, quoted in *Secession Convention*, 393.

10. O. M. Roberts to General Sidney Sherman, Galveston, February 25, 1861, quoted in *Secession Convention*, 393–394.

11. W. N. Bate, *General Sidney Sherman: Texas Soldier, Statesman and Builder* (Waco: Texian Press, 1974), 262–263.

12. "Sherman, Sidney," entry by Julia Beazley, in Walter Prescott Webb, ed., *The Handbook of Texas* (Austin: Texas State Historical Association, 1952), 2:603.

13. Bate, *General Sidney Sherman*, 240–249.

14. Ibid., 259.

15. Sidney Sherman to J. C. Robertson, Galveston, March 6, 1861, quoted in *Secession Convention*, 395.

16. Sidney Sherman to W. H. Ochiltree, Galveston, March 8, 1861, *OR*, 1:610–611.

17. *GDN*, March 5, 1861.

18. Sidney Sherman to J. C. Robertson, Galveston, March 6, 1861, quoted in *Secession Convention*, 395.

19. Charles W. Hayes, *History of the Island and the City of Galveston* (Cincinnati, 1879 [set in type but not released]; Austin: Jenkins Garrett Press, 1974), 1:487–488, 2:709–710 (hereafter cited as *Island and City*).

20. Sidney Sherman to J. C. Robertson, Galveston, March 6, 1861, quoted in *Secession Convention*, 395; Sidney Sherman to W. H. Ochiltree, Galveston, March 8, 1861, *OR*, 1:611.

21. Ezra J. Warner, *Generals in Gray: Lives of the Confederate Commanders* (Baton Rouge: Louisiana State University Press, 1959), 292; William C. Davis, ed., *The Confederate General*, entry by Jeffry D. Wert (n.p.: National Historical Society, 1991), 6:6–7.

22. Stevens to Jefferson Davis, Richmond, June 12, 1861, *OR*, 4:92.

23. Sorley Smith & Co. to Governor Edward Clark, Galveston, April 9, 1861, MS, Papers of Governor Edward Clark.

24. Sidney Sherman to Governor Edward Clark, Galveston, May 22, 1861, MS, Papers of Governor Edward Clark.

25. Sidney Sherman to Gov. Moore of Louisiana, Galveston, April 25, 1861, MS, Sidney Sherman Papers, GTHC.

26. E. C. Wharton to Unknown, "News Office, Galveston," April 9, 1861, *OR*, 1:625.

27. Mayor Thomas Joseph to Governor Edward Clark, Galveston, undated, attaching Resolution dated April 12, 1861, MS, Papers of Governor Edward Clark.

28. Sidney Sherman to Governor Edward Clark, Galveston, April 17, 1861, MS, Papers of Governor Edward Clark.

29. Sidney Sherman to Governor Edward Clark, Galveston, May 22, 1861, MS, Papers of Governor Edward Clark.

30. Mrs. A. M. Fitch to P. C. Tucker, Galveston, June 25, 1861, MS, Tucker Family Papers, GTHC.

31. S. Cooper to Capt. J. M. Galt, Adjutant and Inspector General's Office, Montgomery, April 17, 1861, *OR*, 1:626.

32. S. Cooper to Colonel Earl Van Dorn, Adjutant and Inspector General's Office, Montgomery, April 11, 1861, *OR*, 1:623; General Orders No. 1, San Antonio, April 21, 1861, *OR*, 1:628.

33. Hayes, *Island and City*, 1:498.

3. WARMING UP FOR WAR

1. S. Cooper to Colonel Earl Van Dorn, Adjutant and Inspector General's Office, Montgomery, April 11, 1861, *OR*, 1:623.

2. Robert G. Hartje, *Van Dorn: The Life and Times of a Confederate General* (Nashville: Vanderbilt University Press, 1967), 83; Rudolf Coreth to Family, Mouth of the St. Bernard River, November 10, 1861, quoted in Minetta Altgelt Goyne, *Lone Star and Double Eagle: Civil War Letters of a German-Texas Family* (Fort Worth: Texas Christian University Press, 1982), 22.

3. John S. Ford to J. C. Robertson, Brownsville, February 25, 1861, *OR*, 53:655; James J. Day, "Leon Smith: Confederate Mariner," *East Texas Historical Journal* 3 (March 1965): 34–35.

4. Naval History Division, Navy Department, *Civil War Naval Chronology: 1861–1865* (Washington, D.C.: U.S. Government Printing Office, 1971), I-2.

5. Mrs. Samuel Posey, "Capture of the Star of the West," *Confederate Veteran* 32 (May 1924): 174.

6. "Keeping Green Memories and Traditions of Days of '61," *GDN*, January 23, 1916.

7. Hartje, *Van Dorn*, 85.

4. THE ISLAND CITY CHOOSES SIDES

1. O. M. Roberts, *Texas*, vol. 15 of *Confederate Military History: Extended Edition* (1899; reprint, Wilmington, N.C.: Broadfoot Publishing Co., 1989), 30–32.

2. *Secession Convention*, 95–96.

3. Hayes, *Island and City*, 1:488; Fornell, *The Galveston Era*, 288–289.

4. *Secession Convention*, 89.

5. Hayes, *Island and City*, 1:490.

6. Houston to Colonel Waite, Austin, March 29, 1861, *OR*, 1:551.

7. Thomas North, *Five Years in Texas; or, What You Did Not Hear during the War from January 1861 to January 1866* (Cincinnati: Elm Street Printing Co., 1871), 93.

8. Ibid., 94.

9. Ibid.

10. Eugene C. Barker and Amelia W. Williams, eds., *The Writings of Sam Houston*, (Austin: University of Texas, 1943), 8:300–301.

5. CITY IN THE SEA

1. Sherman to Governor Edward Clark, Galveston, April 30, 1861, MS, Papers of Governor Edward Clark.

2. Ibid.

3. Hayes, *Island and City*, 1:495.

4. Ibid., 1:497.

5. S. Sherman to "The Volunteer Troops of the City and County of Galveston," June 25, 1861, undated newspaper article in Sherman Family Scrapbook, GTHC; J. S. Sydnor et al. to Governor Edward Clark, Galveston, June 25, 1861, MS, Papers of Governor Edward Clark.

6. Van Dorn to His Wife, Galveston, July 23, 1861, quoted in *A Soldier's Honor: With Reminiscences of Major-General Earl Van Dorn by His Comrades* (New York: Abbey Press, 1902), 53.

7. J. S. Sydnor et al. to Governor Edward Clark, Galveston, June 25, 1861, MS, Papers of Governor Edward Clark.

8. William Pitt Ballinger Diary, entry for February 27, 1862, TS, GTHC, 5.

6. THE BLOCKADE BEGINS

1. Virginia Eisenhour, *Galveston: A Different Place*, 4th ed. (Galveston: V. Eisenhour, 1989), 51; Douglas Zwiener and Elisabeth Darst, *A Guide to Historic Galveston* (Galveston: n.p., 1966), 2; Howard Barnstone, *The Galveston That Was* (1966; reprint, Houston: Rice University Press, 1993), 23–24.

2. JOLO Observatory Record Book, April 22–December 27, 1861, MS, GTHC (hereafter cited as JOLO).

3. JOLO, May 7, 1861.

4. Ibid., May 12 and 22, 1861.

5. Ibid., entry for September 2, 1861.

6. Ibid., entry for June 20, 1861.

7. Tim Finn Autobiography, entry for July 3, 1861, MS, CAH.

8. J. J. Sydnor to Governor Edward Clark, Galveston, July 6, 1861, MS, Papers of Governor Edward Clark.

9. Lewis R. Hamersly, *The Records of the Living Officers of the U.S. Navy and Marine Corps* (Philadelphia: J. B. Lippincott & Co., 1870), 36.

10. Robert Collins Suhr, "Firing the Norfolk Navy Yard," *America's Civil War* (November 1996): 52–57.

11. Captain James Alden to Flag-Officer William Mervine, Off Galveston, July 8, 1861, *ORN*, 16:576–577.

12. "The Blockade: Five Prizes Captured!", *The Civilian*, undated, Civil War Scrapbook No. 76-0041 [small volume], GTHC.

13. William Mervine to Commander James Alden, Flagship *Colorado*, Off Fort Pickens, *ORN*, 16:588.

14. JOLO, entry for August 2, 1861.

15. Ben C. Stuart, "Some True Tales of Sixty-One," *GDN*, July 2, 1911; Philip C. Tucker III Narrative, TS, CAH, 87.

16. Frank Moore, ed., *The Rebellion Record: A Diary of American Events* (New York: G. P. Putnam, 1862), 2:484–485.

17. Tim Finn Autobiography, entry for August 3, 1861, MS, CAH.

18. Hayes, *Island and City*, 1:498.

19. "Battle of Galveston Topic of Discussion," *GDN*, January 9, 1911.

20. Peggy Gregory, copyist, *Record of Interments of the City of Galveston* (Houston: n.p., 1976), 21.

21. Arthur Lynn (British Consul) et al. to Captain James Alden, August 5, 1861, *ORN*, 16:605–606.

22. Alden to Lynn et al., August 6, 1861, *ORN*, 16:606–607.

23. Colonel J. C. Moore to Messrs. Lynn et al., Galveston, August 6, 1861, newspaper article mounted in JOLO, 130.

24. James Alden to Flag-Officer Mervine, U.S.S. *South Carolina*, Off Galveston, August 10, 1861, *ORN*, 16:607–608.

25. G. V. Fox to Commander James Alden, Navy Department, September 12, 1861, *ORN*, 16:610.

26. J. J. Hendley et al. to J. J. Sydnor, August 6, 1861, JOLO.

27. Alwyn Barr, "Texas Coastal Defense," *SWHQ* 65 (July 1961): 6–7.

28. James Alden to Flag-Officer William Mervine, U.S.S. *South Carolina*, Off Galveston, September 13, 1861, *ORN*, 16:665–666.

29. Tim Finn Autobiography, entries for August and September of 1861.

7. A PESSIMISTIC ASSESSMENT

1. The biographical information about Paul O. Hebert is from Warner, *Generals in Gray*, 131–132; and Davis, *The Confederate General*, entry by Terry L. Jones, 3:84–85.

2. P. O. Hebert to Governor Edward Clark, Galveston, September 16, 1861, *OR*, 4:105–106; General Orders No. 1, Galveston, September 18, 1861, *OR*, 4:106.

3. P. O. Hebert to the Secretary of War, Galveston, September 27, 1861, *OR*, 4:112.

4. General Orders No. 19, Galveston, October 2, 1861, *OR*, 4:113.

5. Samuel Boyer Davis to Colonel John C. Moore, Galveston, November 4, 1861, *OR*, 4:131.

6. Address to the Men of Texas by General P. O. Hebert, Galveston, October 7, 1861, *OR*, 4:115–116.

7. Sackfield Maclin to General P. O. Hebert, Galveston, October 19, 1861, *OR*, 4:125.

8. P. O. Hebert to J. P. Benjamin, Galveston, October 24, 1861, *OR*, 4:126–127.

9. P. O. Hebert to J. P. Benjamin, Galveston, August 31, 1861, *OR*, 4:130–131.

10. P. O. Hebert to J. P. Benjamin, Galveston, October 24, 1861, *OR*, 4:126–127.

11. P. O. Hebert to J. P. Benjamin, Galveston, November 15, 1861, *OR*, 4:139–140.

12. C. Richard King, ed., "Andrew Neill's Galveston Letters," *Texana* 3 (Fall 1965): 204.

13. Francis R. Lubbock, *Six Decades in Texas or Memoirs of Francis Richard Lubbock, Governor of Texas in War-time, 1861–63*, ed. C. W. Raines (Austin: Ben C. Jones & Co., 1900), 348.

14. Thomas Joseph to F. R. Lubbock, Galveston, December 16, 1861, Papers of Governor F. R. Lubbock, Texas State Archives at Austin.

15. Lubbock, *Six Decades in Texas*, 349–350.

16. Ibid., 350, 380.

17. David S. Kennard to Father and Mother, Virginia Point, November 28, 1861, MS, Claude Elliot Memorial Collection, Special Collections, University of Houston Libraries.

18. Charlie G. Collings to Unidentified Family Member, Galveston, December 2, 1861, MS, Amerman-Collings Family Collection, Houston Metropolitan Research Center, Houston Public Library.

19. Charlie G. Collings to Unidentified Family Member, Galveston, December 9, 1861, MS, Amerman-Collings Family Collection.

20. Charlie G. Collings to Unidentified Family Member, Galveston, December 31, 1861, MS, Amerman-Collings Family Collection.

8. THOMAS CHUBB AND THE *ROYAL YACHT*

1. Fremantle, *The Fremantle Diary*, 54.

2. "Death of Thomas Chubb," *GDN*, August 27, 1890; Lewis Publishing Co., *History of Texas Together with a Biographical History of the Cities of Houston and Galveston* (Chicago: Lewis Publishing Company, 1895), 333.

3. General Orders No. 4, Headquarters Department of Texas, San Antonio, May 3, 1861, *OR*, 1:632.

4. H. N. Duble to Cecelia Chubb, Galveston, July 4, 1861, MS, H. N. Duble Papers, GTHC; Lubbock, *Six Decades in Texas*, 318–319.

5. Agreements Regarding the Services of the Schooner *Royal Yacht* and Its Crew, Galveston, October 9–10, 1861, *ORN*, 16:844.

6. Henry Eagle to Flag-Officer William W. McKean, U.S. Frigate *Santee*, Off Galveston Bar, October 19, 1861, *ORN*, 16:733–734.

7. James G. Wilson and John Fiske, eds., *Appleton's Cyclopedia of American Biography* (New York: D. Appleton and Co., 1888; republished, Detroit: Gale Research Co., 1968), 2:287–288.

8. Henry Eagle to Clerk of the District Court, Southern District of New York, U.S. Frigate *Santee*, Off Galveston Bar, October 27, 1861, *ORN*, 16:748–749.

9. Hamersly, *The Records of Living Officers of the U.S. Navy and Marine Corps*, 108; Philip C. Tucker III, "Schooner Royal Yacht Played Interesting Role during the Civil War; Formed Part of Confederate Fleet Defending Galveston Harbor," *Galveston Tribune*, January 5, 1929; Mitchell S. Goldberg, "A Federal Raid into Galveston Harbor, November 7–8, 1861: What Really Happened?", *SWHQ* 76 (July 1972): 58–70.

10. Jouett to Henry Eagle, U.S. Frigate *Santee*, Off Galveston Bar, November 14, 1861, *ORN*, 16:757–758; Goldberg, "A Federal Naval Raid," 76:58–70.

11. Henry Eagle to Lieutenant James E. Jouett et al., U.S. Frigate *Santee*, Off Galveston Bar, November 7, 1861, *ORN*, 16:756.

12. Tucker, "Schooner *Royal Yacht* Played Interesting Role during the Civil War."

13. Jouett to Hon. R. W. Thompson, Washington, D.C., May 13, 1879, quoted in Goldberg, "A Federal Naval Raid," 76:63. The account of the raid on November 7 and 8 is taken almost completely from the letters of Lieutenant Jouett and Gunner William W. Carter, which are quoted in the article cited in this note and are found in Letters Received by the Secretary of the Navy from Commanding Officers of Squadrons, 1841–1886, Microcopy, M-89, Roll No. 119.

14. Abstract of the Log of the *Santee*, November 7–8, 1861, *ORN*, 16:759.

15. General Order of Flag-Officer McKean, U.S. Flagship *Niagara*, December 7, 1861, *ORN*, 16:758.

16. Gideon Welles to Flag-Officer William McKean, Navy Department, December 23, 1861, *ORN*, 16:758–759.

17. Goldberg, "A Federal Naval Raid," 76:58–59.

18. William W. Hunter to P. O. Hebert, Galveston, November 11, 1861, *ORN*, 16:760–761.

19. Ibid.

20. William W. Hunter to General P. O. Hebert, Steamer *Bayou City*, Galveston, November 8, 1861, *ORN*, 16:759–760.

21. Abstract of the Log of the *Santee*, November 8, 1861, *ORN*, 16:759.

22. "Death of Thomas Chubb," *GDN*, August 27, 1890.

23. Tucker, "Schooner Royal Yacht Played Interesting Role during the Civil War."

24. E. P. Petty to Margaret, Galveston, April 2, 1862, quoted in Norman D. Brown, ed., *Journey to Pleasant Hill: The Civil War Letters of Captain Elijah P. Petty, Walker's Texas Division, C.S.A.* (San Antonio: University of Texas Institute of Texas Cultures, 1982), 1:44.

25. Hayes, *Island and City*, 1:507.

26. Logbook of the *Royal Yacht*, 1862–1863, MS, GTHC; Charles K. Bowen, "The

Royal Yacht, She Was Not Destroyed by Admiral Jouett as His Report Says," *GDN*, August 5, 1894.

27. Tim Finn Autobiography, entry for August 5, 1861.

28. Bosson, *History of the 42nd Regiment*, 418.

29. Ben C. Stuart, "First Submarine Torpedo Vessel," *GDN*, August 29, 1909.

9. THE THREAT OF BOMBARDMENT

1. C. G. Collings to Unidentified Family Member, Galveston, December 11, 1861, MS, Amerman-Collings Family Collection.

2. E. P. Petty to Ella, Galveston, March 24, 1862, quoted in N. D. Brown, *Journey to Pleasant Hill*, 1:40.

3. Henry L. Ingram, comp., *Civil War Letters of George W. and Martha F. Ingram* (College Station: Texas A&M University Press, 1973), 14–15.

4. Ballinger to "Mother," Houston, January 13, 1862, MS, William Pitt Ballinger Papers, GTHC.

5. Johnson, *Red River Campaign*, 7–18.

6. Andrew to G. V. Fox, Boston, November 27, 1861, *OR*, 15:412–413.

7. George B. McClellan to B. F. Butler, Headquarters of the Army, February 23, 1862, quoted in James Parton, *General Butler in New Orleans: History of the Administration of the Department of the Gulf* (New York: Mason Brothers, 1864), 192–194.

8. S. F. Du Pont et al. to Gideon Welles, Washington, September 3, 1861, *ORN*, 16:654.

9. Gideon Welles to David G. Farragut, Navy Department, January 9, 1862, *ORN*, 18:5.

10. Patricia L. Faust, ed., *Historical Times Illustrated Encyclopedia of the Civil War* (New York: Harper & Row, 1986), 254.

11. David D. Porter, "The Opening of the Lower Mississippi," *Battles and Leaders of the Civil War: Grant-Lee Edition* (1887; reprint, Harrisburg, Pa.: Archive Society, 1991), 2:26.

12. D. G. Farragut to Captain H. Eagle, U.S.S. *Hartford*, South West Pass, March 12, 1862, *ORN*, 18:60.

13. J. P. Benjamin to General P. O. Hebert, February 24, 1862, *OR*, 9:700.

14. J. P. Benjamin to Governor F. R. Lubbock, Richmond, March 17, 1862, Papers of Governor F. R. Lubbock.

15. Special Orders No. 471, Headquarters Military District of Galveston, May 14, 1862, *OR*, 9:709.

16. D. G. Farragut to Eagle, U.S. Flagship *Hartford*, Off the City of New Orleans, May 2, 1862, *ORN*, 18:463.

17. Henry Eagle to the Military Commandant, quoted in Joseph J. Cook to General P. O. Hebert, Galveston, May 17, 1862, *OR*, 9:710.

18. P. O. Hebert to Colonel Cook, Houston, May 17, 1862, *OR*, 9:711.

19. Joseph J. Cook to P. O. Hebert, Galveston, May 18, 1862, *OR*, 9:711.

20. Henry Eagle to the Foreign Consuls Residents of the Town of Galveston, U.S. Frigate *Santee*, May 19, 1862, quoted in J. J. Cook to P. O. Hebert, *OR*, 9:711.

21. Henry Eagle to the Foreign Consuls, U.S. Frigate *Santee*, May 22, 1862, quoted in Hayes, *Island and City*, 1:508.

22. P. O. Hebert to Colonel J. J. Cook, Houston, May 19, 1862, *OR*, 9:712.

23. Proclamation of Major and Provost-Marshal J. C. Massie, Galveston, May 23, 1862, quoted in Hayes, *Island and City*, 1:510.

24. Brig. General T. B. Howard to Colonel J. Y. Dashiell, Galveston, MS, May 19, 1862, First Brigade Correspondence.

25. Lubbock, *Six Decades in Texas*, 387.

26. Henry Eagle to D. G. Farragut, U.S. Frigate *Santee*, Off Galveston Bar, June 4, 1862, *ORN*, 18:536.

27. J. F. Smith to Justina Rowzee, Galveston, June 28, 1862, TS, John F. Smith Letters, CAH.

28. Hayes, *Island and City*, 1:513–514.

29. J. C. Massie to Governor F. R. Lubbock, Galveston, July 30, 1862, MS, Papers of Governor F. R. Lubbock.

30. Carland Elaine Crook, "Benjamin Theron and French Designs in Texas during the Civil War," *SWHQ* 68 (April 1965): 432–433.

31. Crook, "Benjamin Theron," 68:442–446.

32. P. O. Hebert to Governor F. R. Lubbock, San Antonio, August 28, 1862, *OR*, 9:733–734.

33. North, *Five Years in Texas*, 105–106.

10. CAPTURED BY FERRYBOATS

1. D. G. Farragut to Gideon Welles, Flagship *Hartford*, New Orleans, July 29, 1862, *ORN*, 19:98.

2. A. A. Hoehling, *Damn the Torpedoes! Naval Incidents of the Civil War* (Winston-Salem, N.C.: John F. Blair, 1989), 27–28.

3. Tony Gibbons, *Warships and Naval Battles of the Civil War* (New York: Gallery Books, 1989), 84, 166; Paul H. Silverstone, *Warships of the Civil War Navies* (Annapolis, Md.: Naval Institute Press, 1989), 49–52.

4. H. A. Trexler, "The *Harriet Lane* and the Blockade of Galveston," *SWHQ* 35 (October 1931): 109.

5. Remo Salta, "Guardians of the Coast," *America's Civil War* (March 1994): 36–38.

6. W. E. Ehrman, "The *Harriet Lane* — Fighting Lady of the Civil War," *Bulletin of the U.S. Coast Guard Academy Alumni Association* (September/October 1980): 22.

7. Cobb to Augustus Schell, Custom Collector, New York City, October 26, 1859, quoted in Fornell, *The Galveston Era*, 262–263.

8. David P. Marvin, "The *Harriet Lane*," *SWHQ* 39 (July 1935): 16–17.

9. Salta, "Guardians of the Coast," 36; Philip C. Tucker III, "The United States Gunboat *Harriet Lane*," *SWHQ*, 21 (April 1918): 360–361.

10. Hoehling, *Damn the Torpedoes!*, 28.

11. Marvin, "The *Harriet Lane*," 39:18.

12. David D. Porter to Flag-Officer McKean, U.S.S. *Harriet Lane*, Mississippi River, April 25, 1862, *ORN*, 17:233.

13. Report of David D. Porter, U.S.S. *Harriet Lane*, Forts Jackson and St. Philip, April 30, 1862, *ORN*, 18:362.

14. D. D. Porter to Edward Higgins, U.S.S. *Harriet Lane*, Mississippi River, April 26, 1862, *ORN*, 18:436; Edward Higgins to D. D. Porter, Headquarters Forts Jackson and St. Philip, April 27, 1862, *ORN*, 18:437.

15. David D. Porter, "The Opening of the Lower Mississippi," 2:50.

16. Articles of Capitulation, April 28, 1862, *ORN*, 18:438; Charles G. Hearn, *The Capture of New Orleans: 1862* (Baton Rouge: Louisiana State University Press, 1995), 253–254.

17. Porter, "The Opening of the Lower Mississippi," 2:51.

18. D. D. Porter to Gideon Welles, U.S.S. *Harriet Lane*, Pensacola, May 10, 1862, *ORN*, 18:478–479.

19. D. G. Farragut to Gideon Welles, U.S. Flagship *Hartford*, Above Vicksburg, July 2, 1862, *ORN*, 18:609–610.

20. D. D. Porter to D. G. Farragut, U.S.S. *Octorara*, Vicksburg, July 3, 1862, *ORN*, 18:639.

21. W. B. Renshaw to Gideon Welles, U.S.S. *Westfield*, Mississippi River, July 23, 1862, *ORN*, 19:29; W. B. Renshaw to Gideon Welles, U.S.S. *Westfield*, New Orleans, July 29, 1862, *ORN*, 19:32.

22. W. B. Renshaw to Gideon Welles, U.S.S. *Westfield*, New Orleans, July 29, 1862, *ORN*, 19:98–99.

23. D. G. Farragut to Gideon Welles, Flagship *Hartford*, Mississippi River, August 15, 1862, *ORN*, 19:157–158; G. Welles to D. G. Farragut, Navy Department, August 26, 1862, *ORN*, 19:170.

24. Except where specifically attributed to another source, this account of the Union capture of Galveston is based on a comparison of the principal Union and Confederate accounts of this encounter. W. B. Renshaw to D. G. Farragut, U.S.S. *Westfield*, Off Galveston, October 8, 1862, *ORN*, 19:255–260; J. J. Cook to R. M. Franklin, Headquarters, Fort Hebert, October 9, 1862, *ORN*, 19:262–263.

25. P. O. Hebert to James Deshler, San Antonio, October 15, 1862, *OR*, 15:147.

26. Telegram from X. B. Debray to Major T. S. Moise, Virginia Point, October 5, 1862, *ORN*, 19:261.

27. X. B. Debray to J. J. Cook, Galveston, October 5, 1862, *ORN*, 19:261.

28. J. J. Cook to R. M. Franklin, Fort Hebert, October 9, 1862, *ORN*, 19:263.

29. X. B. Debray to J. J. Cook, Fort Hebert, October 10, 1862, *OR*, 15:150–151.

30. Hayes, *Island and City*, 1:522.

31. Tucker Narrative, TS, 98; MS, 138–139, CAH.

32. William Pitt Ballinger Diary, entry for October 4, 1862, TS, GTHC, 78–79.

33. Henry O. Gusley Diary, entry for October 9, 1862, *GDN*, October 28, 1863.

34. W. B. Renshaw to D. G. Farragut, U.S.S. *Westfield*, Galveston, October 8, 1862, *ORN*, 19:259.

35. X. B. Debray to Samuel Boyer Davis, Houston, October 19, 1862, *OR*, 15:836–837.

36. Samuel Boyer Davis to X. B. Debray, San Antonio, November 3, 1862, *OR*, 15:855.

37. X. B. Debray to Samuel Boyer Davis, Houston, November 6, 1862, *OR*, 15: 856–857.

38. J. Y. Dashiell to H. S. Lubbock, October 10, 1862, MS, J. Y. Dashiell Papers, GTHC; F. R. Lubbock to W. W. Hunter, Houston, October 16, 1862, MS, Papers of Governor F. R. Lubbock.

39. F. R. Lubbock to P. O. Hebert, Executive Department, October 15, 1862, MS, Papers of Governor F. R. Lubbock.

40. Lubbock, *Six Decades in Texas*, 421.

41. W. W. Hunter to C. M. Mason, C.S. Schooner *Dodge*, Off San Jacinto, September 14, 1862, *ORN*, 19:788; W. W. Hunter to S. R. Mallory, C.S. Schooner *Dodge*, Off San Jacinto, November 2, 1862, *ORN*, 19:801–802.

42. D. G. Farragut to Gideon Welles, Flagship *Hartford*, Pensacola Bay, October 15, 1862, *ORN*, 19:253–254.

43. D. G. Farragut to Benjamin J. Butler, Flagship *Hartford*, Pensacola Bay, October 14, 1862, *ORN*, 19:300.

44. D. G. Farragut to W. B. Renshaw, Flagship *Hartford*, Pensacola Bay, October 14, 1862, *ORN*, 19:260–261.

45. D. G. Farragut to W. B. Renshaw, Flagship *Hartford*, Pensacola Bay, October 28, 1862, *ORN*, 19:319.

46. J. M. Wainwright to B. F. Butler, U.S.S. *Harriet Lane*, Galveston, November 4, 1862, quoted in *GDN*, January 21, 1863.

47. Hayes, *Island and City*, 1:535–548.

48. Donald S. Frazier, *Cottonclads!: The Battle of Galveston and the Defense of the Texas Coast* (Fort Worth: Ryan Place Publishers, 1996), 26, 29.

49. J. M. Wainwright to Caroline Mason, U.S.S. *Harriet Lane*, Galveston, November 18, 1862, MS, J. M. Wainwright Papers, GTHC.

50. J. Berkemeier to W. B. Renshaw, Galveston, October 20, 1862, *ORN*, 19:310.

51. W. B. Renshaw to J. Berkemeier, U.S.S. *Westfield*, October 22, 1862, *ORN*, 19:310–311.

52. Henry O. Gusley Diary, entry for November 16, 1862, quoted in *GDN*, November 4, 1863.

53. Henry O. Gusley Diary, entries for October 25 and November 26, 1862, quoted in *GDN*, November 4, 1863.

54. Hayes, *Island and City*, 1:541–542.

55. Ben C. Stuart, "Lone Star Rifles," *GDN*, July 21, 1907.

56. Ben C. Stuart, "History of Galveston," Chapter 24, 8–9, and "Military," 49–50, MS, B. C. Stuart Papers, GTHC.

57. Hayes, *Island and City*, 1:542.

58. Ibid., 1:545.

59. "House Which Played Almost Tragic Part in Civil War to Be Torn Down," *GDN*, February 17, 1929.

60. Hayes, *Island and City*, 1:546.

61. D. G. Farragut to W. B. Renshaw, Flagship *Hartford*, Off New Orleans, December 12, 1862, *ORN*, 19:404.

62. D. G. Farragut to W. B. Renshaw, Flagship *Hartford*, Off New Orleans, December 15, 1862, *ORN*, 19:409–410.

11. THE INFANTRY ARRIVES

1. Henry Greenleaf Pearson, *The Life of John Andrew: Governor of Massachusetts, 1861–1865* (Boston: Houghton, Mifflin and Company, 1904); Faust, *Historical Times Illustrated Encyclopedia*, 17.

2. Faust, *Historical Times Illustrated Encyclopedia*, 479.

3. Except where specifically noted otherwise, the material contained in this chapter on the Forty-Second Massachusetts Regiment is taken from Bosson, *History of the 42nd Regiment*. Biographical material on members of the regiment is primarily derived from *Massachusetts Soldiers, Sailors, and Marines in the Civil War* (Norwood, Mass.: Norwood Press, 1932), 4:153–228. Chronological details about this regiment's service can also be found in *Supplement to the Official Records of the Union and Confederate Armies*, serial no. 41 (Wilmington, N.C.: Broadfoot Publishing Co., 1996), 340–361.

4. Speech of E. Jarvis Baker, 1882, Dorchester, Massachusetts, Benj. Stone Jr. Post, G.A.R., E. Jarvis Baker Memoir, CAH, 2.

5. Jarvis Baker Memoir, 3.

6. Ezra J. Warner, *Generals in Blue: Lives of the Union Commanders* (Baton Rouge: Louisiana State University Press, 1964), 17–18.

7. Johnson, *Red River Campaign*, 19–26.

8. H. W. Halleck to N. P. Banks, Washington, D.C., November 9, 1862, *OR*, 15: 590–591.

9. Edwin W. Stanton to A. J. Hamilton, Washington, D.C., November 14, 1862, *OR*, Series 3, 2:782.

10. N. P. Banks to Major-General Halleck, New Orleans, December 18, 1862, *OR*, 15:613.

11. Alexander Hobbs Diary, entry for November 27, 1862, MS, Woodson Center, Fondren Library, Rice University.

12. Bosson, *History of the 42nd Regiment*, 23–24.

13. Jarvis Baker Memoir, 8.

14. Julius P. Varney to Wife, Camp at Carrolton, Louisiana, January 19, 1863, Book 42, Lewis Leigh Collection, U.S. Army Military History Institute, Carlisle Barracks, Pennsylvania.

15. Bosson, *History of the 42nd Regiment*, 46–47.

16. General Order No. 1, On Board the U.S. Transport *Shetucket*, December 6, 1862, MS, Orville W. Leonard Papers, Massachusetts Historical Society.

17. James Miller Diary, entries for December 10–11, 1862, MS, Massachusetts Historical Society.

18. Bosson, *History of the 42nd Regiment*, 44–45.

19. Richard A. Atkins and Helen Fiske Atkins, eds., *Civil War Journal of George M. Fiske of Medfield, Massachusetts* (Syracuse, N.Y.: n.p., 1962), 7.

20. Thornton A. Jenkins to H. H. Bell, U.S. Steam Sloop *Oneida*, Off Mobile, December 17, 1862, *ORN*, 19:414; Bosson, *History of the 42nd Regiment*, 39.

21. Atkins and Atkins, *Civil War Journal of George M. Fiske*, 11.

22. Report of W. B. Renshaw, U.S.S. *Westfield*, Off Galveston, October 8, 1862, *ORN*, 19:260.

23. D. G. Farragut to B. F. Butler, Flagship *Hartford*, Pensacola Bay, October 28, 1862, *ORN*, 19:317–318.

24. Bosson, *History of the 42nd Regiment*, 70–71.

25. Atkins and Atkins, *Civil War Journal of George M. Fiske*, 13.

26. Report of I. S. Burrell, Galveston, December 29, 1862, *OR*, 15:204–205.

27. Emil Neumann to Sister, Fort Eagle Grove, December 9, 1862, MS, Woodson Research Center, Fondren Library, Rice University.

28. "Another Yankee Journal of the Events That Transpired from December 25th to the Recapture of Galveston," *GDN*, January 30, 1863.

29. Jarvis Baker Memoir, 14–15.

30. Alexander Hobbs Diary, December 28, 1862, Woodson Research Center, Fondren Library, Rice University.

31. Bosson, *History of the 42nd Regiment*, 84–85.

12. THE PRINCE AND HIS PLAYERS

1. Special Orders No. 237, Richmond, October 10, 1862, *OR*, 15:826.

2. Thomas M. Settles, "The Military Career of John Bankhead Magruder," (Ph.D. diss., Texas Christian University, 1972), 19. Unless otherwise indicated, the biographical material on General Magruder is taken from this excellent work, which is well deserving of wider publication.

3. Ruth A. Gallaher, "Albert Miller Lea," *Iowa Journal of History and Politics* (July 1935): 198–199; W. T. Block, "A Towering East Texas Pioneer: A Biographical Sketch of Colonel Albert Miller Lea," *East Texas Historical Journal* 32 (Fall 1993): 23–24.

4. "Monument to General J. B. Magruder," *Confederate Veteran* 5 (April 1897; reprint, National Historical Society, n.d.): 171.

5. Daniel H. Hill, "Lee's Attacks North of the Chickahominy," *Battles and Leaders of the Civil War*, vol. 2, pt. 1:362n.

6. James Longstreet, *From Manassas to Appomattox: Memoirs of the Civil War in America* (Philadelphia: J. B. Lippincott Company, 1896), 20.

7. Thomas Jackson Arnold, *Early Life and Letters of General Thomas J. Jackson* (New York: Fleming H. Revell Co., 1916), 93, 95–96.

8. Report of J. B. Magruder, Galveston, February 26, 1863, *OR*, 15:212.

9. Address of Benjamin S. Ewell before the Magruder-Ewell Camp, n.d., TS, from Library of Congress, B. S. Ewell Papers, GTHC.

10. Magruder to Colonel L. T. Wigfall(?), Yorktown, Virginia, June 12, 1861, MS, J. B. Magruder Papers, Chicago Historical Society; Magruder to R. S. Garnett, Bethel Church, June 10, 1861, *OR*, 2:91–92; Douglas Southall Freeman, *Lee's Lieutenants* (New York: Charles Scribner's Sons, 1942), 1:17.

11. *Richmond Dispatch*, June 13, 1861.

12. J. B. Magruder to G. W. Randolph, Yorktown, March 24, 1862, *OR*, vol. 11, pt. 3: 392–393.

13. Baker P. Lee, "Magruder's Peninsula Campaign in 1862," *SHSP* 19 (January 1891): 64; Stephen W. Sears, *To the Gates of Richmond: The Peninsula Campaign* (New York: Ticknor & Fields, 1992), 37–38.

14. C. Vann Woodward, ed., *Mary Chesnut's Civil War* (New Haven, Conn.: Yale University Press, 1981), 401.

15. W. J. Wood, *Battles of the Revolutionary War: 1775–1781* (New York: Da Capo Press, 1955), 288.

16. Special Orders No. 118, Richmond, May 23, 1862, *OR*, vol. 11, pt. 3:540.

17. Special Orders No. 120, Richmond, May 26, 1862, *OR*, vol. 11, pt. 3:551.

18. Hill, "Lee's Attacks North of the Chickahominy," *Battles and Leaders of the Civil War*, vol. 2, pt. 1:361–362.

19. Sears, *To the Gates of Richmond*, 216–217.

20. Gary W. Gallagher, "The Fall of Prince John Magruder," *Civil War* 19 (August 1989): 11–12.

21. General A. L. Long, "Memoir of General John Bankhead Magruder," *SHSP* 12 (January–February 1884): 110.

22. Joseph L. Brent, *Memoirs of the War between the States* (New Orleans: Fontana Printing Co., 1940), 190–192; Gallagher, "The Fall of Prince John Magruder," 19:12.

23. Sears, *To the Gates of Richmond*, 269–270.

24. Joseph P. Cullen, *The Peninsula Campaign: 1862* (New York: Bonanza Books, 1973), 137.

25. R. E. Lee to J. B. Magruder, Headquarters, Department of Northern Virginia, June 29, 1862, *OR*, vol. 11, pt. 2:687.

26. Freeman, *Lee's Lieutenants*, 1:586–587.

27. Report of J. B. Magruder, Richmond, August 12, 1862, *OR*, vol. 11, pt. 2: 667–668.

28. Rev. P. G. Robert, "Justice to General Magruder," *SHSP* 5 (May 1878): 249–250.

29. Freeman, *Lee's Lieutenants*, 1:598.

30. R. H. Chilton to J. B. Magruder, in the vicinity of Malvern Hill, July 1, 1862, *OR*, vol. 11, pt. 2:677.

31. A. G. Dickinson to J. B. Magruder, July 1, 1862, *OR*, vol. 11, pt. 2:677–678.

32. Paul D. Casdorph, *Prince John Magruder: His Life and Campaigns* (New York: John Wiley & Sons, 1996), 104.

33. Daniel H. Hill, "McClellan's Change of Base and Malvern Hill," *Battles and Leaders of the Civil War*, vol. 2, pt. 2:394.

34. J. B. Magruder to G. W. Randolph, Battlefield at Crew's Farm, Virginia, July 2, 1862, *OR*, vol. 11, pt. 3:630.

35. Special Field Orders issued by R. H. Chilton, Headquarters, Department of Northern Virginia, July 3, 1862, *OR*, vol. 11, pt. 3:630; J. B. Magruder to G. W. Randolph, Richmond, July 5, 1862, *OR*, 13:851–852.

36. Jefferson Davis to Brigadier-General French, Richmond, July 13, 1862, *OR*, vol. 11, pt. 3:641.

37. John Lamb, "Malvern Hill—July 1, 1862," *SHSP* 25 (1897): 217; Freeman, *Lee's Lieutenants*, 1:607–610.

38. Report of J. B. Magruder with Exhibits, Richmond, August 12, 1862, *OR*, vol. 11, pt. 2:660–679.

39. R. E. Lee to G. W. Randolph, Headquarters, Department of Northern Virginia, August 14, 1862, *OR*, vol. 11, pt. 2:679.

40. Kenneth H. Williams, "Prince without a Kingdom: The Recall of John Bankhead Magruder," *Civil War History* (March 1995): 6–7; Lynda Crist and Mary Dix, eds., *The Papers of Jefferson Davis* (Baton Rouge: Louisiana State University Press, 1995), 8: 296–297.

41. J. B. Magruder to Jefferson Davis, Fairfield Race Course, August 13, 1862, *OR*, vol. 11, pt. 2:687; original in collection of Chicago Historical Society.

42. Special Orders No. 164, Richmond, July 16, 1862, *OR*, 13:855.

43. Special Orders No. 237, Richmond, October 10, 1862, *OR*, 15:826; Crist and Dix, *The Papers of Jefferson Davis*, 8:413.

44. R. E. Lee to P. O. Hebert, Richmond, May 26, 1862, *OR*, 9:713.

45. E. Kirby Smith to R. W. Johnson, Shreveport, January 15, 1864, *OR*, vol. 34, pt. 2:870.

46. Ralph A. Wooster, *Texas and Texans in the Civil War* (Austin: Eakin Press, 1995), 65.

47. Charles W. Trueheart to His Mother, Lynchburg, Virginia, February 21, 1863, TS, Trueheart Family Papers, GTHC.

48. John S. Ford, *RIP Ford's Texas*, ed. Stephen B. Oates, (Austin: University of Texas Press, 1963), 343; Letter from L. Q. C. Lamar to Davis, San Antonio, December 31, 1862, quoted in Crist and Dix, *The Papers of Jefferson Davis*, 8:591.

49. Freeman, *Lee's Lieutenants*, 1:15–16.

50. J. B. Magruder to E. Kirby Smith, Beaumont, September 26, 1863, *OR*, vol. 26, pt. 2:261.

13. FROM GLORIETA TO GALVESTON

1. Donald S. Frazier, *Blood and Treasure: Confederate Empire in the Southwest* (College Station: Texas A&M University Press, 1995), 23–24.

2. Proclamation by J. R. Baylor, Governor and Colonel Commanding, Mounted Rifles, C.S. Army, Mesilla, August 1, 1861, *OR*, 4:20–21; J. R. Baylor to T. A. Washington, Dona Ana, Arizona [New Mexico], September 21, 1861, *OR*, 4:17–20.

3. Frazier, *Blood and Treasure*, 79–80; Odie Faulk, *General Tom Green: "A Fightin' Texan"* (Waco: Texian Press, 1963); Curtis W. Milbourn, "Brigadier General Thomas Green of Texas," *East Texas Historical Journal* 32, no. 1 (1994): 3–5; Roberts, *Confederate Military History*, 15:231–233.

4. Frazier, *Blood and Treasure*, 78–79; Paul I. Kliger, "The Confederate Invasion of New Mexico," *Blue & Gray Magazine* (June 1994): 49.

5. Kliger, "The Confederate Invasion of New Mexico," 19.

6. Frazier, *Blood and Treasure*, 180–181, 250.

7. Kliger, "The Confederate Invasion of New Mexico," 49.

8. William C. Whitford, *The Battle of Glorieta Pass: The Colorado Volunteers in the Civil War* (1906; reprint, Glorieta, N.Mex.: Rio Grande Press, 1991), 98–127.

9. Frazier, *Blood and Treasure,* 264.

10. Ibid., 294–295; S. S. Anderson to H. H. Sibley, Little Rock, October 24, 1862, *OR,* 15:843.

11. This discussion of A. P. Bagby's Court of Inquiry is taken from Martin Hardwick Hall, "The Court-Martial of Arthur Pendleton Bagby, C.S.A.," *East Texas Historical Journal* 19, no. 2 (Fall 1981): 60–67.

12. Theophilus Noel, *Autobiography and Reminiscences of Theophilus Noel* (Chicago: Theo. Noel Company, 1904), 99.

13. G. W. Randolph to J. B. Magruder, War Department, Richmond, November 7, 1862, *OR,* 15:857; M. H. McWillie to War Department, Richmond, January 10, 1863, *OR,* 15:940–942.

14. Frazier, *Blood and Treasure,* 294–295; J. R. Baylor to J. B. Magruder, Houston, December 29, 1862, *OR,* 15:914–919.

15. James Reily to H. H. Sibley, Houston, January 31, 1863, *OR,* 15:968.

16. S. S. Anderson to J. B. Magruder, Little Rock, November 26, 1862, *OR,* 15:879.

17. E. P. Turner to A. M. Jackson, Houston, December 23, 1862, *OR,* 15:905.

18. James Reily to H. H. Sibley, Houston, January 31, 1863, *OR,* 15:968.

19. J. B. Magruder to S. Cooper, Houston, December 9, 1862, *OR,* 15:894–895; J. B. Magruder to S. S. Anderson, Houston, December 8, 1862, *OR,* 15:894.

20. J. B. Magruder to S. S. Anderson, Houston, December 9, 1862, *OR,* 15:895–896; J. B. Magruder to S. S. Anderson, Houston, December 12, 1862, *OR,* 15:897; J. B. Magruder to S. S. Anderson, Houston, December 19, 1862, *OR,* 15:902.

21. J. B. Magruder to F. R. Lubbock, Houston, December 21, 1862, *OR,* 15: 903–904.

22. S. S. Anderson to J. B. Magruder, Little Rock, January 2, 1863, *OR,* 15:922.

23. J. B. Magruder to S. Cooper, Houston, December 9, 1862, *OR,* 15:894–895.

14. PRINCE JOHN PLANS HIS NEXT PRODUCTION

1. X. B. Debray to S. B. Davis, Houston, November 6, 1862, *OR,* 15:856–857.

2. F. R. Lubbock to X. B. Debray, November 29, 1862, quoted in Lubbock, *Six Decades in Texas,* 424.

3. C. G. Forshey to J. B. Magruder, Rutersville, December 2, 1862, *OR,* 15:885–886; "Military Education in Civil Institutions: An Address Delivered by Professor C. G. Forshey at Galveston, July 4, 1855," Caleb G. Forshey Papers, GTHC.

4. Hayes, *Island and City,* 2:549.

5. Report of J. B. Magruder, Galveston, February 26, 1863, *OR,* 15:212.

6. Settles, "The Military Career of John Bankhead Magruder," 238.

7. These letters are found in *OR,* 15:884–913.

8. J. B. Magruder to S. S. Anderson, Houston, December 12, 1862, *OR,* 15:897; J. B. Magruder to S. S. Anderson, Houston, December 19, 1862, *OR,* 15:902.

9. Lubbock, *Six Decades in Texas,* 432n.

10. James E. Day, "Leon Smith: Confederate Mariner," *East Texas Historical Journal* 3 (March 1965): 34.

11. C. G. Forshey to X. B. Debray, December 25, 1862, *OR*, 15:908; "Summary of Summaries," TS of diary summaries by Caleb G. Forshey, entry for December 25, 1862, Daughters of the Republic of Texas Library at the Alamo.

12. Hayes, *Island and City*, 2:550.

13. Julius G. Kellersberger, *Memoirs of an Engineer in the Confederate Army in Texas*, trans. Helen S. Sundstrom (n.p.: n.p., 1957), 24.

14. Joseph Edmund Wallis to Wife Kate, Eagle Grove, November 3, 1862, MS, Wallis Family Papers, GTHC.

15. Jimmie Black to Wife, Headquarters Co. "I," Cook's Regiment of Artillery, Virginia Point, December 1, 1862, TS, Black Family Papers, Holt-Atherton Department of Special Collections, University of Pacific Libraries, University of the Pacific, Stockton, California.

16. Henry M. Trueheart to Sister Mary, Office Provost Marshal, Galveston, January 22, 1863, TS, Trueheart Family Papers, GTHC.

17. Jimmie Black to Wife, Virginia Point, December 31, 1862, TS, Black Family Papers.

18. C. G. Forshey to X. B. Debray, December 25, 1862, *OR*, 15:908.

19. "Battle of Galveston Described by Veteran," *GDN*, January 5, 1914.

20. Faulk, *General Tom Green*, 49, quoting "An Address by Governor Richard B. Hubbard upon the Presentation of Tom Green's Portrait," n.d., MS, Miscellaneous Speeches and Addresses, Texas State Archives at Austin.

21. Texas Horsemen of the Sea Manuscript, Galley Proofs, Gal. 3, GTHC; "Battle of Galveston Described by Veteran," *GDN*, January 5, 1914.

22. Oscar Haas, "Teenage Joseph Faust Recounts Experience in Steamboat Battle," *New Braunfels Herald*, July 3, 1962.

23. Hayes, *Island and City*, 2:551.

24. Lubbock, *Six Decades in Texas*, 433.

25. Hayes, *Island and City*, 2:553.

15. THE BATTLE OF KUHN'S WHARF

1. Lubbock, *Six Decades in Texas*, 434.

2. Hayes, *Island and City*, 2:553.

3. Tucker Narrative, TS, CAH, 114.

4. Letter from Leonidas J. Story to Augustus M. Hill, February 21, 1908, included in Augustus M. Hill, "Incidents of Banks Campaign: Mansfield and Pleasant Hill," TS, Augustus M. Hill Papers, CAH.

5. Woodward, *Mary Chesnut's Civil War*, 352.

6. Henry M. Trueheart to Sister Mary, Office Provost Marshal, Galveston, January 22, 1863, TS, Trueheart Family Papers, GTHC; Barnstone, *The Galveston That Was*, 183.

7. Report of J. B. Magruder, Galveston, February 26, 1863, *OR*, 15:213.

8. Ibid., 15:214.

9. Hayes, *Island and City*, 2:553.

10. Report of Thomas Gonzales to Colonel X. B. Debray, Galveston, January 6, 1863, quoted in John H. Brown, *Indian Wars and Pioneers of Texas* (Austin: L. E. Daniell, 189?), 297–298; Paul Freier, "Thomas Gonzales," *Port Lavaca Wave*, March 12, 1982.

11. J. B. Magruder to S. Cooper, Galveston, February 26, 1863, *OR*, 15:218.

12. Hayes, *Island and City*, 2:555; Bosson, *History of the 42nd Regiment*, 95.

13. Joseph J. Cook to Messrs. D. Landes et al., Headquarters of Artillery, Galveston, April 17, 1863; "More of the Battle of Galveston," *GDN*, May 6, 1863.

14. Report of J. B. Magruder, Galveston, February 26, 1863, *OR*, 15:214.

15. Letter from Adjutant Charles A. Davis, quoted in "The Fight of the 42nd," *Boston Journal*, January 20, 1863.

16. Hayes, *Island and City*, 2:571; S. T. Fontaine to Editor, *Galveston News*, January 6, 1863, article in Sherman Family Scrapbook, GTHC.

17. Noel, *Autobiography and Reminiscences*, 102–103.

18. Ibid., 103.

19. Ibid., 102.

20. Theophilus Noel, *A Campaign from Santa Fe to the Mississippi, Being a History of the Old Sibley Brigade* (1865; reprint, Houston: Stagecoach Press, 1961), 64.

21. Report of General John B. Magruder, Galveston, February 26, 1863, *OR*, 15:213; Robert M. Franklin, *Battle of Galveston* (Galveston: San Luis Press, 1975), 7.

22. Hayes, *Island and City*, 2:592.

23. Report of General John B. Magruder, Galveston, February 26, 1863, *OR*, 15:214.

24. J. E. Wallis to Kate, Eagle Grove, January 20, 1863, Wallis Family Papers, GTHC.

25. Mamie Yeary, comp., *Reminiscences of the Boys in Gray* (1912; reprint, Dayton, Ohio: Morningside, 1986), entry for Elijah Barr, 40.

26. Ziegler, "General E. B. Nichols, Early Merchant, Helped Magruder Retake City from Federals"; Hayes, *Island and City*, 2:555.

27. Ronnie C. Tyler and Lawrence R. Murphy, eds., *The Slave Narratives of Texas* (Austin: Encino Press, 1974), 100.

28. Bosson, *History of the 42nd Regiment*, 93.

29. W. Randolph Howell Diary, entry for January 1, 1863, MS, Randolph Howell Papers, CAH.

30. Henry M. Trueheart to Sister Mary, Office Provost Marshal, Galveston, January 22, 1863, TS, Trueheart Family Papers, GTHC, 2.

31. W. P. Doran, "Reminiscences of the War by 'Sioux,'" *GDN*, August 6, 1876.

32. W. P. Doran, "A 35th Anniversary, the War Correspondent of the News Indulges in a Few Reminiscences," *GDN*, February 22, 1896.

33. Bosson, *History of the 42nd Regiment*, 96–97.

34. Ibid., 93–94.

35. Statement of Colonel Isaac S. Burrell, Houston, January 23, 1863, *OR*, 15:226.

36. "Some Details and Incidents of the Naval & Land Engagement at Galveston," *GDN*, January 5, 1863, article contained in Civil War Scrapbooks, GTHC.

37. P. C. Headley, *Massachusetts in the Rebellion: A Record of the Historical Position of the Commonwealth and the Services of the Leading Statesmen, the Military, the Colleges, and the People, in the Civil War of 1861–65* (Boston: Walker, Fuller & Co., 1886), 410.

38. Jarvis Baker Memoir, CAH, 25.

39. Bosson, *History of the 42nd Regiment*, 114.

16. COTTONCLAD VICTORY

1. Answers of Henry S. Lubbock, C.S.A. Prize Commission Proceedings, TS, GTHC, 6–7.

2. Franklin, *Battle of Galveston*, 6.

3. C. H. McGill, "Battle of Galveston," *GDN*, January 1, 1906.

4. Statement of Captain McCormick, quoted in Hayes, *Island and City*, 2:556.

5. Report of a Galveston correspondent to the *Houston Telegraph*, n.d., quoted in *ORN*, 19:469.

6. Leon Smith to E. P. Turner, Velasco, August 9, 1863, *ORN*, 20:835.

7. Answers of Henry S. Lubbock, C.S.A. Prize Commission Proceedings, TS, GTHC, 6–7.

8. Answers of William H. Sangster, C.S.A. Prize Commission Proceedings, TS, GTHC, 15; Report of a Galveston correspondent to the *Houston Telegraph*, n.d., quoted in *ORN*, 19:469.

9. Answers of Henry S. Lubbock, C.S.A. Prize Commission Proceedings, TS, GTHC, 7.

10. Lee C. Harby, "The Battle of Galveston," *GDN*, February 7, 1897; Bosson, *History of the 42nd Regiment*, 101.

11. Hayes, *Island and City*, 2:557.

12. Franklin, *Battle of Galveston*, 9.

13. Report of a Galveston correspondent to the *Houston Telegraph*, n.d., quoted in *ORN*, 19:469; Hayes, *Island and City*, 2:558.

14. Answers of Henry S. Lubbock, C.S.A. Prize Commission Proceedings, TS, GTHC, 9–10.

15. D. G. Farragut to W. B. Renshaw, Flagship *Hartford*, Off New Orleans, December 12, 1862, *ORN*, 19:404.

16. "The Recapture of Galveston: Graphic Description of the Naval Engagement," *Boston Journal*, January 17, 1863.

17. W. S. Long to D. C. Houston, New Orleans, January 10, 1863, *ORN*, 19:460; W. L. Burt to Major-General Banks, n.d., *ORN*, 19:456.

18. Hayes, *Island and City*, 2:563; Lubbock, *Six Decades in Texas*, 446.

19. Jarvis Baker Memoir, 24.

20. Lubbock, *Six Decades in Texas*, 444–445.

21. C. G. Collings to Sister, Galveston, January 2, 1862 [1863], MS, Amerman-Collings Papers, Houston Metropolitan Research Center, Houston Public Library.

22. Lubbock, *Six Decades in Texas*, 445.

23. Answers of Henry S. Lubbock, C.S.A. Prize Commission Proceedings, TS, GTHC, 9–10.

24. A. T. Spear to D. G. Farragut, U.S. Schooner *Corypheus*, Off Sabine Pass, January 2, 1863, *ORN*, 19:438; D. G. Farragut to A. T. Spear, Flagship *Hartford*, Off New Orleans, January 14, 1863, *ORN*, 19:451.

25. Proceedings of Court of Inquiry, U.S. Steam Sloop *Hartford*, Off New Orleans, January 12, 1863, *ORN*, 19:449–450.

26. Lubbock, *Six Decades in Texas*, 446.

27. Report of a Galveston correspondent to the *Houston Telegraph*, n.d., quoted in *ORN*, 19:470.

28. Hayes, *Island and City*, 2:565–566.

29. J. B. Magruder to S. Cooper, Galveston, February 26, 1863, *OR*, 15:216; P. C. Tucker III, "History of Galveston," TS, Tucker Family Papers, CAH, 118–121.

30. Acheson, *35,000 Days in Texas*, 53.

31. Davis to Magruder, Richmond, January 28, 1863, *OR*, 15:211.

32. Lubbock, *Six Decades in Texas*, 453.

33. General Orders No. 56, San Antonio, March 30, 1863, *OR*, 15:221; Joint Resolution of the Congress of the Confederate States of America, February 25, 1863, *Statutes at Large of the Confederate States of America, Passed at the Third Session of the First Congress* (Richmond: R. H. Smith, 1863), 166.

34. Jedediah Hotchkiss, *Make Me a Map of the Valley: The Civil War Journal of Stonewall Jackson's Topographer*, ed. Archie P. McDonald (Dallas: Southern Methodist University, 1973), 107.

35. Gary E. Wilson, ed., "Diary of a Union Prisoner," *Southern Studies* 23 (Spring 1984): 105.

36. Farragut to Acting Rear-Admiral Bailey, Mississippi River above Port Hudson, April 22, 1863, *ORN*, 20:157.

37. Letter of February 13, 1863, quoted in Loyall Farragut, *The Life of David Glasgow Farragut, First Admiral of the United States Navy, Embodying His Journal and Letters* (New York: D. Appleton and Company, 1879), 309.

38. G. V. Fox to S. F. Dupont, February 12, 1863, quoted in Robert Means Thompson, ed., *Confidential Correspondence of Gustavus Vasa Fox* (New York: De Vinne Press, 1920), 1:178–179.

39. "The Affair at Galveston," *New York Tribune*, January 19, 1863.

40. D. G. Farragut to Gideon Welles, Flagship *Hartford*, New Orleans, January 29, 1863, *ORN*, 19:440.

41. Gideon Welles, *Diary of Gideon Welles: Secretary of the Navy under Lincoln and Johnson* (Boston: Houghton Mifflin Company, 1911), 1:220

42. General Order No. 28, January 7, 1864, *ORN*, 19:463–464.

43. N. P. Banks to E. M. Stanton, New Orleans, January 7, 1863, *OR*, 15:642–643; N. P. Banks to Major-General Halleck, New Orleans, January 7, 1863, *ORN*, 19:454–455.

44. N. P. Banks to Secretary of War, New York, April 6, 1865, *OR*, vol. 26, pt. 1:7.

17. AFTER THE BATTLE

1. Bosson, *History of the 42nd Regiment*, 110.

2. Ibid., 109.

3. Report from Galveston, May 2, 1863, *GDN*, May 6, 1863.

4. Atkins and Atkins, *Civil War Journal of George M. Fiske,* 19.

5. Alexander Hobbs Diary, entry for January 1, 1863, Woodson Research Center, Fondren Library, Rice University.

6. Dorman H. Winfrey, ed., "Two Battle of Galveston Letters," *SWHQ* 65 (October 1961): 254–256.

7. "St. Ursula's Convent in Galveston Was First Base Hospital in Texas; Tribute Paid to Sisters' Heroism," *GDN,* October 2, 1921.

8. Alice H. Cromie, *A Tour Guide to the Civil War,* 2d ed. (New York: E. P. Dutton & Co., 1975), 47.

9. Ben C. Stuart, "The Seamy Side of Civil Strife: Son Dies in Father's Arms," *GDN,* December 12, 1909; "Men Prominent in Texas Are Buried Here," *Galveston Tribune,* January 11, 1935.

10. David D. Porter, *Incidents and Anecdotes of the Civil War* (New York: D. Appleton and Company, 1886), 111.

11. Azile L. L. Lea, "The Cost of War: An Incident of the Battle of Galveston," TS, Lea (Pryor) Items (1850–1964), CAH.

12. D. G. Farragut to Edward Lea, Flagship *Hartford,* Off New Orleans, January 1, 1863, *ORN,* 19:479.

13. Stuart, "The Seamy Side of Civil Strife."

14. Acheson, *35,000 Days in Texas,* 53–54.

15. Leon Smith to the *New York Herald,* Havana, December 8, 1864, quoted in J. Thomas Scharf, *History of the Confederate States Navy* (Albany, N.Y.: Joseph McDonough, 1894), 519–520.

18. A TRAP FAILS TO CLOSE

1. Hayes, *Island and City,* 2:580–582.

2. J. B. Magruder to S. Cooper, Galveston, February 26, 1863, *ORN,* 19:477.

3. Franklin, *Battle of Galveston,* 2.

4. Ben C. Stuart, "Two Types of Old Time Texas Courage," *GDN,* January 2, 1910.

5. C. M. Mason to E. P. Turner, Galveston, January 8, 1863, *ORN,* 19:827–828.

6. E. J. Davis to W. P. Doran, Austin, August 3, 1876, E. J. Davis Papers, GTHC.

7. "Captain Payne Returned Home—His Account of His Capture, etc.," *GDN,* April 29, 1863.

8. Stuart, "Two Types of Old Time Texas Courage"; Ben C. Stuart, "A War Incident," *GDN,* August 1, 1886.

9. Proclamation of J. B. Magruder, Galveston, January 5, 1863, *ORN,* 19:465.

10. J. P. Benjamin to A. Paul et al., Richmond, February 7, 1863, *ORN,* 19:836; Sarah Woolfolk Wiggins, ed., *The Journals of Josiah Gorgas: 1857–1878* (Tuscaloosa: University of Alabama Press, 1995), 56.

11. D. G. Farragut to Gideon Welles, Flagship *Hartford,* Off New Orleans, January 3, 1863, *ORN,* 19:481.

12. D. G. Farragut to Admiral Bailey, n.p., January 7, 1863, *ORN,* 19:499.

13. D. G. Farragut to J. Alden, Flagship *Hartford,* Off New Orleans, January 5, 1863, *ORN,* 19:489–490.

19. STILL ANOTHER DISASTER OFF GALVESTON

1. H. H. Bell to G. Welles, U.S. Steam Sloop *Brooklyn*, Off Galveston, January 13, 1863, *ORN*, 19:508–509.

2. Frederick H. Thompson to Joseph Thompson, Galveston, January 10, 1863, *ORN*, 19:505.

3. William M. Armstrong to Thaddeus Armstrong, Virginia Point, January 12, 1863, MS, T. C. Armstrong Papers, GTHC.

4. Report of H. C. Blake, U.S. Consulate, Kingston, Jamaica, January 21, 1863, *ORN*, 2:19; Raphael Semmes, *Memoirs of Service Afloat during the War between the States* (Baltimore: Kelly, Piet & Co., 1869), 543.

5. R. Semmes to S. R. Mallory, C.S.S. *Alabama*, Bahia, May 12, 1863, *ORN*, 2: 683–685.

6. J. R. Soley, *The Blockade and the Cruisers* (1887; reprint, Wilmington, N.C.: Broadfoot Publishing Company, 1989), 196–198; Report of H. C. Blake, U.S. Consulate, Kingston, Jamaica, January 21, 1863, *ORN*, 2:18–20; L. H. Partridge to D. G. Farragut, U.S. Steam Sloop *Brooklyn*, Galveston, January 12, 1863, *ORN*, 2:21–22.

7. Excerpts from Diary of Commodore H. H. Bell, entries for January 11–12, 1863, *ORN*, 19:737.

8. "The Naval Fight," *GDN*, January 21, 1863; H. M. Trueheart to Cally and Sister Mary, Galveston, January 26 and 30, 1863, quoted in Edward B. Williams, ed., *Rebel Brothers: The Civil War Letters of the Truehearts* (College Station: Texas A&M University Press, 1995), 162–165.

9. Excerpts from Diary of Commodore H. H. Bell, entry for January 12, 1863, *ORN*, 19:737–738.

10. D. G. Farragut to H. H. Bell, Flagship *Hartford*, New Orleans, January 15, 1863, *ORN*, 19:525–526.

11. D. G. Farragut to H. H. Bell, Flagship *Hartford*, New Orleans, January 20, 1863, *ORN*, 19:544; D. G. Farragut to G. Welles, Flagship *Hartford*, New Orleans, January 21, 1863, *ORN*, 19:552–553.

20. AN ENTRENCHED CAMP

1. H. H. Bell to J. B. Magruder, U.S. Steam Sloop *Brooklyn*, Off Galveston, January 20, 1863, *ORN*, 19:546–547.

2. H. H. Bell to J. B. Magruder, U.S. Steam Sloop *Brooklyn*, Off Galveston, January 21, 1863, *ORN*, 19:550; Proclamation of H. H. Bell, Off Galveston, January 21, 1863, *ORN*, 19:550–551.

3. Cecelia Labadie Diary Fragment, January 29, 1863, M. A. Williams Papers, GTHC.

4. H. H. Bell to D. G. Farragut, U.S. Steam Sloop *Brooklyn*, Off Galveston, January 21, 1863, *ORN*, 19:592.

5. Ibid., 19:595–596.

6. Gregory, *Record of Interments of the City of Galveston*, 25–27; J. E. Wallis to Kate, Galveston, April 3, 1863, Wallis Family Papers, GTHC.

7. James Jones to Zenas Bartlett, quoted in Frank Calvert Oltorf, *The Marlin Compound: Letters of a Singular Family* (Austin: University of Texas Press, 1968), 109.

8. Kellersberger, *Memoirs of an Engineer*, 28.

9. Ibid., 28–29.

10. Henry O. Gusley, "Yankee Notebook — Continued," *GDN*, October 28, 1863.

11. Kellersberger, *Memoirs of an Engineer*, 29.

12. Cecilia Labadie Diary Fragment, January 29, 1863, M. A. Williams Papers, GTHC.

13. Lubbock, *Six Decades in Texas*, 486.

14. Adele B. Looscan, "How the Shaft of a Federal Vessel Was Converted into Cannon by the Confederates," MS, Briscoe (Mary Jane Harris) and Looscan (Adele Lubbock Briscoe) Papers, CAH.

15. Report of J. N. Barney, C.S.S. *Harriet Lane*, Galveston, February 13, 1863, *ORN*, 19:839.

16. Ibid., 19:838–840; Report of J. N. Barney, Houston, February 23, 1863, *ORN*, 19:842–844.

17. Answers of Henry Lubbock, C.S.A. Prize Commission Records, TS, GTHC, 12.

18. S. R. Mallory to James A. Seddon, Navy Department, Richmond, March 31, 1863, *ORN*, 20:807.

19. J. B. Magruder to W. R. Boggs, Houston, June 25, 1863, *ORN*, 20:831.

20. W. R. Scurry to E. P. Turner, Houston, April 23, 1863, *ORN*, 20:151.

21. Yeary, *Reminiscences of the Boys in Gray*, 754–755; "Henry Martyn Trueheart Dies in Pennsylvania," *GDN*, August 20, 1914.

22. "Letter from Galveston," *GDN*, April 3, 1863.

23. Hayes, *Island and City*, 2:591.

24. "Memoirs of Henry Martyn Trueheart, Galveston, Texas, and Copies of Old Letters: 1843–1865," Trueheart Family Papers, GTHC, 9.

25. John W. Lockhart to Wife, Eagle Grove, February 14, 1863, John W. Lockhart Papers, GTHC.

26. General Orders No. 24, Houston, *OR*, 15:979.

27. Hayes, *Island and City*, 2:596.

28. Fremantle, *Fremantle Diary*, 55.

29. Thomas J. League to Mary D. League, Virginia Point, November 6, 1862, MS, Thomas Jefferson League Papers, GTHC.

30. Simon Kuykendall to Family, Galveston, March 11, 1863, MS, Simon Kuykendall Papers, GTHC.

31. John Jones to Wife, Camp Groce, January 26, 1863, quoted in Oltorf, *The Marlin Compound*, 114.

32. Gregory, *Record of Interments of the City of Galveston*, 35.

33. General Order No. 197 regarding Court Martial of Earnest Haase, issued in Houston, November 10, 1863, Amerman-Collings Family Collection, Houston Metropolitan Research Center, Houston Public Library; Emil Neumann to Sister, Galveston, November 22, 1863, MS, Neumann Papers, Woodson Research Center, Fondren Library, Rice University.

34. Hayes, *Island and City*, 2:595.

35. X. B. Debray to A. N. Mills, Galveston, August 1, 1863, *OR*, vol. 26, pt. 2: 132–133.

36. E. F. Gray to R. M. Franklin, Galveston, August 4, 1863, *OR*, vol. 26, pt. 1:241.

37. X. B. Debray to A. N. Mills, Galveston, August 11, 1863, *OR*, vol. 26, pt. 1: 242–243; X. B. Debray to A. N. Mills, Galveston, August 12, 1863, *OR*, vol. 26, pt. 1: 244; X. B. Debray to E. P. Turner, Galveston, August 12, 1863, *OR*, vol. 26, pt. 1:243.

38. P. N. Luckett to E. P. Turner, Galveston, August 13, 1863, *OR*, vol. 26, pt. 1: 245–246.

39. X. B. Debray to A. N. Mills, Galveston, August 1, 1863, *OR*, vol. 26, pt. 2: 132–133.

40. Hayes, *Island and City*, 2:600–601.

41. J. B. Magruder to W. R. Boggs, Near Millican, September 4, 1863, *OR*, vol. 26, pt. 2:203–204.

42. William Pitt Ballinger Diary, August 31, 1863, TS, GTHC, 99.

43. "Return of the Forty-Second Regiment," *Boston Journal*, August 10, 1863.

44. This account of the Battle at Sabine Pass is taken from Wooster, *Texas and Texans in the Civil War*, 87–92; Alwyn Barr, "Sabine Pass, September 1863," *Texas Military History* 2 (February 1962): 17–22; and Frank X. Tolbert, *Dick Dowling at Sabine Pass* (New York: McGraw-Hill Book Co., 1962).

45. Report of J. Bankhead Magruder to S. Cooper, Sabine Pass, September 27, 1863, *OR*, vol. 26, pt. 1:305–306.

46. Wooster, *Texas and Texans in the Civil War*, 134–135; Alwyn Barr, "Texas Coastal Defense," 27–29.

47. V. Sulakowski to E. P. Turner, Galveston, October 8, 1863, *OR*, vol. 26, pt. 2: 296–297.

48. Civil War Scrapbooks, small vol. 76-0043, GTHC.

21. TREATED LIKE A CONQUERED CITY

1. Hayes, *Island and City*, 2:607–608.

2. *Flake's Bulletin*, January 16, 1864, quoted in Hayes, *Island and City*, 2:609.

3. Hayes, *Island and City*, 2:612.

4. William Tyler to Captain Spencer, Galveston, August 16, 1864, Record Book of Confederate Correspondence: 1863–1865, MS, Ashbel Smith Papers, CAH, 142.

5. Hayes, *Island and City*, 2:625–626.

6. Ibid., 2:621.

7. Report of "Item" from Galveston, June 7, 1864, *Galveston Tri-Weekly News*, June 10, 1864.

8. Rebecca W. Smith and Marion Mullins, eds., "The Diary of H. C. Medford, Confederate Soldier, 1864," *SWHQ* 34 (October 1930): 128–129.

9. General Order No. 1, Headquarters 1st Sub-District, April 15, 1864, General and Special Orders: 1863–1865, MS, Ashbel Smith Papers, CAH, 60.

10. Warner, *Generals in Gray*, 128–129; Davis, *The Confederate General*, 3:74–75.

11. Hayes, *Island and City*, 2:612.

12. D. R. Wood to Wife, Galveston, January 21, 1864, quoted in *El Campanario: Publication of the Texas Old Missions and Forts Restoration Association* 25 (February 1994): 1–2.

13. Special Order No. 4, Headquarters 1st Sub-District, April 18, 1864, General and Special Orders: 1863–1865, MS, Ashbel Smith Papers, CAH, 220–221.

14. Resolution of April 23, 1864, quoted in Hayes, *Island and City*, 2:613–614.

15. J. M. Hawes to J. B. Magruder, Galveston, April 26, 1864, *OR*, vol. 34, pt. 3:794.

16. Hayes, *Island and City*, 2:617; Ben C. Stuart, "War Time Incidents," *GDN*, June 23, 1907; "Item," Galveston, June 11, 1864, *GDN*, June 17, 1864.

17. Hayes, *Island and City*, 2:618.

18. General Order No. 24, Headquarters 1st Sub-District, June 22, 1864, General and Special Orders: 1863–1865, MS, Ashbel Smith Papers, CAH, 77–78.

19. P. C. Tucker III, "History of Galveston," TS, Tucker Narrative, CAH, 129; Letter from "Justice," Galveston, March 4, 1864, quoted in *Houston Daily Telegraph*, March 8, 1864.

20. Smith and Mullins, "The Diary of H. C. Medford," 34:120–121.

21. Ibid., 34:121.

22. Advertisement by Colonel George Wythe Baylor, *Houston Daily Telegraph*, February 18, 1864.

23. Smith and Mullins, "The Diary of H. C. Medford," 34:129–130.

24. Ibid., 34:126–127.

25. Gregory, *Record of Interments of the City of Galveston*, 34–40; Hayes, *Island and City*, 2:624.

26. Ashbel Smith to William A. Smith, Galveston, October 10, 1864, Record Book of Confederate Correspondence: 1863–1865, MS, Ashbel Smith Papers, CAH, 164.

27. Letter from Smith to Dr. [illegible], October 15, 1864, Ashbel Smith Papers, CAH.

28. Circular No. 30, October 3, 1864, Record Book of Confederate Correspondence: 1863–1865, MS, Ashbel Smith Papers, CAH, 158.

29. Hayes, *Island and City*, 2:610.

30. J. M. Hawes to Brigadier-General Slaughter, Galveston, May 3, 1864, Record Book of Confederate Correspondence: 1863–1865, MS, Ashbel Smith Papers, CAH, 122.

31. N. A. Blume to Charles H. Brown, U.S.S. *Virginia*, Off Galveston, January 11, 1865, *ORN*, 21:773; D. Augustin, Prize Commissioner, to Secretary of the Navy, New Orleans, January 5, 1865, *ORN*, 21:773–774.

22. RUNNING THE BLOCKADE

1. J. B. Marchand to James S. Palmer, U.S. Steam Sloop *Lackawanna*, Off Galveston, April 11, 1864, *ORN*, 21:183; Marcus W. Price, "Ships That Tested the Blockade of the Gulf Ports, 1861–1865," *American Neptune* 11 (October 1951): 262–263.

2. J. C. Wallis to Ed, Galveston, April 6, 1865, Wallis Family Papers, GTHC.

3. J. B. Marchand to A. P. Cooke, U.S. Steam Sloop *Lackawanna*, Off Galveston, April 12, 1864, *ORN*, 21:185.

4. William Watson, *The Adventures of a Blockade Runner; or Trade in Time of War* (London: T. Fisher Unwin, 1892), 249–258.

5. William F. Hutchinson, M.D., "Life on the Texan Blockade," a paper read before the Rhode Island Soldiers and Sailors Historical Society, *Military Order of the Loyal Legion of the United States* 35 (April 17, 1883; reprint, Wilmington, N.C.: Broadfoot Publishing Company, 1993): 34–35.

6. Ben C. Stuart, "Some True Stories of the Blockade: A Risky but Highly Profitable Business Carried On during the Civil War," *GDN*, July 16, 1911.

7. Stephen R. Wise, *Lifeline of the Confederacy: Blockade Running during the Civil War* (Columbia: University of South Carolina Press, 1988), 214.

8. Hayes, *Island and City*, 2:599.

9. Rufus Jameson to Sarah Jameson, Indianola, August 23, 1862, Rufus Jameson Papers, GTHC.

10. Tucker, "Schooner *Royal Yacht* Played Interesting Role during the Civil War"; Frederic S. Hill to Gideon Welles, U.S. Bark *William G. Anderson*, Off Galveston, April 17, 1863, *ORN*, 20:142–143.

11. John D. Hayes, "Escape of '*Harriet Lane*' from Island Recalled," *GDN*, May 1, 1970; Captain J. B. Marchand to Rear-Admiral D. G. Farragut, U.S. Steam Sloop *Lackawanna*, Off Galveston, May 5, 1864, *ORN*, 21:226–227.

12. J. B. Magruder to W. R. Boggs, Houston, January 6, 1864, *OR*, vol. 34, pt. 2:836; E. K. Smith to J. B. Magruder, Shreveport, January 23, 1864, *OR*, vol. 34, pt. 2: 907–908; J. B. Magruder to J. A. Seddon, In Field, Monticello, September 29, 1864, *OR*, vol. 41, pt. 3:963–964.

13. D. G. Farragut to Gideon Welles, Flagship *Hartford*, Off New Orleans, January 3, 1863, *ORN*, 19:481.

14. D. G. Farragut to unnamed, U.S. Flagship *Tennessee*, Off New Orleans, April 5, 1864, *ORN*, 21:223.

15. D. G. Farragut to J. B. Marchand, U.S. Flagship *Tennessee*, Off New Orleans, April 11, 1864, *ORN*, 21:224.

16. J. B. Marchand to D. G. Farragut, U.S. Steam Sloop *Lackawanna*, Off Galveston, April 14, 1864, *ORN*, 21:224–225.

17. Report of John Irwin, U.S.S. *Katahdin*, Off Galveston, May 3, 1864, *ORN*, 21: 227–229.

18. D. G. Farragut to J. B. Marchand, U.S.S. *Hartford*, Pensacola, May 13, 1864, *ORN*, 21:231; D. G. Farragut to J. Irwin, U.S.S. *Hartford*, Pensacola, May 13, 1864, *ORN*, 21:231.

19. Gideon Welles to D. G. Farragut, Navy Department, June 8, 1864, *ORN*, 21:232.

20. H. S. Stellwagen to Gideon Welles, U.S. Ship *Constellation*, Havana, December 14, 1864, *ORN*, 3:394.

21. Dr. J. O. Dyer, "Blockade Runners Defy Federal Fleet, and Galveston Is Kept in Communication with Outside," *GDN*, November 26, 1922.

22. Hutchinson, "Life on the Texan Blockade," 34–35.

23. Price, "Ships That Tested the Blockade of the Gulf Ports," 271; Jesse A. Ziegler, "Yankee Fleet No Match for Crude Cotton Clads," *Houston Post*, June 27, 1937.

24. George F. Emmons to J. S. Palmer, U.S.S. *Lackawanna*, Off Galveston, February 8, 1865, *ORN*, 22:32–33; M. B. Woolsey to George F. Emmons, U.S.S. *Princess Royal*, Off Galveston, February 10, 1865, *ORN*, 22:34–35; C. E. McKay to M. B. Woolsey, U.S.S. *Princess Royal*, Off Galveston, February 10, 1865, *ORN*, 22:35–36; William A. Ward, "The Saga of the *Will O' The Wisp:* The Story of a Confederate Blockade Runner," *In Between* 164 (November 1983): 1.

25. B. F. Sands to H. K. Thatcher, U.S.S. *Fort Jackson*, Off Galveston, May 24, 1865, *ORN*, 22:197; J. A. Johnstone to B. F. Sands, U.S.S. *Cornubia*, Off Galveston, May 25, 1865, *ORN*, 22:197–198.

26. Thomas E. Taylor, *Running the Blockade: A Personal Narrative of Adventures, Risks, and Escapes during the American Civil War* (1896; reprint, Bowie, Md.: Heritage Books, 1991), 155–156.

27. Ibid., 157.

28. "Blockade Runners Gave Island Plenty of Excitement," *GDN*, April 11, 1942.

23. THE "CLOSING ACT OF THE REBELLION"

1. J. G. Walker to Pendleton Murrah, Houston, January 23, 1865, Papers of Governor P. Murrah, Texas State Archives at Austin.

2. J. R. M. Mullany to George F. Emmons, U.S.S. *Bienville*, Off Galveston, February 8, 1865, *ORN*, 22:30.

3. Henry Wilson to B. F. Sands, U.S.S. *Cayuga*, Off Galveston, March 27, 1865, *ORN*, 22:124–125.

4. General Orders No. 6, Headquarters, District of Texas, New Mexico, and Arizona, Houston, February 23, 1865, C.S.A. Galveston, 1861–1865 Collection, GTHC.

5. *Flake's Bulletin* of March 5, 1865, quoted in Hayes, *Island and City*, 2:631; *GDN*, March 8, 1865.

6. General Order No. 22, Headquarters Defenses of Galveston, April 14, 1865, General and Special Orders of Confederate Officers: 1863–1865, MS, Ashbel Smith Papers, CAH, 437.

7. Elizabeth Silverthorne, *Ashbel Smith of Texas: Pioneer, Patriot, Statesman, 1805–1886* (College Station: Texas A&M University Press, 1982), 37–96.

8. Ibid., 147–170.

9. James H. M'Neilly, "Col. Ashbel Smith, of Texas," *Confederate Veteran* 27 (December 1919): 463–464.

10. Joseph E. Chance, *From Shiloh to Vicksburg: The Second Texas Infantry* (Austin: Eakin Press, 1984), 164.

11. James A. Stevens, "Col. Ashbel Smith of Texas," *Confederate Veteran* 28 (January 1920): 38.

12. Ben C. Stuart, "Old War Records: Some Not Favorable," *GDN*, October 13, 1907.

13. Ashbel Smith to Captain E. P. Turner, Headquarters Defenses of Galveston, May 15, 1865, Record Book of Confederate Correspondence, 1863–1865, Ashbel Smith Papers, CAH, 435–436; J. B. Magruder to E. Kirby Smith, Houston, May 16, 1865, *OR*, vol. 48, pt. 2:1308; J. F. Smith to Cousin, Galveston, May 19, 1865, TS, John F. Smith Letters, CAH.

14. Civil War Diary of Wright Smith Andrews, entry for May 22, 1865, TS, Sam Houston Regional Library & Research Center, Liberty, Texas.

15. Ben C. Stuart, "War Time Incidents: Military Banish Women," *GDN*, June 23, 1907.

16. Stuart, "Some True Stories of the Blockade."

17. E. Kirby Smith to Soldiers of the Trans-Mississippi Army, Shreveport, April 21, 1865, *OR*, vol. 48, pt. 2:1284.

18. J. B. Magruder to E. Kirby Smith, Houston, April 28, 1865, *OR*, vol. 48, pt. 2: 1289.

19. J. B. Magruder to the People and Army of Texas, Houston, May 4, 1865, *OR*, vol. 48, pt. 2:1294.

20. Statement of J. B. Magruder quoted from *Houston Telegraph*, n.d., in William W. White, "The Disintegration of an Army: Confederate Forces in Texas, April–June 1865," *East Texas Historical Journal* 26 (Fall 1988): 42.

21. John C. Walker, "Reconstruction in Texas," *SHSP* 24 (January–December 1896): 45.

22. J. B. Magruder to the People and Army of Texas, Houston, May 19, 1865, quoted in Hayes, *Island and City*, 2:633.

23. E. P. Turner to A. Smith, Houston, May 21, 1865, *OR*, vol. 48, pt. 2:1316–1317.

24. Robert L. Kerby, *Kirby Smith's Confederacy: The Trans-Mississippi South, 1863–1865* (Tuscaloosa: University of Alabama Press, 1972), 422–423.

25. *GDN*, June 7, 1865.

26. Telegrams from J. B. Magruder to E. Kirby Smith, Houston, May 22, 24, and 26, 1865, MS, Chicago Historical Society.

27. Ashbel Smith to B. Sands, Galveston, May 22, 1865, *ORN*, 22:198.

28. J. B. Magruder to Ashbel Smith and W. P. Ballinger, Houston, May 24, 1865, MS, J. B. Magruder Papers, GTHC; J. B. Magruder to People of Texas, Houston, May 26, 1865, *OR*, vol. 48, pt. 2:1319–1320.

29. J. B. Magruder to B. F. Sands, Houston, May 27, 1865, *ORN*, 22:206.

30. "Reminiscences of the Last Vestige of a Lost Cause," H. A. Wallace Recollections, 1865, TS, CAH.

31. W. F. Keeler to Anna, Off Galveston, May 30, 1865, quoted in Robert W. Daly, ed., *Aboard the USS Florida: 1863–1865 — The Letters of Paymaster William Frederick Keeler, U.S. Navy to His Wife, Anna*, Naval Letter Series, vol. 2 (Annapolis, Md.: United States Naval Institute, 1968), 223–224.

32. Terms of a Military Convention, New Orleans, May 26, 1865, *OR*, vol. 48, pt. 2:600–601.

33. C. T. Christensen to E. J. Davis, New Orleans, May 27, 1865, *OR*, vol. 48, pt. 2:621.

34. William Pitt Ballinger Diary, entries for May 30–June 25, 1865, TS, GTHC, 72–89.

35. A. Smith and W. P. Ballinger to E. R. S. Canby, New Orleans, May 30, 1865, *OR*, vol. 48, pt. 2:675–676.

36. E. J. Davis to W. P. Doran, August 3, 1876, and August 26, 1876, E. J. Davis Papers, GTHC; "Surrender of the Trans-Mississippi Department," *Galveston Tri-Weekly News*, Houston, June 7, 1865.

37. E. J. Davis to W. P. Doran, August 3, 1876, August 7, 1876, and August 26, 1876, E. J. Davis Papers, GTHC.

38. Alice Murphy, "Rebel Leader Discovered by Kin," *Houston Post*, July 13, 1967.

39. H. K. Thatcher to Gideon Welles, U.S. Flagship *R. R. Cuyler,* Off Galveston, June 8, 1865, *ORN,* 22:216–217.

40. "Editorial Correspondence," *GDN,* June 9, 1865; Hayes, *Island and City,* 2:641.

41. "Editorial Correspondence," *Galveston Tri-Weekly News,* June 9, 1865.

42. Benjamin F. Sands, *From Reefer to Rear-Admiral: Reminiscences and Journal Jottings* (New York: Frederick A. Stokes Company, 1899), 278.

43. Donald J. Lehman, *Lucky Landmark: A Study of a Design and Its Survival* (Washington, D.C.: GSA Public Buildings Service, 1973), 4, 33.

EPILOGUE

1. William Pitt Ballinger Diary, entries for July 11 and 14, 1865, TS, GTHC, 92–93.

2. General Orders No. 3, Headquarters, District of Texas, Galveston, June 19, 1865, *OR,* vol. 48, pt. 2:929.

3. Hayes, *Island and City,* 2:649.

4. William Pitt Ballinger Diary, entries for August 25–September 1, 1865, TS, GTHC, 101–109.

5. "Remains of Gen. Wigfall," *GDN,* February 20, 1874; "The Funeral of Gen. Wigfall," *GDN,* February 22, 1874; Alvy L. King, *Louis T. Wigfall: Southern Fire-eater* (Baton Rouge: Louisiana State University Press, 1970).

6. "Death of Gen. Braxton Bragg," *GDN,* September 28, 1876; "Death of Gen. Bragg: Particulars of His Sudden Taking Off," *GDN,* September 28, 1876.

7. "Gen. Grant and Party: Entertainment at the Tremont Hotel Last Night," *GDN,* March 25, 1880.

8. "Wainwright's Sword: A Lady in Galveston Has One for the Commodore's Daughter," *GDN,* January 5, 1895; "Lieut. Jouett, Who Led Civil War Raid on Galveston Harbor, Was Cousin of Group Commander," *Galveston Tribune,* January 5, 1929; *Webster's New Biographical Dictionary* (Springfield, Mass.: Merriam-Webster Inc., 1988), 1034.

9. "The *Harriet Lane,*" *GDN,* November 26, 1872; W. P. Doran, "The *Harriet Lane:* Some Unwritten History about the Fate of This Noted Vessel," *GDN,* May 22, 1895; Trexler, "The *Harriet Lane* and the Blockade of Galveston," 35:109, 122–123; "Sidewheeler *Harriet Lane* Built in 1857," *GDN,* February 22, 1970; Marvin, "The *Harriet Lane,*" 39:15, 20.

10. "Old Frigate to Junk Heap," undated, *GDN,* Morgan Family Papers, GTHC.

11. Day, "Leon Smith: Confederate Mariner," 45–46.

12. J. B. Magruder to Isaac Burrell, Boston, October 24, 1869, Autograph Collection, MOLLUS–Massachusetts Commandery Collection, vol. 3, p. 214, U.S. Army Military History Institute, Carlisle Barracks, Pennsylvania.

BIBLIOGRAPHY

MANUSCRIPTS AND ARCHIVAL MATERIALS

Center for American History, University of Texas at Austin:
E. Jarvis Baker Memoir
William Pitt Ballinger Diaries
William Pitt Ballinger Papers
Briscoe (Mary Jane Harris) and Looscan (Adele Lubbock Briscoe) Papers
Civil War Miscellany
Confederate States of America Records
Eberstadt Collection
Tim Finn Autobiography
Oscar Haas Papers
Augustus M. Hill Papers
Milton G. Howe Papers
W. Randolph Howell Papers
Lea (Pryor) Items
Ashbel Smith Papers
John F. Smith Letters
Philip C. Tucker III Narrative
Philip C. Tucker III Papers
H. A. Wallace Recollections
Chicago Historical Society:
J. B. Magruder Papers
Daughters of the Republic of Texas Library at the Alamo:
Alexander-Lewis Family Papers
Summary of Diaries Written by Caleb G. Forshey between July 12, 1838, and
    May 24, 1878
Galveston and Texas History Center, Rosenberg Library, Galveston:
Annals of the Propagation of the Faith
T. C. Armstrong Papers
W. P. Ballinger Diary
W. P. Ballinger Papers
Beers Family Papers
D. Bradbury Papers
Anne Ammons Brindley and Walter E. Grover Papers
British Consular Records
D. G. Burnet Papers
Civil War Scrapbooks
H. Clark Papers
C.S.A. Army, Texas Dept. Records
C.S.A. Galveston Collection
C.S.A. Prize Commission Records

William Maury Darst Papers
J. Y. Dashiell Papers
E. J. Davis Papers
Dege's Light Artillery Records
C. F. A. Dieckmann Papers
H. N. Duble Papers
J. O. Dyer Scrapbooks
B. S. Ewell Papers
Federal Writers Project Records
Caleb G. Forshey Papers
Robert Lee Gary Papers
Gonzales Family Papers
G. W. Grover Papers
J. J. Hendley Papers
Rufus Jameson Papers
JOLO Observatory Records
Simon Kuykendall Papers
Cecelia Labadie Diary
Labadie-Tucker Family Papers
Thomas Jefferson League Papers
S. G. S. Lee Papers
John W. Lockhart Papers
J. B. Magruder Papers
Morgan Family Papers
A. Nathan Papers
R. N. Oliver Papers
A. Pichard Papers
Royal Yacht Records
H. Sampson Papers
S. Sherman Papers
Sherman Family Scrapbook
B. C. Stuart Papers
Texas Horsemen of the Sea Manuscript
John Grant Tod Papers
Trueheart Family Papers
Tucker Family Papers
Union Soldier Diary
J. M. Wainwright Papers
Wallis Family Papers
M. A. Williams Papers
Holt-Atherton Department of Special Collections, University of Pacific Libraries,
Stockton, California:
Black Family Papers
Houston Metropolitan Research Center, Houston Public Library:
Amerman-Collings Family Collection

Sam Houston Regional Library & Research Center, Liberty, Texas:
  Wright Smith Andrews Diary
University of Houston Libraries, Special Collections:
  Claude Elliot Memorial Collection
Howard-Tilton Memorial Library, Tulane University, Special Collections Division:
  W. W. Hunter Papers
  Louisiana Historical Association Collection
Library of the Boston Athenaeum:
  Petition to Abraham Lincoln for Exchange of Officers Held as Prisoners in Texas,
    1864
Massachusetts Historical Society, Boston, Massachusetts:
  Orville W. Leonard Papers
  James Miller Diary
Naval Historical Collection, Naval War College, Newport, Rhode Island:
  John B. Marchand Journals
Peabody Essex Museum, Salem, Massachusetts:
  John E. Goodhue Papers
Texas State Archives, Austin, Texas:
  First Brigade Correspondence
  Miscellaneous Speeches and Addresses
  Papers of Governor Edward Clark
  Papers of Governor F. R. Lubbock
  Papers of Governor P. Murrah
  Annie Charlotte Terrill, "Life of Ebenezer B. Nichols," San Antonio, Texas,
    June 1935
U.S. Army Military History Institute, Carlisle Barracks, Pennsylvania:
  Lewis Leigh Collection
  MOLLUS–Massachusetts Commandery Collection
Woodson Research Center, Fondren Library, Rice University, Houston, Texas:
  Alexander Hobbs Diary
  Emil Neumann Papers

BOOKS

Acheson, Sam. *35,000 Days in Texas: A History of the Dallas News and Its Forbears.* New
  York: Macmillan Company, 1938.
Alberts, Don E. *Rebels on the Rio Grande: The Civil War Journal of A. B. Peticolas.*
  Albuquerque: Merit Press, 1993.
Allardice, Bruce S. *More Generals in Gray.* Baton Rouge: Louisiana State University
  Press, 1995.
Armstead, Bert Carson. "Galveston during the Civil War." Master's thesis, Texas
  Southern University, 1974.
Arnold, Thomas Jackson. *Early Life and Letters of General Thomas J. Jackson.* New York:
  Fleming H. Revell Co., 1916.

Atkins, Richard A., and Helen Fiske Atkins, eds. *Civil War Journal of George M. Fiske of Medfield, Massachusetts.* Syracuse N.Y.: n.p., 1962.

Barker, Eugene C., and Amelia W. Williams, eds. *The Writings of Sam Houston.* 8 vols. Austin: University of Texas, 1928–1943.

Barnstone, Howard. *The Galveston That Was.* 1966. Reprint, Houston: Rice University Press, 1993.

Barr, Alwyn. "Confederate Artillery in the Trans-Mississippi." Master's thesis, University of Texas at Austin, 1961.

Bate, W. N. *General Sidney Sherman: Texas Soldier, Statesman and Builder.* Waco: Texian Press, 1974.

Battles and Leaders of the Civil War: Grant-Lee Edition. 4 vols. 1887. Reprint, Harrisburg, Pa.: Archive Society, 1991.

Blessington, J. P. *The Campaigns of Walker's Texas Division.* Austin: Pemberton Press, 1968.

Bosson, Charles P. *History of the Forty-Second Regiment, Infantry, Massachusetts Volunteers, 1862, 1863, 1864.* Boston: Mills, Knight & Co., 1886.

Bowden, J. J. *The Exodus of Federal Forces from Texas.* 1861. Reprint, Austin: Eakin Press, 1986.

Bowen, Nancy Head. "A Political Labyrinth: Texas in the Civil War — Questions in Continuity." Ph.D. diss., Rice University, 1974.

Brent, Joseph L. *Memoirs of the War between the States.* New Orleans: Fontana Printing Co., 1940.

Brown, John H. *Indian Wars and Pioneers of Texas.* Austin: L. E. Daniell, 189?.

Brown, Norman D., ed. *Journey to Pleasant Hill: The Civil War Letters of Captain Elijah P. Petty, Walker's Texas Division, C.S.A.* 2 vols. San Antonio: University of Texas Institute of Texas Cultures, 1982.

Buenger, Walter L. *Secession and the Union in Texas.* Austin: University of Texas Press, 1984.

Campbell, Randolph B. *An Empire for Slavery: The Peculiar Institution in Texas, 1821–1865.* Baton Rouge: Louisiana State University Press, 1989.

Carse, Robert. *Blockade: The Civil War at Sea.* New York: Rinehart & Co., 1958.

Cartwright, Gary. *Galveston: A History of the Island.* New York: Atheneum, 1991.

Casdorph, Paul D. *Prince John Magruder: His Life and Campaigns.* New York: John Wiley & Sons, 1996.

Chance, Joseph E. *From Shiloh to Vicksburg: The Second Texas Infantry.* Austin: Eakin Press, 1984.

Confederate Veteran, 1893–1932. 40 vols. Reprint, Harrisburg, Pa.: National Historical Society, n.d.

Crist, Lynda, and Mary Dix, eds. *The Papers of Jefferson Davis.* 9 vols. Baton Rouge: Louisiana State University Press, 1995.

Cromie, Alice H. *A Tour Guide to the Civil War,* 2d ed. New York: E. P. Dutton & Co., 1975.

Cullen, Joseph P. *The Peninsula Campaign: 1862.* New York: Bonanza Books, 1973.

Current, Richard N., ed. *Encyclopedia of the Confederacy.* 4 vols. New York: Simon & Schuster, 1993.

Daly, Robert W., ed. *Aboard the USS Florida: 1863–1865 — The Letters of Paymaster*

William Frederick Keeler, U.S. Navy to His Wife, Anna. Naval Letter Series, vol. 2. Annapolis, Md.: United States Naval Institute, 1968.

Davis, William C., ed. *The Confederate General.* 6 vols. n.p.: National Historical Society, 1991.

Debray, Xavier B. *A Sketch of Debray's (26ᵗʰ) Regiment of Texas Cavalry.* Austin: Von Boeckman, 1884.

Eisenhour, Virginia. *Galveston: A Different Place,* 4th ed. Galveston: V. Eisenhour, 1989.

Farragut, Loyall. *The Life of David Glasgow Farragut, First Admiral of the United States Navy, Embodying His Journal and Letters.* New York: D. Appleton and Company, 1879.

Faulk, Odie. *General Tom Green: "A Fightin' Texan".* Waco: Texian Press, 1963.

Faust, Patricia L., ed. *Historical Times Illustrated Encyclopedia of the Civil War.* New York: Harper & Row, 1986.

Ford, John S. *RIP Ford's Texas.* Edited by Stephen B. Oates. Austin: University of Texas Press, 1963.

Fornell, Earl W. *The Galveston Era: The Texas Crescent on the Eve of Secession.* Austin: University of Texas Press, 1961.

Forrest, Douglas F. *Odyssey in Gray: A Diary of Confederate Service.* Edited by William N. Still. n.p.: Virginia State Library, 1979.

Franklin, Robert M. *Battle of Galveston.* Galveston: San Luis Press, 1975.

Frazier, Donald S. *Blood and Treasure: Confederate Empire in the Southwest.* College Station: Texas A&M University Press, 1995.

———. *Cottonclads!: The Battle of Galveston and the Defense of the Texas Coast.* Fort Worth: Ryan Place Publishers, 1996.

Freeman, Douglas Southall. *Lee's Lieutenants.* 3 vols. New York: Charles Scribner's Sons, 1942.

Freeman, Martha Doty, and Sandra L. Hannum. *A History of Fortifications at Fort San Jacinto, Galveston, Texas.* Austin: Prewitt & Associates, 1991.

Fremantle, Arthur J. L. *The Fremantle Diary, Being the Journal of Arthur James Lyon Fremantle, Coldstream Guards, On His Three Months in the Southern States.* Edited by Walter Lord. Boston: Little Brown and Company, 1954.

Gallaway, B. P., ed. *Texas: The Dark Corner of the Confederacy,* 3d ed. Lincoln: University of Nebraska Press, 1994.

Garner, Ruby Lee. "Galveston during the Civil War." Master's thesis, University of Texas at Austin, 1927.

Gibbons, Tony. *Warships and Naval Battles of the Civil War.* New York: Gallery Books, 1989.

Goyne, Minetta Altgelt. *Lone Star and Double Eagle: Civil War Letters of a German-Texas Family.* Fort Worth: Texas Christian University Press, 1982.

Gregory, Peggy, copyist. *Record of Interments of the City of Galveston.* Houston: n.p., 1976.

Hamersly, Lewis R. *The Records of the Living Officers of the U.S. Navy and Marine Corps.* Philadelphia: J. B. Lippincott & Co., 1870.

Hartje, Robert G. *Van Dorn: The Life and Times of a Confederate General.* Nashville: Vanderbilt University Press, 1967.

Hasskarl, Robert A., and Captain Lief R. Hasskarl. *Waul's Texas Legion, 1862–1865.* Ada, Okla.: n.p., 1985.

Hayes, Charles W. *History of the Island and the City of Galveston.* 2 vols. Cincinnati, 1879 (set in type but not released); Austin: Jenkins Garrett Press, 1974.

Headley, P. C. *Massachusetts in the Rebellion: A Record of the Historical Position of the Commonwealth and the Services of the Leading Statesmen, the Military, the Colleges, and the People, in the Civil War of 1861–65.* Boston: Walker, Fuller & Co., 1886.

Hearn, Charles G. *The Capture of New Orleans: 1862.* Baton Rouge: Louisiana State University Press, 1995.

Henson, Margaret Swett. *Samuel May Williams: Early Texas Entrepreneur.* College Station: Texas A&M University Press, 1976.

Hoehling, A. A. *Damn the Torpedoes! Naval Incidents of the Civil War.* Winston-Salem, N.C.: John F. Blair, 1989.

Hooverstol, Paeder Joel. "Galveston in the Civil War." Master's thesis, University of Houston, 1950.

Hotchkiss, Jedediah. *Make Me a Map of the Valley: The Civil War Journal of Stonewall Jackson's Topographer.* Edited by Archie P. McDonald. Dallas: Southern Methodist University, 1973.

Ingram, Henry L., comp. *Civil War Letters of George W. and Martha F. Ingram.* College Station: Texas A&M University Press, 1973.

Johnson, Ludwell H. *Red River Campaign: Politics and Cotton in the Civil War.* Kent, Ohio: Kent State University Press, 1993.

Kellersberger, Julius G. *Memoirs of an Engineer in the Confederate Army in Texas.* Translated by Helen S. Sundstrom. n.p.: n.p., 1957.

Kelly, Ruth Evelyn. "'Twixt Failure and Success': The Port of Galveston in the 19th Century." Master's thesis, University of Houston, 1975.

Kerby, Robert L. *Kirby Smith's Confederacy: The Trans-Mississippi South, 1863–1865.* Tuscaloosa: University of Alabama Press, 1972.

King, Alvy L. *Louis T. Wigfall: Southern Fire-eater.* Baton Rouge: Louisiana State University Press, 1970.

Ladd, Kevin. *Chambers County Texas in the War between the States.* Baltimore: Gateway Press, 1994.

Lehman, Donald J. *Lucky Landmark: A Study of a Design and Its Survival.* Washington, D.C.: General Services Administration Public Buildings Service, 1973.

Lewis Publishing Co. *History of Texas Together with a Biographical History of the Cities of Houston and Galveston.* Chicago: Lewis Publishing Company, 1895.

Longstreet, James. *From Manassas to Appomattox: Memoirs of the Civil War in America.* Philadelphia: J. B. Lippincott Company, 1896.

Lubbock, Francis R. *Six Decades in Texas or Memoirs of Francis Richard Lubbock, Governor of Texas in War-time, 1861–63.* Edited by C. W. Raines. Austin: Ben C. Jones & Co. Printers, 1900.

McComb, David G. *Galveston: A History.* Austin: University of Texas Press, 1986.

Massachusetts Soldiers, Sailors, and Marines in the Civil War. 4 vols. Norwood, Mass.: Norwood Press, 1932.

Moore, Frank, ed. *The Rebellion Record: A Diary of American Events*. 11 vols. New York: G. P. Putnam, 1862.

Moretta, John A. "William Pitt Ballinger: Public Servant, Private Pragmatist." Ph.D. diss., Rice University, 1985.

Morgan, William Manning. *Trinity Protestant Episcopal Church, Galveston, Texas, 1841–1953: A Memorial History*. Houston: Anson Jones Press, 1954.

Noel, Theophilus. *Autobiography and Reminiscences of Theophilus Noel*. Chicago: Theo. Noel Company, 1904.

———. *A Campaign from Santa Fe to the Mississippi, Being a History of the Old Sibley Brigade*. 1865. Reprint, Houston: Stagecoach Press, 1961.

North, Thomas. *Five Years in Texas; or, What You Did Not Hear during the War from January 1861 to January 1866*. Cincinnati: Elm Street Printing Co., 1871.

Nott, Charles C. *Sketches in Prison Camp: A Continuation of Sketches of the War*, 3d ed. New York: Anson D. F. Randolph, 1865.

Nunn, Dr. W. C. *Ten More Texans in Gray*. Hillsboro, Tex.: Hill Junior College Press, 1980.

Oltorf, Frank Calvert. *The Marlin Compound: Letters of a Singular Family*. Austin: University of Texas Press, 1968.

Parks, Joseph H. *General Edmund Kirby Smith, C.S.A.* Baton Rouge: Louisiana State University Press, 1954.

Parton, James. *General Butler in New Orleans: History of the Administration of the Department of the Gulf*. New York: Mason Brothers, 1864.

Pearson, Henry Greenleaf. *The Life of John Andrew: Governor of Massachusetts, 1861–1865*. 2 vols. Boston: Houghton, Mifflin and Company, 1904.

Porter, David D. *Incidents and Anecdotes of the Civil War*. New York: D. Appleton and Company, 1886.

Richardson, Willard and D. *The Texas Almanac for 1861, with Statistics, Historical and Biographical Sketches, &c, Relating to Texas*. Galveston: The Galveston News, 1861.

Roberts, O. M. *Texas*, vol. 15 of *Confederate Military History: Extended Edition*. 1899. Reprint, Wilmington, N.C.: Broadfoot Publishing Co., 1989.

Sands, Benjamin F. *From Reefer to Rear-Admiral: Reminiscences and Journal Jottings*. New York: Frederick A. Stokes Company, 1899.

Scharf, J. Thomas. *History of the Confederate States Navy*. Albany, N.Y.: Joseph McDonough, 1894.

Sears, Stephen W. *George B. McClellan: The Young Napoleon*. New York: Ticknor & Fields, 1988.

———. *To the Gates of Richmond: The Peninsula Campaign*. New York: Ticknor & Fields, 1992.

Semmes, Raphael. *Memoirs of Service Afloat during the War between the States*. Baltimore: Kelly, Piet & Co., 1869.

Settles, Thomas M. "The Military Career of John Bankhead Magruder." Ph.D. diss., Texas Christian University, 1972.

Shackelford, George G. *George Wythe Randolph and the Confederate Elite*. Athens: University of Georgia, 1996.

Silverstone, Paul H. *Warships of the Civil War Navies.* Annapolis, Md.: Naval Institute Press, 1989.

Silverthorne, Elizabeth. *Ashbel Smith of Texas: Pioneer, Patriot, Statesman, 1805–1886.* College Station: Texas A&M University Press, 1982.

Soley, J. R. *The Blockade and the Cruisers.* 1887. Reprint, Wilmington, N.C.: Broadfoot Publishing Company, 1989.

Spell, Timothy D. "John Bankhead Magruder: Defender of the Texas Coast, 1863." Master's thesis, Lamar University, 1981.

Spencer, John. *Terrell's Texas Cavalry: Wild Horsemen of the Plains in the Civil War.* Burnet, Tex.: Eakin Press, 1982.

Taylor, Thomas E. *Running the Blockade: A Personal Narrative of Adventures, Risks, and Escapes during the American Civil War.* 1896. Reprint, Bowie, Md.: Heritage Books, 1991.

Thompson, Robert Means, ed. *Confidential Correspondence of Gustavus Vasa Fox.* 2 vols. New York: De Vinne Press, 1920.

Tolbert, Frank X. *Dick Dowling at Sabine Pass.* New York: McGraw-Hill Book Co., 1962.

Trammell, Camilla Davis. *Seven Pines: Its Occupants and Their Letters, 1825–1872.* Dallas: Southern Methodist University Press, 1986.

Tyler, Ronnie C., and Lawrence R. Murphy, eds. *The Slave Narratives of Texas.* Austin: Encino Press, 1974.

Van Dorn, Earl. *A Soldier's Honor: With Reminiscences of Major-General Earl Van Dorn by His Comrades.* New York: Abbey Press, 1902.

Waller, John L. *Colossal Hamilton of Texas.* El Paso: Texas Western Press, 1968.

Warner, Ezra J. *Generals in Blue: Lives of the Union Commanders.* Baton Rouge: Louisiana State University Press, 1964.

———. *Generals in Gray: Lives of the Confederate Commanders.* Baton Rouge: Louisiana State University Press, 1959.

Watson, William. *The Adventures of a Blockade Runner; or Trade in Time of War.* London: T. Fisher Unwin, 1892.

Webb, Prescott, ed. *The Handbook of Texas.* 3 vols. Austin: Texas State Historical Association, 1952.

Webster's New Biographical Dictionary. Springfield, Mass.: Merriam-Webster Inc., 1988.

Welles, Gideon. *The Diary of Gideon Welles: Secretary of the Navy under Lincoln and Johnson.* 3 vols. Boston: Houghton Mifflin Company, 1911.

Whitford, William C. *The Battle of Glorieta Pass: The Colorado Volunteers in the Civil War.* 1906. Reprint, Glorieta, N.Mex.: Rio Grande Press, 1991.

Wiggins, Sarah Woolfolk, ed. *The Journals of Josiah Gorgas: 1857–1878.* Tuscaloosa: University of Alabama Press, 1995.

Williams, Edward B., ed. *Rebel Brothers: The Civil War Letters of the Truehearts.* College Station: Texas A&M University Press, 1995.

Wilson, James G., and John Fiske, eds. *Appleton's Cyclopedia of American Biography.* 7 vols. New York: D. Appleton and Co., 1888. Republished, Detroit: Gale Research Co., 1968.

Winkler, Ernest W., ed. *Journal of the Secession Convention of Texas.* Austin: Austin Printing Company, 1912.

Wise, Stephen R. *Lifeline of the Confederacy: Blockade Running during the Civil War.* Columbia: University of South Carolina Press, 1988.

Wood, W. J. *Battles of the Revolutionary War: 1775–1781.* New York: Da Capo Press, 1955.

Woodward, C. Vann, ed. *Mary Chesnut's Civil War.* New Haven, Conn.: Yale University Press, 1981.

Wooster, Ralph A. *Texas and Texans in the Civil War.* Austin: Eakin Press, 1995.

Wooten, Dudley G. *A Comprehensive History of Texas: 1685 to 1897.* 2 vols. Dallas: William G. Scarff, 1898.

Wright, Marcus J., comp. *Texas in the War, 1861–1865.* Edited by Harold Simpson. Hillsboro, Tex.: Hill Junior College Press, 1965.

Yearns, W. Buck, ed. *The Confederate Governors.* Athens: University of Georgia Press, 1985.

Yeary, Mamie, comp. *Reminiscences of the Boys in Gray.* 1912. Reprint, Dayton, Ohio: Morningside, 1986.

Young, Kevin R. *To the Tyrants Never Yield: A Texas Civil War Sampler.* Plano, Tex.: Wordware Publishing, Inc., 1992.

Zwiener, Douglas, and Elisabeth Darst. *A Guide to Historic Galveston.* Galveston: n.p., 1966.

NEWSPAPERS

Boston Journal

The Civilian

Flake's Bulletin

Galveston News and *Galveston Daily News*

Galveston Tri-Weekly News

Galveston Tribune

Houston Daily Telegraph

Houston Post

New Braunfels Herald

New York Tribune

Port Lavaca Wave

Richmond Dispatch

ARTICLES AND JOURNALS

Angel, William D., Jr. "Vantage on the Bay: Galveston and the Railroads." *East Texas Historical Journal* 22, no. 1 (1984): 3–18.

Barr, Alwyn. "Sabine Pass, September 1863." *Texas Military History* 2 (February 1962): 17–22.

———. "Texas Coastal Defense." *SWHQ* 65 (July 1961): 1–31.

———. "Texas' Confederate Field Artillery." *Texas Military History* 1 (August 1961): 1–12.

Block, W. T. "A Towering East Texas Pioneer: A Biographical Sketch of Colonel Albert Miller Lea." *East Texas Historical Journal* 32, no. 2 (1993): 23–33.

Crook, Carland Elaine. "Benjamin Theron and French Designs in Texas during the Civil War." *SWHQ* 68 (April 1965): 432–454.

Cumberland, Charles C. "The Confederate Loss and Recapture of Galveston, 1862–1863." *SWHQ* 51 (October 1947): 109–130.

Darst, Maury. "Artillery Defenses of Galveston, 1863." *Military History of Texas and the Southwest* 12, no. 1 (1975): 63–67.

———. "Robert Hodges, Jr.: Confederate Soldier." *East Texas Historical Journal* 9 (March 1971): 20–49.

Day, James J. "Leon Smith: Confederate Mariner." *East Texas Historical Journal* 3 (March 1965): 34–49.

Ehrman, W. E. "The *Harriet Lane*—Fighting Lady of the Civil War." *Bulletin of the U.S. Coast Guard Academy Alumni Association* (September/October 1980): 22–25.

El Campanario: Publication of the Texas Old Missions and Forts Restoration Association 25 (February 1994): 1–2.

Ellis, L. Tuffly. "Maritime Commerce in the Far Western Gulf." *SWHQ* 77 (October 1973): 167–226.

Fontaine, Sidney. "Battle of Galveston—The *Harriet Lane*." *Confederate Veteran* 18 (January 1910): 29.

Frazier, Donald S. "Sibley's Texans and the Battle of Galveston." *SWHQ* 99 (October 1995): 174–198.

Gaines, John, ed. "Historical Notes on Galveston." *Texana* 3 (Summer 1965): 154–176.

Gallagher, Gary W. "The Fall of Prince John Magruder." *Civil War* 19 (August 1989): 9–15.

Gallaher, Ruth A. "Albert Miller Lea." *Iowa Journal of History and Politics* (July 1935): 195–241.

Goldberg, Mitchell S. "A Federal Raid into Galveston Harbor, November 7–8, 1861: What Really Happened?" *SWHQ* 76 (July 1972): 58–70.

Grimsley, Mark. "Inside a Beleaguered City: A Commander and Actor—Prince John Magruder." *CWTI* 21 (September 1982): 14–17, 32–35.

Hall, Martin Hardwick. "The Court-Martial of Arthur Pendleton Bagby, C.S.A." *East Texas Historical Journal* 19, no. 2 (Fall 1981): 60–67.

Hutchinson, William F., M.D. "Life on the Texan Blockade." Paper read before the Rhode Island Soldiers and Sailors Historical Society. *Military Order of the Loyal Legion of the United States* 35 (April 17, 1883; reprint, Wilmington, N.C.: Broadfoot Publishing Company, 1993): 1–41.

Jones, Virgil C. "The Battle of Galveston Harbor." *CWTI* 5 (February 1967): 28–38.

King, C. Richard, ed. "Andrew Neill's Galveston Letters." *Texana* 3 (Fall 1965): 203–217.

Kliger, Paul I. "The Confederate Invasion of New Mexico." *Blue & Gray Magazine* (June 1994): 8–20, 48–60.

Lamb, John. "Malvern Hill—July 1, 1862." *SHSP* 25 (January–December 1897): 208–221.

Lea, Albert M. "Autobiography of A. M. Lea." *Freeborn County Standard* (March 13, 1889).

Lee, Baker P. "Magruder's Peninsula Campaign in 1862." *SHSP* 19 (January 1891): 60–65.

Long, General A. L. "Memoir of General John Bankhead Magruder." *SHSP* 12 (January–February 1884): 105–110.

M'Neilly, James H. "Col. Ashbel Smith, of Texas." *Confederate Veteran* 27 (December 1919): 463–465.

Marvin, David P. "The *Harriet Lane*." *SWHQ* 39 (July 1935): 15–20.

Milbourn, Curtis W. "Brigadier General Thomas Green of Texas." *East Texas Historical Journal* 32, no. 1 (1994): 3–11.

Minnesota Historical Society. "Albert Miller Lea." *Minnesota History Bulletin* 35 (August 1923): 204–205.

Moretta, John. "William Pitt Ballinger and the Travail of Texas Secession." *Houston Review: History and Culture of the Gulf Coast* 11, no. 1 (1989): 3–26.

Posey, Mrs. Samuel. "Capture of the Star of the West." *Confederate Veteran* 32 (May 1924): 174.

Price, Marcus W. "Ships That Tested the Blockade of the Gulf Ports, 1861–1865." *American Neptune* 11 (October 1951): 262–290; 12 (July 1952): 229–238; 13 (April 1953): 154–161; 15 (January 1955): 97–131.

Robert, Rev. P. G. "Justice to General Magruder." *SHSP* 5 (May 1878): 249–250.

Rozek, Barbara J. "Galveston Slavery." *Houston Review: History and Culture of the Gulf Coast* 15, no. 2 (1993): 67–101.

Salta, Remo. "Guardians of the Coast." *America's Civil War* (March 1994): 34–40.

Smith, Rebecca W., and Marion Mullins, eds. "The Diary of H. C. Medford, Confederate Soldier, 1864." *SWHQ* 34 (October 1930): 106–140; 34 (January 1931): 203–230.

Stevens, James A. "Col. Ashbel Smith of Texas." *Confederate Veteran* 28 (January 1920): 38.

Suhr, Robert Collins. "Firing the Norfolk Navy Yard." *America's Civil War* (November 1996): 52–57, 98.

Trexler, H. A. "The *Harriet Lane* and the Blockade of Galveston." *SWHQ* 35 (October 1931): 109–123.

Tucker, Philip C., III. "The United States Gunboat *Harriet Lane*." *SWHQ* 21 (April 1918): 360–380.

Walker, John C. "Reconstruction in Texas." *SHSP* 24 (January–December 1896): 41–57.

Ward, William A. "The Saga of the *Will O' The Wisp:* The Story of a Confederate Blockade Runner." *In Between* 164 (November 1983): 1–4.

White, William W. "The Disintegration of an Army: Confederate Forces in Texas, April–June 1865." *East Texas Historical Journal* 26 (Fall 1988): 40–47.

Williams, Edward B., ed. "A 'Spirited Account' of the Battle of Galveston, January 1, 1863." *SWHQ* 99 (October 1995): 200–215.

Williams, Kenneth H. "Prince without a Kingdom: The Recall of John Bankhead Magruder." *Civil War History* (March 1995): 5–21.

Wilson, Gary E., ed. "Diary of a Union Prisoner." *Southern Studies* 23 (Spring 1984): 103–119.

———. "The Ordeal of William H. Cowdin and the Officers of the Forty-Second

Massachusetts Regiment: Union Prisoners in Texas." *East Texas Historical Journal* 23 (Spring 1985): 16–26.

Winfrey, Dorman H., ed. "Two Battle of Galveston Letters." *SWHQ* 65 (October 1961): 251–257.

Wise, Stephen R. "Greyhounds and Cavaliers of the Sea: Confederate Blockade Running during the Civil War." *Journal of Confederate History* 4 (1989): 61–76.

Young, Jo. "The Battle of Sabine Pass." *SWHQ* 52 (April 1949): 398–409.

GOVERNMENT DOCUMENTS

Letters Received by the Secretary of the Navy from Commanding Officers of Squadrons, 1841–1886, Microcopy, M-89, Roll No. 119.

Naval History Division, Navy Department. *Civil War Naval Chronology: 1861–1865.* Washington, D.C.: U.S. Government Printing Office, 1971.

Official Records of the Union and Confederate Navies in the War of the Rebellion. 31 vols. Washington, D.C.: Government Printing Office, 1899–1908.

Statutes at Large of the Confederate States of America, Passed at the Third Session of the First Congress. Richmond: R. H. Smith, 1863.

Supplement to the Official Records of the Union and Confederate Armies. Wilmington, N.C.: Broadfoot Publishing Co., 1996.

The War of the Rebellion: A Compilation of the Official Records of the Union and Confederate Armies. 128 vols. Washington, D.C.: Government Printing Office, 1880–1901.

INDEX

Alabama, C.S.S., 142; building of, 144; engagement with *Hatteras*, 143–147
Alamo, 15
Alaska Territory, 187
Albuquerque, New Mexico, 101
Alcohol, 43, 97, 99, 102, 110, 135, 153, 155
Alden, James: initiates blockade, 31; fails to destroy *Merrimack*, 31; capture of Wharton, 32; controversy with consuls, 34; capture of *Anna Taylor*, 36; capture of *Harriet Lane*, 142
Ammunition, 84, 125, 180–181
Anderson, Robert, 183
Andrew, John A., 51, 73–74
Anna Ryan, 32
Anna Taylor, 36
Ansteadt, Rev. Father, 177
Appomattox, Virginia, 179
Arizona, Confederate Territory of, 100
Arkansas, 52, 186
Arkansas (Confederate ram), 61
Armistead, Lewis A., 95–96
Army of Northern Virginia, 18, 28, 93–97, 179. *See also* Lee, Robert E.
Army of the Potomac, 92. *See also* McClellan, George B.
Army of the Trans-Mississippi, 93, 99, 157, 179; and surrender, 181–182, 187
Artillery: failed attempt to manufacture, 50; deployed at Galveston, 115; use of wrong cartridges, 125; made out of shafts, 151
Ashton Villa, 121
Austin, Charles W., 174
Austin, Texas, 18, 54
Austria, 70

Bagby, Arthur Pendleton, 102, 111–112
Baker, Jarvis, 76, 86
Baker, Mr., 161
Ballinger, William Pitt, 23; meets with Sam Houston, 28; trip to Richmond,

35, 50–51, 66, 105; proposal to arm slaves, 158; surrender negotiations, 181–182; pardons, 184–185
Baltimore, Maryland, 87
Band, 165
Banks, Nathaniel P.: assessment of Galveston's importance, 5; biographical information, 76–77, 83; shifts blame for capture, 133–134; on importance of Galveston, 134; 1863 invasion of Texas, 159
Banks Expedition, 76–77, 103, 133, 145
Banshee (II), 174
Barnett, Thomas, 70–72
Barney, Joseph N., 151–152
Barnum, P. T., 78
Battery Robinett, 138
Battle of Galveston. *See* Galveston, Battle of
Baylor, John Robert, 100; Apache plan, 103; service in Battle of Galveston, 116
Baylor's Second Texas Mounted Rifles, 101
Bayou City, C.S.S.: chartered by State of Texas, 68; acquired by Confederacy, 68; guns mounted, 108, 112, 121; cotton-clad attack at Galveston, 124–128; death of A. R. Wier, 125; rams *Harriet Lane*, 125; death of Lea, 136; sinking in 1864, 167
Beaufort, South Carolina, 81
Beef, 71–72, 164. *See also* Cattle
Bell, George, 45
Bell, Henry H.: ordered to Galveston, 142; failed attempt to capture Galveston, 143–147; shells Galveston, 148–149
Belle, 167
Benjamin, Judah P., 38, 52, 55
Big Bethel, Battle of, 91–92, 99
Blake, Homer C., 144–146
Blockade: proclamation of, 29; strategy of, 32; lifting of, 142

Blockade runners: types of, 170; last, 179
Blockade running, 168–175; profits from, 170; statistics on success of, 173
Blockading ships, depicted, 169
Blume, N. A., 167
Boarding pike, 45
Bolivar Point, 1, 19, 44
Bosson, Charles P., 73, 78
Boston, Massachusetts, 31, 42, 158, 186–187
Bragg, Braxton, 13, 99, 162, 185
Branch, Jacob, 120
Brazoria County, Texas, 177
Brazos River, 157, 159
Brazos Santiago, Texas: capture of, 10; defensive positions at, 11; captured arms, 17, 159
Bread riot of 1864, 164
British consul, 12
Broadway, 33
Brooke naval rifle, 94
Brooklyn, New York, 78
Brooklyn, U.S.S., 142–143, 148
Brown, John, 73
Brownsville, Texas, 10
Buchanan, James, 58
Burrell, Charles, 129
Burrell, Isaac: election as colonel, 74; photograph of, 75; selection of officers, 76; drilling of regiment, 78; ordered to Galveston, 83; fortification of wharf, 84–86; Battle of Kuhn's Wharf, 115–123; surrender, 122–123; request for truce, 123; meets Magruder, 135; postwar meeting with Magruder, 187
Burrows, Hiram, 102
Butchers, 71–72, 154
Butler, Benjamin F., 51, 69, 72, 77, 91, 163

California, 90, 107
Cambria: attempted capture by Confederates, 140–142, 182
Campbell, Robert C., 23
Camp followers, 163

Canby, Edward R. S., 101, 181
Caney River, 177
Cannons, wooden, 62, 149–151
Carrolton, Louisiana, 82
Carter, William W., 44–47
Cattle, 39, 54, 101, 153, 164–165
Cavallo, 131
Cemetery, Episcopal, 66, 138, 149, 188
Central Wharf, 179
Charles Osgood, 79–80
Charleston Harbor, 58, 81
Chesnut, Mary Boykin Miller, 92, 114
Chickahominy River, 93–94
Chilton, Robert H., 95, 97
China Fleet, 168
Chubb, Thomas: meeting with blockaders, 31; biographical information, 42; operation at Indianola, 42; meeting with blockaders, 42; capture of the *Royal Yacht*, 43–48; imprisoned in Fort Lafayette, 48; release from prison, 49
Churubusco, Battle of, 90
Clark, Edward, 19, 28
Clark, Harvey, 112
Clear Creek, 27
Clifton, U.S.S., 57, 59, 80, 127, 130–131, 159
Coal, 152
Coast Guard, 13, 58
Cobb, Howell, 58
Coffee, 36, 41
Collings, Charlie, 41
Committee on Public Safety: creation of, 8; appointment of agent, 9; reports to, 10, 12, 17; assessment of defenses, 13; early actions, 13; Schooner *Dodge*, 14
Commodore, 77
Constitution, 31
Consuls, foreign, 12, 34, 53, 55–56, 70, 142, 148, 171
Contreras, Battle of, 90
Cook, Joseph J., 53, 63–64; evacuation notice by, 65; leads attack on Kuhn's Wharf, 116

Cook's Regiment of Heavy Artillery, 106, 156
Cooper, Samuel, 97
Corinth, Mississippi, 138, 177
Cornmeal, 156
Corpus Christi, Texas, 90
Corypheus, U.S.S., 117
Cotton, 2, 86, 108–109, 119, 167, 170–171, 174, 176
Cottonclads, 108, 124–126
Court of Inquiry, 79, 102, 133
Crime, 155, 160–161, 184
Curfew, 161
Customhouse, U.S., 69, 105, 118, 122, 140; photograph of, 119; site of bread riot, 164, 183, 185

Daniel Webster, 11
Dart, 33
Davidson's Battalion, 111
Davis, Edmund J.: avoids capture, 140–142; at surrender of Trans-Mississippi, 182, 187
Davis, Jefferson, 13, 18–19, 39, 55, 97, 100, 103, 124, 132
Davis Guards, 116; at Battle of Sabine Pass, 159
Debray, Xavier B.: taking charge in Galveston, 63; possibility of attack on Houston, 67; plan to recapture Galveston, 67–68, 105; dispute over captured hats, 152–153; appointed to command, 154; mutiny of his troops, 156–157
Dege's Battery, 176
Delta, 43
Denbigh, 173
Desertions, 176, 178
"Dignified Resignation," 184
Discharges, 180
Disease, 162, 166
District of Texas, New Mexico, and Arizona, Confederate, 87, 98, 100, 176
Dodge, 112. *See also Henry Dodge*
Dona Ana, 102
Doran, William P., 122

Dowling, Dick [Richard William]: at Battle of Galveston, 116; at Battle of Sabine Pass, 159
Drunkenness, 153, 155

Eagle, Henry: biographical information, 43; capture of *Royal Yacht*, 43–47; seizure of *Delta*, 43; threat to bombard Galveston, 52–54, 62
Eagle Grove, 19–20; fort at, 64, 67, 150
Earthworks, 19
Eldridge, Captain, 27
Elias Pike, 131
Elliot Ritchie, 186
Elmore's Regiment, 116
Emancipation Proclamation, 184
Enfield rifles, 104, 111
Enrica, 144
Entrenched camp, 148, 163
Evacuation notice, 65
Execution, military, 140–142, 177

Falls County, Texas, 149
Faneuil Hall, 158
Farragut, David Glasgow: biographical information, 51–52; assigned to West Gulf Blockading Squadron, 51–52; threatens to seize Galveston, 52–53; bombardment threat, 53–54; orders to Renshaw, 57; praise of mortar flotilla, 60–61; authority over mortar flotilla, 61; reaction to Galveston's capture, 66–68; promises troops, 69; rebukes Renshaw, 72; reaction to Galveston's recapture, 132; promotes Lea, 137–138; questions John Payne, 141; fears *Lane* as cruiser, 142–143; concludes he can't capture Galveston, 147; reacts to escape of *Harriet Lane*, 171–172
Fashion, 22
Faunce, John, 58
Faust, Joseph, 112
Fifth Texas Cavalry, 100, 111
Fifty-First Massachusetts Infantry Regiment, 76

Firewood, 156
First Artillery, U.S., 87
First Texas Mounted Volunteers, U.S.,
  101
Fisher (Galveston's first casualty), 34
Fiske, George, 83, 135
Flake, Ferdinand, 23, 132
Florida (state), 182
Florida, U.S.S., 181
Fontaine, Sidney T., 115
Ford, John S. "RIP," 9; recruiting in sa-
  loons, 10; controversy over supplies,
  12; opinion of Magruder, 99
Forshey, Caleb G., 105–106
Fort Bankhead, 150
Fort Green, 19, 150
Fort Griffin, 159
Fort Hebert, 19, 150
Fortifications, diagram of, 150
Fort Jackson, 19, 59, 150
Fort Jackson, U.S.S., 182
Fort Jefferson, 81
Fort Lafayette, 48
Fort Leavenworth, Kansas, 91, 96
Fort Magruder, 19, 150
Fort Moore, 19, 150
Fort Point, 19, 62, 115, 140, 150, 159
Fortress Monroe, 80, 91–92
Fort Scurry, 19, 150
Fort St. Philip, 59
Fort Sumter, 7, 11, 58, 183
Forty-Second Massachusetts Infantry
  Regiment: imprisonment of, 49; for-
  mation of, 74–75; photo of officers, 75;
  training of, 77–78; trip south, 79–83;
  arrival in Louisiana, 82–83; at Battle
  of Kuhn's Wharf, 115–123; surrender
  of, 122–123; arrival back at Boston,
  158
Foster, Captain, 154
Fourth Texas Cavalry, 100
Fox, Gustavus Vasa, 51, 132–133
Freeman, Douglas Southall, 87, 95
Fremantle, Arthur James, 154

Galveston: description of, 1–4; consequences of Union loss of, 5; defensive
  possibilities of, 18; construction of fortifications on, 20; vote on secession, 23;
  blockade of, 26, 31; first shots of the
  war, 34; troop potential, 38; plan to
  destroy, 39; departure of civilians from,
  50; importance of blockading, 51; civilian problems in, 69; assignment of
  Union troops to, 72; Magruder's reason for attacking, 99; plan to attack,
  105–110; diagram of fortifications at,
  150; criminal activity in, 155; diversion
  of troops from, 157; weather in, 160
Galveston, Battle of, 4; planning for,
  105–112; description of, 113–131;
  drawing of, 121; ends, 131; casualties,
  news coverage, and Union reaction,
  132–134; situation after battle, 135–
  139; monument to, 188
Galveston Artillery Company, 10
Galveston Bay, 1, 18, 29, 67, 160
Galveston Historical Foundation, 29
Galveston Island: map of, 19; problem of
  defending, 38
Galveston News, 3, 17, 50, 122
Garrison, William Lloyd, 73
General Order No. 3, 184
General Rusk, 9, 21–22, 43–44
Gentry, Abram M., 14
German population of Galveston, 1, 21,
  23
Gettysburg, Battle of, 95, 157
Gettysburg of the West, 101
Glorieta Pass, Battle of, 100–102
Gonzales, Thomas, 115
Gonzales Light Battery, 115
Goose Creek, Texas, 49
Gorham, Martin, 79
Gosport Navy Yard, 31
Governor Runnels, 125
Grand Opera House, 186
Granger, Gordon: and Juneteenth, 184–
  185

Grant, Ulysses S., 90, 185
Grappling hooks, 109
Green, Thomas, 100; biographical information, 101; at Bagby court, 102; volunteers for Galveston expedition, 111–112; Union surrender sought by, 130; death of, 186
Greer, John L., 10
Griffin's Battalion, 116
Groton, Connecticut, 77
Grover, George, 71, 127–128, 138, 168–169
Guard house, 41
Gulf Blockading Squadron, 32, 47
Gunboats, 90-day, 57

Hamilton, Andrew Jackson, 77, 79, 133
Hannum, Josiah, 126–127
Harby, Captain, 112
Harriet Lane, U.S.S.: prewar history of, 58; at Hatteras Inlet, 59; operations in Mississippi River, 59; capture of forts below New Orleans, 59–60; capture of Galveston, 62–63; fires at Schirmer house, 71; scouting mission of, 84; observes cottonclads, 113, 121, 124; captured by Confederates, 126; sketch of capture of, 127, 128; Magruder tours, 130; use by Confederates after capture, 131; prisoners from, 132; Northern reaction to capture of, 133; Edward Lea, 136–137, 140; fear of, as cruiser, 142; disposition of, after capture, 151–152, 167; as blockade runner, 170–172; renamed the *Lavinia*, 172; returns to Galveston, 186
Harris & Morgan Line, 26–27, 107, 174
Harrisburg, Texas, 103, 111
Hatteras, U.S.S.: and fight with C.S.S. *Alabama*, 143–145
Hatteras Inlet, North Carolina, 59
Hats, Union Army, 153
Havana, Cuba, 172, 174, 179
Hawes, James Morrison: registers inhabi-

tants, 161; biography, 162; bread riot, 164; yellow fever, 166; relieved, 177
Hayes, Charles W., 160
Hays, Jack, 101
Hebert, Paul O.: biographical information, 37; military strategy of, 38–39; leaks Lubbock's letter, 40; reaction to *Royal Yacht* capture, 48; troop movements of, 52; refuses surrender, 53; seeks transfer from department, 56; abandonment of Galveston, 63–66; abandonment of Virginia Point, 67; replaced, 87
Hempstead, Texas, 103
Hendley, Joseph J., 30
Hendley, "Uncle Billy," 30
Hendley, William, & Co., 29
Hendley Building, 29, 33, 35, 115; photograph of, 30; use by blockade runners, 172–173
Henry Dodge, 13–14, 68, 112
Hill, Bennett H., 7; at Fort Brown, 10
Hill, Daniel H., 91, 94, 96
Hilton Head, South Carolina, 80–81
Hobbs, Alexander, 77–78
Holland, 70
Holmes, Theophilus H., 98
"Horse Marines," 111
"Horsemen of the Sea," 111
Horses, 39, 54, 154, 178
House, Thomas W., 171
Houston, Sam, 15; speech at the Tremont House Hotel, 23–24; breakfast with Ballinger, 28; at San Jacinto, 42; letter from Benjamin Theron, 55, 113, 183
Houston, Sam, Jr., 24
Houston, Texas, 33, 35, 50, 64, 67, 99, 103, 107, 132, 159, 161, 164–165, 171, 181, 188
Hunt, Henry Jackson, 96
Hunter, William W., 38–39, 48, 68
Hurlburt, Samuel B., 64–66
Hutchings Wharf, 115

Ice, 8
Immigration, 1
Indianola, Texas, 21; surrender of
    Federal troops at, 22, 24
Irish population of Galveston, 21
Iron, 2, 14, 149, 170, 183
Iron Battery, 115
Irwin, John, 172
Island City Hotel, 15

Jackson, Thomas J. "Stonewall," 90, 99
Jamaica, 146
James River, 91–92, 94, 96
Jefferson County, Texas, 17
Jenkins' Ferry, Battle of, 186
John F. Carr, 112, 131
Johnson, Andrew, 185
Johnston, Albert Sidney, 162
JOLOs, 29–31, 35
Joseph, Thomas, 40
Jouett, James: capture of *Royal Yacht*,
    43–48, 186
Juneteenth, 184–185

Katahdin, U.S.S., 172
Kennard, David, 41
Kentucky, 162
Key West, Florida, 59, 80–82
Kuhn's Wharf, 73; Burrell ordered to oc-
    cupy, 83–84; photograph of, 85; forti-
    fication of, 86; Battle of, 113–123; dia-
    gram of, 117; Lubbock arrives at, 130;
    damage to, 135, 186

Lackawanna, U.S.S., 172
Laird Shipyards, 144
Lark, 179
Lavinia, 172
Law, Richard, 127; receives surrender
    terms, 128; leaves Galveston Harbor,
    130–131; court-martialed, 133
Lawrence, Kansas, 51
Lea, Albert Miller: 87, 121; son's death
    after battle, 136–138
Lea, Edward, 126, 136–138, 188

Lecompte, 131, 167
Lee, Robert E., 5; Sam Houston's opin-
    ion of, 28; battle plan at Richmond,
    93; instructions at Malvern Hill, 95;
    evaluates Magruder's performance, 97;
    as cause of Magruder's transfer to
    Texas, 98–99, 114; surrenders, 179
Lincoln, Abraham: election of, 7; block-
    ade proclamation by, 25, 29; appoints
    Banks to command, 76, 107; appoints
    military governor of Texas, 133
Linsey, Lieutenant, 160
Little Rock, Arkansas, 103
Liverpool, England, 144
Lockhart, John W., 153
Long Island Sound, 79
Longstreet, James, 95, 99
Looting, 180
Louisiana, 9, 18, 37, 102, 104, 115, 152,
    186
Louisiana, Confederate ironclad, 60
Louisiana State University, 37
Lubbock, Francis R.: inaugurated as
    governor, 39; burning letter, 40–41;
    1862 Tremont speech, 41; letter from
    Benjamin Theron to, 55; relations with
    P. O. Hebert, 56; opposes abandon-
    ment of Galveston, 68; status of Sibley
    Brigade, 103; urges attack on Galves-
    ton, 105, 112; reaction to Galveston's
    recapture, 132; urges use of potatoes,
    152
Lubbock, Henry, 68, 131, 132; captains
    Bayou City, 112; surrender terms of-
    fered by, 126–128; meets Isaac Burrell,
    130; items stolen from, 152
Luckett, Philip N., 156–157
Lucy Gwinn, 112
Lynn, Arthur T., 12

McClellan, George B., 92–94
McCulloch, Henry E., 148, 157, 163
McLeod, Hugh, 26
Magruder, John Bankhead: biographical
    information, 87–91; drinking habits

of, 87–89; photograph of, 88; nickname "Prince John" given to, 89; in Mexican War, 89–90; wins Battle of Big Bethel, 91–92; defends Yorktown, 92–93; initial assignment to Texas, 93; defense of Richmond, 93–94; Battle of Savage's Station, 94–95; Battle of Malvern Hill, 95–96; problems after Malvern Hill, 97–99; assigned to Texas, 98–99; dealings with John R. Baylor, 103; searches for troops, 103–104; designs plan of attack, 105–110; launches attack at Galveston, 113–115; warns residents of Ursuline Convent, 114; tours captured ship, 130; fame after battle, 132; speech to victorious troops, 135; tours captured wharf, 135; orders to Albert Lea, 137; his trap fails to close, 140–142; builds up defenses after battle, 149; reaction to Battle of Sabine Pass, 159; target of mob in 1864, 162; engineers escape of *Harriet Lane*, 171–172; musical staff of, 174; reaction to Lee's surrender, 176; fights army breakup, 179–181; at Trans-Mississippi surrender, 182; postwar career and death of, 187–188

Malvern Hill, Battle of, 95–96, 114, 121

Marchand, John B., 171

Market Street, 155

Martial law, proclamation of, 54

Mary Boardman, 129

Mason, Caroline, 70

Masonic Lodge of Galveston, 66, 138

Massachusetts, 51, 73–74, 76, 158

Massie, J. C., 54

Matagorda, 21

Matagorda Bay, Texas, 21, 70

Maximilian, 187

Medfield, Massachusetts, 74, 82

Medford, Harvey C., 165

Medical care, 136, 166

Menard, J. M. O., 33

Merrimack, U.S.S., 31

Mervine, William, 34

Mesilla, 102

Mexican War, 31, 37, 70, 89–90, 101, 162

Mexico, 183, 187

Mexico City, 90

Millican, Texas, 103

Mississippi River, 23, 59–61, 77, 157

Missouri, C.S.S., 152

Mitchell, Lieutenant John, 44–47

Mobile, Alabama, 60, 134, 168

Mobile Bay, Alabama, 48, 82

Money, Confederate, 86

Monroe (coxswain of *Owasco*), 110

Monterrey, Mexico, 101

Montgomery, Alabama, 17–18

Moore, John C., 20, 34; placed in command, 38

Moore, Thomas O., 13, 18

Morale, 163

Morgan's Point, Texas, 112

Morgan Steamship Line. *See* Harris & Morgan Line

Morgan's Wharf, photograph of, 109

Mormons, 162

Morphine, 94

Mortar flotilla, 57, 59–61, 131

Mosquitoes, 31

Mules, 113

Murrah, Pendleton, 176

Mutiny, 156, 178

Nashville, 58

Navy Department, Confederate, 38, 151

Neptune: guns mounted on, 108; condition of, 112; part of cottonclad attack at Galveston, 124–128; rams *Harriet Lane*, 125

New Braunfels, Texas, 112

New London, U.S.S., 143

New Mexico, 100

New Mexico campaign, 100–104, 182

New Orleans, Louisiana, 2, 9, 19–20, 26, 35, 51, 57; capture of, 59–61, 69, 80–83, 90, 133–134, 141, 158, 163, 168, 181–182

Newspapers, 38, 55, 132–133, 138–139, 177

New York City, 43, 48, 77, 81
New York Herald, 138
New York National Guard armory, 78
New York Tribune, 133
Nichols, E. B., & Co., 27
Nichols, Ebenezer: as representative to
    Secession Convention, 7–8; at Fort
    Brown, 10, 17; capture of supplies, 12;
    begging for arms, 13; action against
    Indianola, 21; seizure of *Nueces*, 27;
    home used as headquarters, 130
Noel, Theophilus, 118
Norfolk, Virginia, 31, 80
North, Thomas, 56
North Carolina, 76
Nuns of the Battlefield Monument,
    136

Ochiltree, William B., 17
"One-Armed Tom," 70–72
Opelousas, Louisiana, 103
Orizaba, 26–27
Owasco, U.S.S.: building of, 57; at New
    Orleans, 59; coxswain of, 110; attacked
    by cottonclads, 126; boarding of, 130,
    148

Paraguay River, 58
Pardons, 185
Payne, John W., 141–142
Pelican Island, 18–19, 69, 83
Pelican Spit, fortifications on, 18–19, 44,
    70, 150
Pemberton, John C., 91
Pensacola, Florida, 60
Petrel, 144
Petty, Captain Elijah, 50
Philadelphia, Pennsylvania, 59, 79
Pierce, Ebenezer W., 91
Pillow, Gideon, 28
Pix Building, 160
Porter, David Dixon, 51, 59, 61, 90, 137
Porter, Fitz John, 11, 93
Port Royal, South Carolina, 81
Postoffice Street, 160

Potato coffee, 41
Potatoes, 152
Prosch, Mr., 161
Pyron, Charles L.: biographical informa-
    tion, 101; at Fort Point, 115
Pyron's Camp, 113
Pyron's Regiment, 116, 154

Quaker guns, 62, 149
Quincy, 79, 81–82

Rail-mounted gun, 94–95, 115, 119, 151
Railroad(s), 51, 99, 149, 151, 180
Railroad bridge, 39, 54, 64, 113, 154
Randolph, George W., 92, 96
Rations, 41, 78, 156, 162, 164–165
Readville, Massachusetts, 76
Receiver, Confederate, 28
Red Fish Reef, 49
Red River Campaign, 5, 159, 186
Religion, 165–166
Renshaw, William B.: ordered to Galves-
    ton, 57, 60, 62; orders destruction of
    Sidney C. Jones, 61; captures Galves-
    ton, 62–63; estimates size of opposing
    force, 66–67; occupation of Galves-
    ton, 69; dealings with foreign consuls,
    70; speech to *Westfield* crew, 70; ignores
    railroad bridge, 85; turns down surren-
    der, 128; blows up *Westfield*, 129
Revenue Service, United States, 13, 58
Revolutionary War, 93
Rice, William Marsh, 8
Richardson, Willard, 3, 50
Richers, Antone, 176
Richmond, Virginia, 28, 35, 38–39, 55,
    91–93, 103, 114, 142, 157
Richmond Dispatch, 92
Rio Grande, 10, 12, 101–102
Roberts, Oran, 15
Rob Roy, 170
Rogers, James H., 13, 17
Rogers, William F., 13–14
Rogers, William P., 138, 177
Rope, 31, 55

Rosenberg Library, Galveston, 29
Roxbury, Massachusetts, 74
Royal Yacht, 31, first meeting with blockaders, 42; capture of, 43–47; restoration of, 48; military career after capture,
49; at Battle of Galveston, 112, 167; as
blockade runner, 170

Sabine Pass, 26, 158
Sabine Pass, Battle of, 5, 116, 158–159
Sabine River, 106, 157
Sachem, U.S.S., 117
Sagamore, 81
Saint Joseph, Missouri, 51
Saloons, 21
Saluria, Texas, 21
San Antonio, Texas, 1; surrender of arse-
nal at, 18, 21, 24, 67, 102
San Bernard River, 159
Sand bars, 152
Sands, Benjamin F.: agrees to informal
truce, 181; enters Galveston, 183
Sangster, William H., 112, 125
San Jacinto, Battle of, 4, 13, 15, 18, 23,
42, 101
Santa Fe, New Mexico, 101–102
Santee, U.S.S., 43–48, 57, 62; returns to
Galveston, 186
Saunders, Thomas, 170
Savage's Station, Battle of, 94–95
Saxon, 79, 82–84, 129
Saxony, 70
Schirmer, Henry, 71
Scott, Winfield, 90
Scurry, William R., 100: biographical in-
formation, 101; at Battle of Glorieta
Pass, 101–102; at Battle of Galveston,
120–121, 130; accepts surrender of
Forty-Second Massachusetts Infantry,
122–123; death of, 186
Scurvy, 61
Scutd-doo, 187
Secession Convention, Texas, 15, 20, 23
Second Regiment of Massachusetts
Volunteer Militia, 74

Second Texas Infantry Regiment, 24,
177–178
Semmes, Raphael: captures *Hatteras*,
144–145
Seven Days' Campaign, 93
Seventh Infantry, U.S., 87
Seventh Texas Cavalry, 100, 111
Seventh Texas Mounted Volunteers, 102
Seventy-Sixth Illinois Regiment, 184
Sheep, 39
Sheridan, Phillip H., 182, 186
Sherman, Sidney: assessment of defenses,
13; appointment as general, 15; biogra-
phical information, 15; portrait of, 16;
assessment of defenses, 17–19; enemy
of Sam Houston, 23; shipping contro-
versies, 26–27; resignation of, 27
Sherman, Sidney (son), 118
Sherman, William T., 37
Shetucket, 79–81
Shiloh, Battle of, 177
Ship Island, 79, 82
Sibley, C. C., 21
Sibley, Henry Hopkins, 100–103; charges
after failed campaign, 102–103
Sibley's Brigade, 102–103; loss of weap-
ons, 104; movements of, 107; as volun-
teers for Galveston expedition, 111–
112; reserve forces at Customhouse, 118
Sidney C. Jones, 61, 129
Signal Corps, Confederate, 160
Slavery: statistics, 1, 42, 70, 73, 120, 149;
proposal to arm slaves, 158, 164; ended,
185
Slave trade, 58
"Slow match," 129
Smith, Ashbel, 24; studies yellow fever,
166; relieves Hawes, 177; biographical
information, 177; handles troop mutiny,
178; at surrender negotiations, 181
Smith, Caleb Blood, 107
Smith, Edmund Kirby, 98, 157, 179, 181
Smith, Leon: capture of the *Star of the
West*, 21–22; saves *Royal Yacht*, 48;
meets Magruder, 91; takes command of

naval expedition, 107; photograph of, 108; supervises cottonclad construction, 108–109; placed in charge of cottonclads, 111; early at Galveston battle, 113; commands cottonclad attack at Galveston, 124–128; captures supply ships, 131–132; unfairly blamed for massacre, 138–139; as *Harriet Lane* commander, 151; at Battle of Sabine Pass, 159; death of, 186–187

Smith, Thomas "Nicaragua," 140–142

Soledad Cos, 36

South Battery, 19, 33, 35, 150

South Carolina, 7, 23

South Carolina, U.S.S., 31–36, 38, 42–43

Southern Steamship Company, 9

Spitfire, 144

Stanley, Thomas, 64

Stanton, Edwin M., 76

Star of the West, U.S.S., 21–22, 26

Stedman, Joseph, 74–75

Stevens, Walter H., 18

St. Pierre, Mother, 118, 136

Strand, 30, 116, 123

Stuart, Ben C., 168, 179

Stuart, J. E. B., 132

Surrender, 182

Susanna, 174–175

Sutton, John S., 100

Sydnor, John, 2, 23–24

Tampico, Mexico, 36, 118

Taylor, Richard, 103

Taylor, Thomas, 173–174

Taylor, Zachary, 90

Telegraph, 132

Terry, Benjamin F., 11

Terry's Texas Rangers, 11

Texas Almanac, 3

Texas Troops. *See names of regiments*

Theron, Benjamin, 55–56

Third Regiment of Texas Infantry, 156

Tides, 110

Tobacco, 2, 86

Topographic Bureau, 89

Torpedo boat, 49

Torpedoes, 166

Tortugas, 81–82

Train, 180

Trans-Mississippi Department, 93, 96–99, 157. *See also* Army of the Trans-Mississippi

Tremont House Hotel, 23–24, 40–41, 49, 166, 183, 185

Tremont Street, 118

Trueheart, Henry M., 121, 152–153

Tucker, Philip C., 138

Twiggs, David E., 11, 17

Twin Sisters, 13, 18

Uniforms, 75–76, 136, 153

Union, 11

Ursuline Convent, 114, 118; used as hospital, 136–137, 148

Valverde, Battle of, 101

Valverde Battery, 101, 107

Vanderbilt, Cornelius, 57, 77

Van Dorn, Earl: assumes command, 21; action against *Star of the West*, 21–22; problems with assignment, 27; requisition for arms, 35; operations at Indianola, 42

Velasco, Texas, 177

Vera Cruz, Mexico, 2, 90

Vicksburg, Mississippi, 60, 91, 103, 157, 177–178

Virginia, 91, 98, 102, 132, 153

Virginia, C.S.S., 31

Virginia, U.S.S., 167

Virginia Point, 19, 66–67, 70–71, 85, 91–96, 98, 105, 113, 165

Vixen, 144

Wainwright, Jonathan M., 60; at Union capture of Galveston, 62–66; liked by civilians, 69–70; advice to Renshaw, 85; killed, 126; funeral of, 138; daughter of, 186

Wainwright, Marie, 186
Walker, John G., 176–177
Walker, William, 140
Wallis, Joseph E., 120
War Department, Confederate, 56
War of 1812, 51
Warwick River, 92
Washington, D.C., 89, 91, 99, 136, 185
Washington, George, 93
Weather, 159–160
Welles, Gideon: reaction to capture of
  Royal Yacht, 47–48, reaction to *Harriet
  Lane's* escape, 133, 171–172
Westfield, U.S.S.: operations as part of
  mortar flotilla, 57–60; scurvy on, 61;
  capture of Galveston, 62–63; Ren-
  shaw's speech on, 70; aground during
  the battle, 128; destruction of, 129–
  130; salvage of guns from, 151
West Gulf Blockading Squadron, 51

West Point Military Academy, 37, 87, 90,
  136, 162
Wharton, John A., 32
Wier, Armand R.: volunteers, 106–107;
  commands gun, 112; killed at Galves-
  ton, 125
Wigfall, Louis T., 185
William G. Anderson, 170
Williams, Samuel May, 9
Williamsburg, New York, 77
Willis, Peter, 161
Will-o'-the-Wisp, 173
Worcester County, Massachusetts, 74

Yellow fever, 63–64, 166
Yorktown, Virginia: defense of, 92–94;
  Washington at, 93; Magruder remem-
  bers, 115

Zephine, 170